Jacoba van Heemskerck

Truly Modern

HIRMER

1 **Compositie** |
Composition 1916
Woodcut on paper
25,4 × 19 cm (sheet)
Kunstmuseum Den Haag

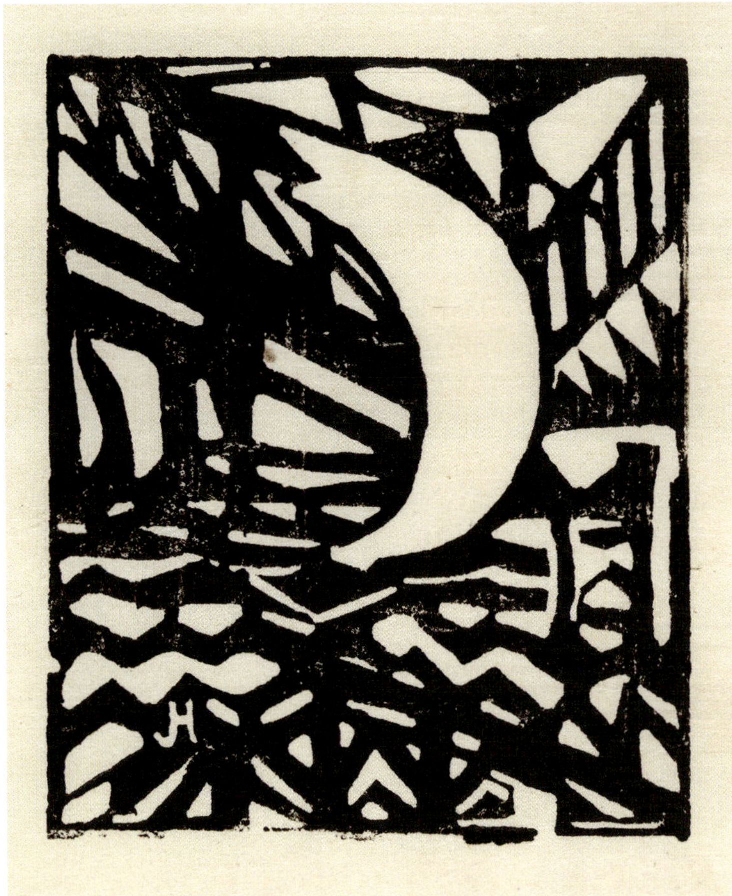

Contents

Preface

Jacoba van Heemskerck was an artist with a strong will and a determination to make a work of international importance. The fact that, as a female artist, she might meet with opposition did not deter her. Her work developed in the early years of the twentieth century, against the backdrop of a flourishing and progressive art scene in the Netherlands. Along with artists like Piet Mondrian and Jan Sluijters, and under the protective wings of Jan Toorop, she emerged as part of the Dutch avant-garde. Their colourful and expressive paintings brought a breath of fresh air to Dutch art, which until that point had been dominated by the mainly dark paintings of the nineteenth century.

Both Piet Mondrian and Jacoba van Heemskerck first encountered the Cubism of Pablo Picasso and Georges Braque at an international exhibition in Amsterdam in 1911. Van Heemskerck and Mondrian realised that to be truly modern they would have to leave the Netherlands and find a place to work abroad. Contemporaries like Sluijters were less adventurous, and they eventually fell back into a comfortable bourgeois style. While Mondrian's journey took him to Paris, Van Heemskerck was drawn to Berlin. There, she sought out close contact to Herwarth Walden and her work featured frequently in his magazine and avant-garde movement Der Sturm. She expressly presented herself in Germany as an alternative to Mondrian and Theo van Doesburg, whom she believed gravitated more towards France.

Kunstmuseum Den Haag has the world's largest collection of Van Heemskerck's works, including paintings, works on paper, mosaics, and stained-glass windows. This rich collection is a powerful counterpoint to the one by Piet Mondrian in our museum. These two artists cannot be viewed in isolation from each other. Their development ran parallel for some years, during which time they also influenced each other. Both were attracted to theosophy and anthroposophy. Following Wassily Kandinsky's example, however, Van Heemskerck developed a lyrical abstraction which remained expressive in terms of her use of colour and her linework, and far removed from Mondrian's geometric abstraction.

I am delighted that many of Jacoba van Heemskerck's works are now on display in Germany. For their cordial and collegial cooperation, I am grateful to my colleagues: Sebastian Möllers from Museen Stade for the initiative; Christina Végh from Kunsthalle Bielefeld for her participation; Helga Gutbrod for showing it at Edwin Scharff Museum in Southern Germany; and to their teams. Jacoba van Heemskerck's work was created largely as a reflection of and in dialogue with developments in art in Germany in the early twentieth century. Now her work is returning there, and I hope that it will inspire young artists living in Germany and serve as an example to them. For the public of our neighbouring country, this exhibition and publication will probably represent their first encounter with Van Heemskerck, but I am certain they will come away with a deeper understanding of her work and of Northern European art in the early to mid-twentieth century. A period which, on reflection, can be regarded as one of the most interesting in the development of art.

Benno Tempel
Director, Kunstmuseum Den Haag

Foreword

Over a period of less than two decades, Jacoba van Heemskerck created a powerful oeuvre that includes paintings, drawings, woodcuts, mosaics and works in glass. It distinguishes the artist as one of the major modernists. The rhythmic composition of the pictorial space, black contouring, and an intensive use of colour characterise her landscapes, harbour scenes, and organic, abstract, formal advancements. They reflect her thoughts about the spiritual impact in art, making her one of the outstanding modern Expressionists. In turning to anthroposophy, however, Van Heemskerck set herself apart from other Expressionist artists. For her, art was not just the expression of subjective emotions, but also a path towards knowledge—primarily concerning the effects of light and colour on viewers. Ultimately, she achieved her goal of creating 'radiantly, spiritual' colours in her works in glass. Van Heemskerck's search for spirituality, as well as her rejection of the notion that nature and the universe are determined purely by materialism and positivism, are what make her works highly relevant today, when we are again being challenged under different auspices to perceive the complexity of the world as a whole.

This exhibition grew out of an initial partnership between the Kunstmuseum Den Haag and the Museen Stade, then joined by the Kunsthalle Bielefeld. The Edwin Scharff Museum became a third venue in the South of Germany. Behind this international cooperation is the intention to shed light on Van Heemskerck's role in the events of the art world exactly a century ago, as well as on her impact on the Netherlands and Germany, and ultimately to bring a nearly forgotten modernist artist back into public consciousness. Thanks to the Kunstmuseum Den Haag's extensive collection and its generosity as a lender, Jacoba van Heemskerck's oeuvre can, after almost forty years, once again be seen in Germany.

After her early career in the Netherlands as part of the circle around Piet Mondrian, among others, Jacoba van Heemskerck joined the avant-garde movement known as Der Sturm in 1913; she remained a member and one of the artists most frequently exhibited by Herwarth and Nell Walden in Berlin until 1923. After an introduction to the artist's life and work by the show's two curators, Luisa Pauline Fink and Henrike Mund, this catalogue delves into the spiritual dimensions of Van Heemskerck's body of work. Laura Stamps, curator of modern and contemporary art at the Kunstmuseum Den Haag, focuses on the significance of theosophy and anthroposophy in the artist's work. Jacqueline van Paaschen, author of the catalogue raisonné and a longtime Van Heemskerck expert, points out her connections to Freemasonry in her essay. Van Heemskerck's multifaceted collaborations with Der Sturm is the object of Anne Lorenz's research, a scientist currently working with the research project *DER STURM. Digitale Quellenedition zur Geschichte der internationalen Avantgarde* (Der Sturm: Digital Source Edition of the History of the International Avant-Garde) at the Akademie der Wissenschaften und der Literatur in Mainz. She is the first to assess the correspondence between Van Heemskerck and Herwarth and Nell Walden using computerised analytics.

We would like to take this opportunity to thank Benno Tempel, Daniel Koep, and

Doede Hardeman of the Kunstmuseum Den Haag for partnering with us on the show and the catalogue, as well as for their generous support and enthusiasm for reintroducing Jacoba van Heemskerck to Germany. Without the scientific expertise of Laura Stamps and the assistance of Vivien Entius, the catalogue could not have been realised in its current form. In addition, we are grateful to Erica Jonkman, the collection coordinator, and conservator Leonoor Speldekamp for their tireless efforts in ensuring the works were ready to be loaned. We also thank Marjolein Prinse, Hanneke Modderkolk, Frans Peterse and Erwin Sutedjo, who cooperated in helping to get all of the artworks on the road. Here, we are heartily obliged to the entire team at the Kunstmuseum Den Haag for their consistently collegial, reliable, and cheerful cooperation.

In addition, we would like to thank all of the authors for their research, having enriched this catalogue with their substantial essays, as well as Sue McDonnell and Allison Moseley for the reliable translations, and Keonaona Peterson for her careful copyediting. We also thank Tania Müller for her accurate research on the list of exhibitions. Further thanks go to Eef Overgaauw, head of the manuscript department at the Staatsbibliothek zu Berlin, Preußischer Kulturbesitz, for allowing us to borrow the *Sturm* magazines and Jacoba van Heemskerck's archival materials. We are also thankful to the Ita Wegman Institut in Arlesheim, Switzerland, which entrusted us with the 1917 manuscript from Willem Zeylmans van Emmichoven's estate, so that it could be translated for the first time from Dutch into German and English. Moreover, the catalogue could not have been published in its current form without Els Kerreman's judicious graphic design. Many thanks to her for the pleasant collaboration, as well as to Kerstin Ludolph and Hannes Halder of Hirmer Verlag, who assisted with the catalogue from the start.

Penultimately, we would not have been able to realise either the exhibition or the catalogue without the generous support of numerous sponsors. Neither would have been possible at the Museen Stade without the Brougier-Seisser-Cleve-Werhahn Stiftung and the ZEIT-Stiftung Ebelin und Gerd Bucerius, or at the Kunsthalle Bielefeld without the Kulturstiftung pro Bielefeld. Concerning the catalogue, we would expressly like to thank the Ernst von Siemens Kunststiftung, particularly Martin Hoernes.

Lastly, we are grateful to the two curators, Luisa Pauline Fink and Henrike Mund. Together, they conceived both the show and the catalogue, preparing them over the course of many meetings and working closely as a team, especially with Daniel Koep at the Kunstmuseum Den Haag, to produce them. We are pleased to be able to demonstrate the relevance of Jacoba van Heemskerck's work today outside of the Netherlands and to bring her art to a broader audience here as well.

Sebastian Möllers, Christina Végh and Helga Gutbrod
Directors Museen Stade, Kunsthalle Bielefeld, Edwin Scharff Museum

Jacoba van Heemskerck

Luisa Pauline Fink, Henrike Mund

Truly Modern

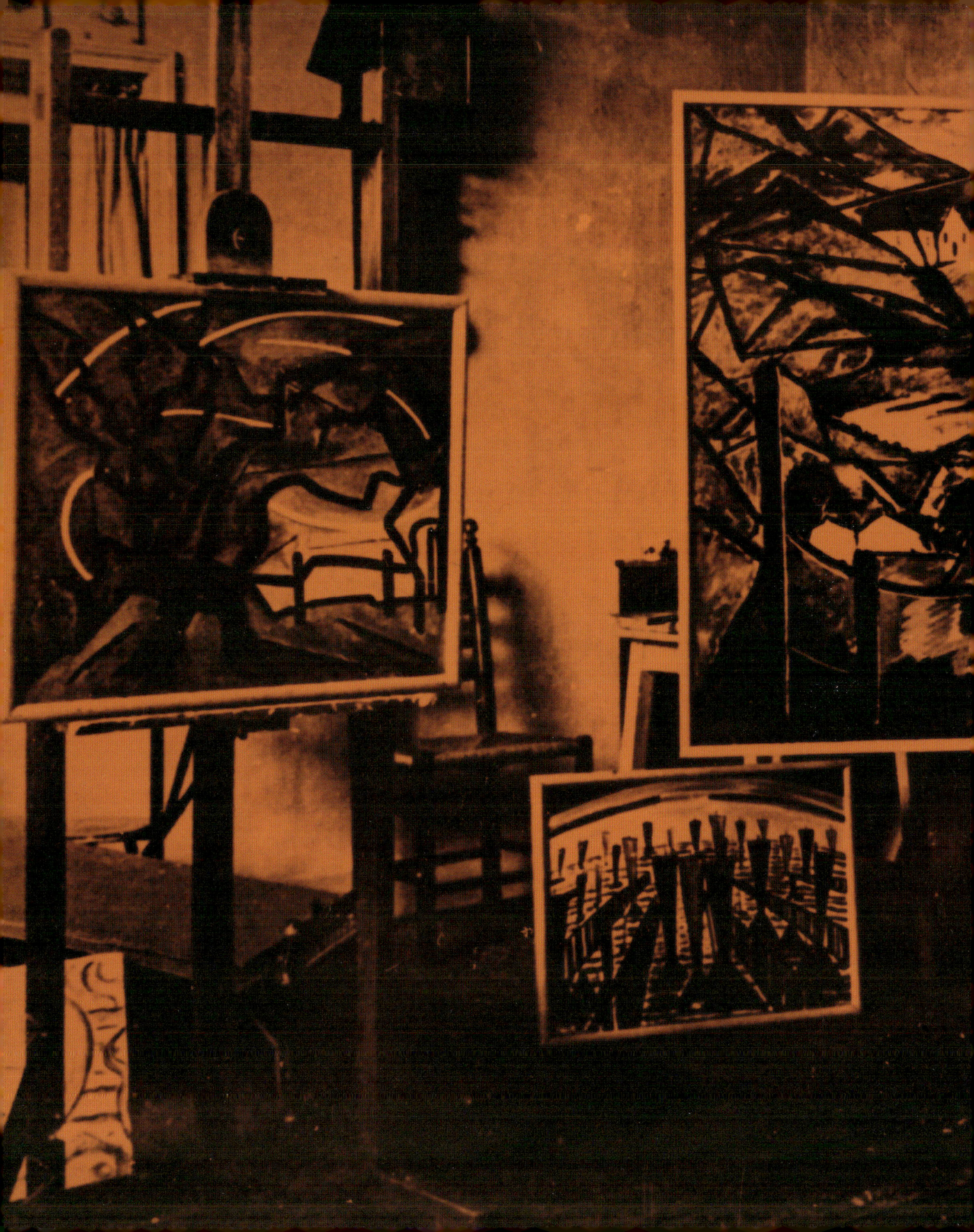

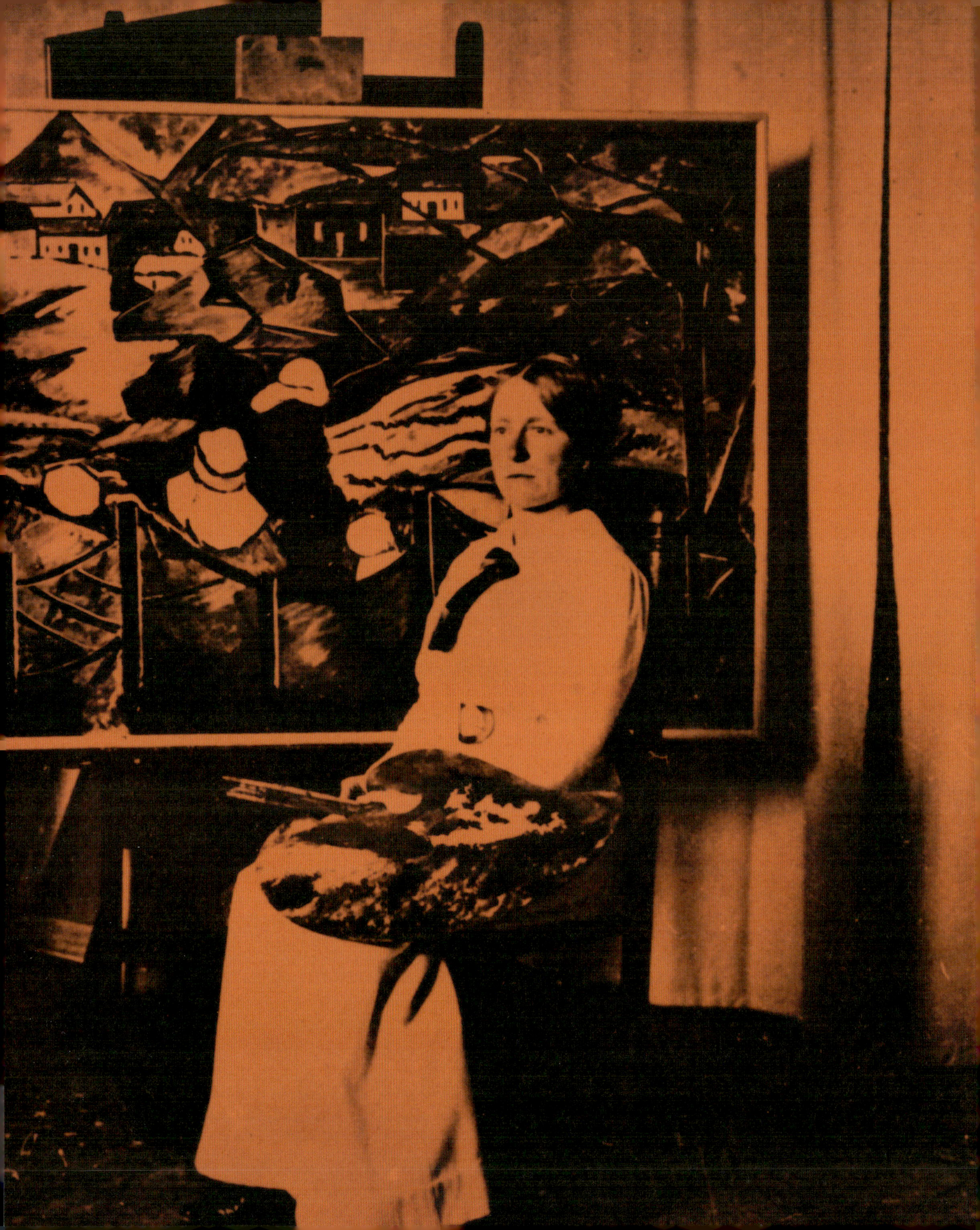

2 Jacoba van Heemskerck in her studio, 1915

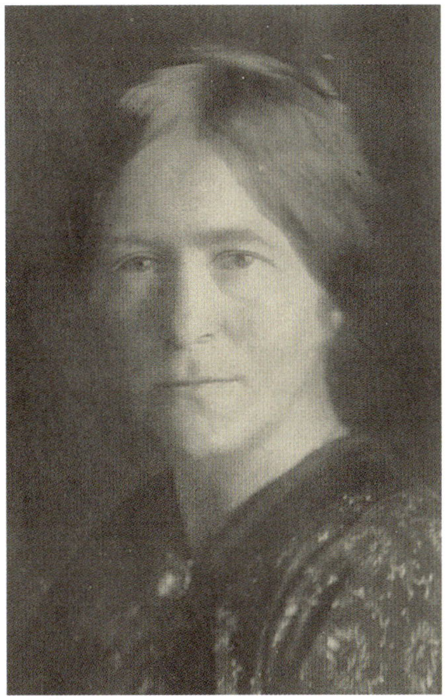

3 Jacoba van Heemskerck, 1915

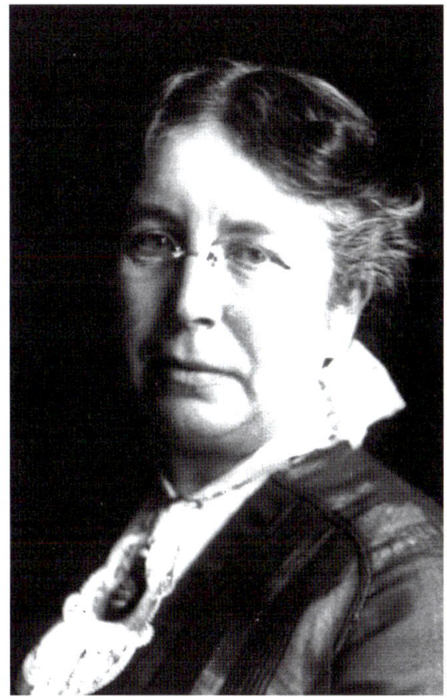

4 Marie Tak van Poortvliet, undated

'Art is my life. [...] I can't do anything about it, I must always be working, I always have something that has to come out,' wrote Jacoba van Heemskerck on 3 March 1915 from The Hague to Herwarth Walden, the founder of Der Sturm in Berlin and one of the foremost promoters of the artistic avant-garde of his time.[1] In fact, the life of Jacoba van Heemskerck was marked by a tireless urge to create. Up until her early death in 1923 at the age of just forty-seven, she worked on the new modern '[art] movement' and was one of its most prominent protagonists.[2] As a member of first the Theosophical and later the Anthroposophical Societies, she consistently aimed to depict the all-encompassing life and the spiritual in the world.

Education and Sojourns in Paris

Jacoba van Heemskerck van Beest was born to an aristocratic Dutch family in The Hague on 1 April 1876.[3] Her father, Jacob Eduard van Heemskerck van Beest, was a navy officer and an admired painter of seascapes who gave her the first drawing lessons. As her later friend and companion Marie Tak van Poortvliet reports, her education at the Koninklijke Academie van Beeldende Kunsten in The Hague from 1897 to 1901 taught her the techniques of painting but could not instruct her in what soon became the goal of her creativity: 'a study of all that which nature contains of spiritual worth, of all that life can teach us of its deep meaning and of the way in which these two factors have an influence on each other'.[4] In order to get on with her art, Van Heemskerck began in September 1900 to take a weekly class with Ferdinand Hart Nibbrig in Laren, an artists' village, where she refined her skills in printmaking and drawing. She produced detailed portraits, mostly of farmers and fishermen.

After the death of her mother in 1901, she and her sister moved to Hilversum, near Utrecht. From then on, it was clear to her that she would have to face life on her own. Perhaps encouraged by Nibbrig, she went to Paris that same year to attend classes at Eugène Carrière's studio. The renowned Symbolist and portraitist had founded his own art school in 1898, and unlike the state-operated École des Beaux-Arts, it allowed more space for artistic individualism and also accepted women as students. André Derain, Henri Matisse, Pablo Picasso and Valentine Val could also be found there. In addition, as home to the buildings that had opened the year before for the World Exposition (such as the Grand Palais, the Petit Palais, and the Pont Alexandre III), Paris was the very embodiment of progress. In particular, the prodigious Grand Palais, made of iron, steel and glass, which had hosted the Salon d'Automne exhibitions since 1904, would have impressed Van Heemskerck. One of her pieces was displayed there in the same year as part of a show produced by the Union des Femmes Peintres et Sculpteurs.

After spending three years commuting back and forth between Paris and Hilversum, Van Heemskerck returned to the Netherlands in 1904. In August 1905 she moved to The Hague to be closer to her friend Marie Tak van Poortvliet, who had become a wealthy woman after the death of her father, the former Dutch Minister of the Interior, Johannes Tak van Poortvliet. It was also during this year that Van Heemskerck began exhibiting her work in the Netherlands. For example, between 1905 and 1911 she took part in the shows put on by the St Lucas artists' association at the Stedelijk Museum in Amsterdam. Each of the pieces on display there sheds light on the development of her art in the early years of her career. Up until 1908 the work shown consisted mainly of realistically drawn or lithographed portraits. The following year she turned to Luminism, a style whose origins were based in French Pointillism, but which in the Netherlands—under the influence of the works of Vincent van Gogh and the Parisian Fauves—resulted in obviously rougher daubs with more intense colour schemes.

Luminist Paintings

By 1889 the Pointillist style of painting, which originated in France, was first presented in the Netherlands at an exhibition by the Brussels-based art group Les XX (Les Vingts) in Amsterdam. Considering that the reserved colours of The Hague School's style of Impressionism still set the tone in art, the show was initially received rather negatively. Above all, the juxtaposition of dots of pure colour, resembling a prismatic dissection of light, which were supposed to be blended by the viewer's eye to create an image and to reveal thereby their full, luminous effect, was dismissed as being too analytical and scientific. The warning was 'that science should not intrude upon the territory of art. Art is an outflow of emotion, of higher emotion. [...] Science, on the other hand, must only account for reason,' as an art critic of the time wrote.[5] It was not until the late 1890s, when leading Dutch painters such as Jan Toorop and Johan Thorn Prikker again turned to this kind of painting, that the style underwent an upturn again in the

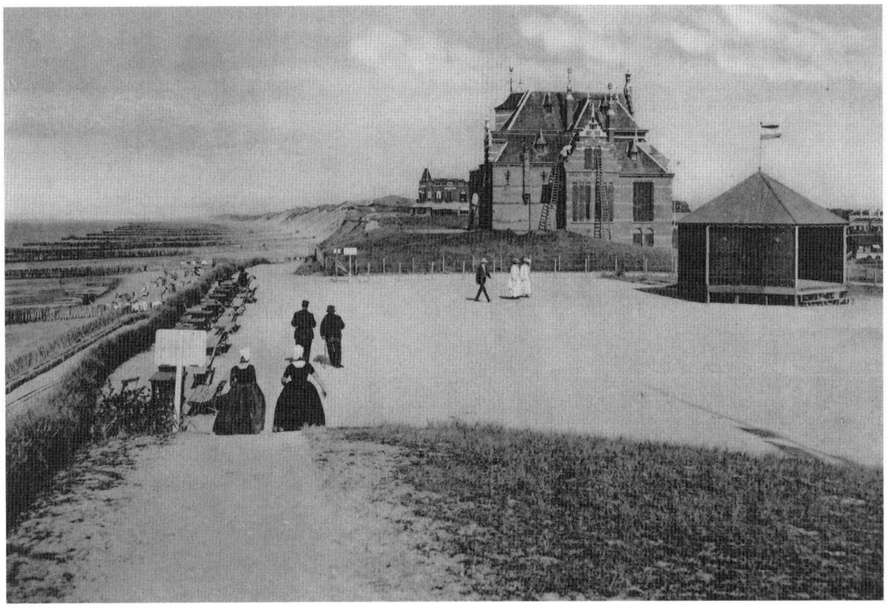

5 Domburg, c.1900

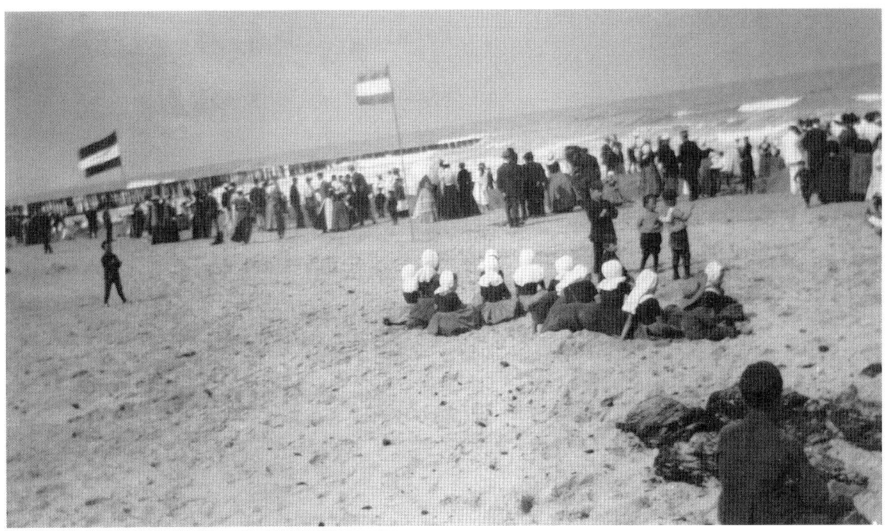

6 Beach in Domburg, Zeeland people, 1904

Netherlands. Further influences came from Vincent van Gogh in 1892, when his work was exhibited for the first time in his own country. The big retrospective of his work at the Stedelijk Museum in Amsterdam in 1905, along with the intensely colourful art of the Fauves, who caused a scandal that same year at the Grand Palais in Paris, resonated widely in the work of Dutch artists. At the St Lucas exhibit in 1908, the term 'Luminism' was first used with reference to the new art.[6]

Jacoba van Heemskerck followed all of this attentively. Finally, the annual stay and artistic exchange with colleagues in Domburg was essential for her advancement in painting. Every year since 1906, she and Marie Tak van Poortvliet had visited the coastal resort on the island of Walcheren, not least for health reasons. After Tak van Poortvliet built the Villa Loverendale there, Domburg became a second home for the two of them during the summer months. Domburg also gradually developed into an artists' town. Jan Toorop had been visiting there annually since 1903, and the artist Mies Elout-Drabbe lived there year-round. Other artists, such as Betsy van Manen, Otto van Rees, Adya van Rees-Dutilh and Cornelis Spoor discovered the resort town for themselves. Beginning in 1908, exhibitions were even presented at the Bath Pavilion. That same summer, Piet Mondrian arrived in Domburg for the first time. In the garden of the Villa Loverendale he produced studies for his famous work *Avond; De rode boom* (*Evening: The Red Tree*, 1908–10), which Tak van Poortvliet, who went on to amass an important collection of art, later acquired.

7 Exhibition room in the Badpaviljoen, Domburg 1908

8 Exhibition Pavillion, Domburg 1911, et al. Jan Toorop, Ferdinand Hart Nibbrig, Jan Heyse, Annie Hall, Jacoba van Heemskerck (with hat and tie in the doorway), Charley Toorop, Marinus Zwart and Marie Tak van Poortvliet (with hat and tie)

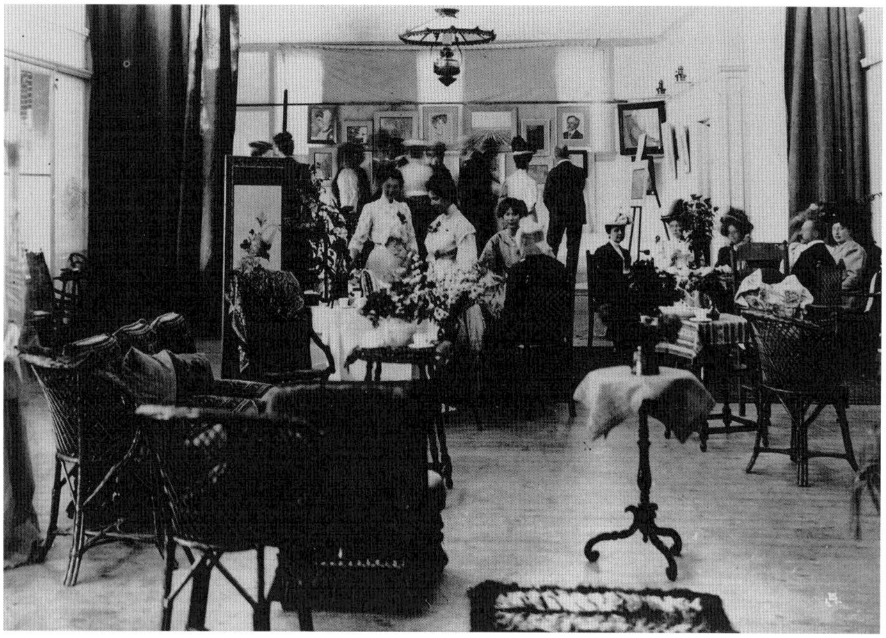

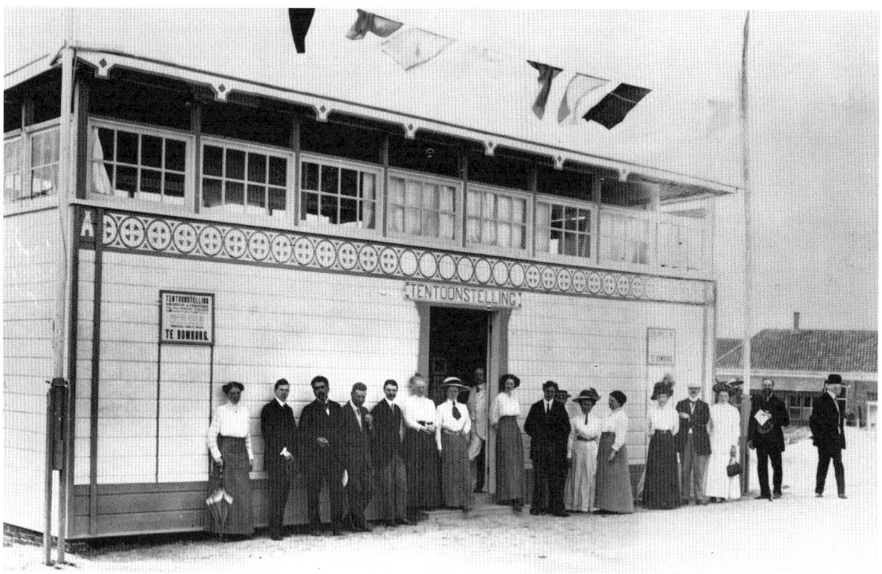

Art as Spiritual Creation

In the following years Van Heemskerck and Mondrian exchanged ideas and thoughts when the two of them were drawing in the area around Domburg. Mondrian, who probably heard Rudolf Steiner lecture in the Netherlands in 1908 and joined the Theosophical Society a year later, expressed his interest in the spiritual dimension of art in 1909, saying that he sought knowledge of the occult in order 'to understand things better through it'.[7] Since the end of the nineteenth century there had been a general receptivity for anything spiritual, mystical and occultic in the Netherlands, and theosophy played a prominent role above all.[8] Cornelis Spoor, for instance, joined the Theosophical Society in 1905, Ferdinand Hart Nibbrig in 1908 and Jacoba van Heemskerck finally in 1910. Over the summer 1909 Charley Toorop, the daughter of Jan Toorop, reported that 'this mad Mondrian' sat in the middle of the beach in his 'Buddha pose'.[9] Around this time Van Heemskerck solidified her lifelong view that art is more than just the reproduction of visible reality. And, in fact, her early Luminist works, composed of dots, not only prove to be the result of a spiritual creation, but their luminosity also points towards a spirtual dimension of life itself behind external manifestations of nature (cat. pp. 74, 75)

The exhibition at St Lucas in the spring of 1910 was ultimately considered a 'triumph of Luminism'.[10] Mondrian was responsible for hanging the works and created two distinct rooms, one 'radical', the other 'moderate'. In the first he displayed his own work alongside that of Jacoba van Heemskerck, Jan Sluijters and Leo Gestel, and in the latter, Cornelis Spoor and Ferdinand Hart Nibbrig. An incensed Sluijters complained to Spoor, it is said, because he thought that Mondrian had 'spoiled' the first room by including works by 'male and female friends'. He (Sluijters) did not want his work to hang amid the 'junk by virginal [aristocratic] misses', in an unmistakable allusion to Jacoba van Heemskerck.[11] In August Van Heemskerck, Mondrian and Sluijters were invited to exhibit with the group Doe Stil Voort at the Museum of Modern Art in Brussels. Van Heemskerck proved capable of asserting herself as an artist to be taken seriously among her male colleagues. In the following three years she also repeatedly exhibited her work with Mondrian and other Dutch artists at the Salon des Indépendants in Paris.

Turning to Cubism

In order to promote a link between Dutch art and international modernism, the artist and critic Conrad Kickert founded the Moderne Kunstkring in November 1910, and it would go on to hold an annual salon every autumn at the Stedelijk Museum in Amsterdam. Mondrian and Sluijters were named to the board, and Jan Toorop became chairman. At the Moderne Kunstkring's first presentation in fall 1911, Kickert exhibited not only the Dutch avant-garde, including Mondrian and Van Heemskerck, but also works by Paul Cézanne, along with Cubist pieces by Georges Braque, Pablo Picasso and the so-called Montparnasse Cubists, such as Henri Le Fauconnier. The aftermath of this show was consequential, for Cubism replaced Luminism as the height of modernism in the Netherlands.

Jacoba van Heemskerck also turned to Cubism. After a brief trip to Paris in May 1912, she painted Cubist-orientated works over the summer in her new studio in the garden of Villa Loverendale. An important interlocutor for her in this matter was Lodewijk Schelfhout, who lived in Paris and was invited by her to Domburg in order to present his works in Jan Toorop's newly opened exhibition pavilion. Unlike Braque and Picasso, Van Heemskerck's concept of Cubism did not envision the simultaneous existence of different perspectives of an object on a single plane, but rather the prismatic, abstract dissection of the entire pictorial space. Besides the rhythmic organization of forms, her primary interest was in the interplay between transparent and opaque sections in the image (cat. pp. 76–79). Light continued to play a major role in her work, despite the predominance of browns, greens and greys.

Der Sturm

That same summer, Herwarth Walden, who had opened his gallery Der Sturm in Berlin in 1912, presented Sturm exhibitions in the Netherlands.[12] The first one took place in August at the Biesing Gallery in The Hague. Walden showed works by the Futurists he had exhibited before in April in Berlin. The show then travelled to Amsterdam and Rotterdam. In November 1912 the gallery Oldenzeel in Rotterdam took on a show of Wassily Kandinsky's work, which Walden had presented in October in Berlin. At the same time the Dutch weekly *De Kunst* published German Expressionist art and Kandinsky's essay *On Understanding Art* (1912). In March 1913 a Franz Marc show followed at the Kunstzalen d'Audretsch in The Hague, organised by Der Sturm.[13] Even though

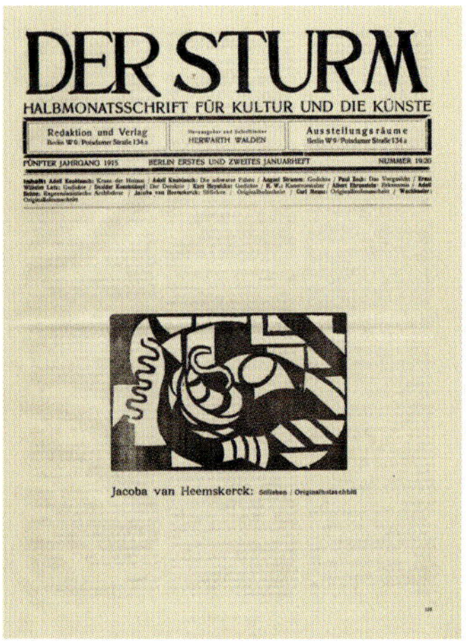

9 *Der Sturm*, vol. 5, no. 19/20 (1915), cover

Jacoba van Heemskerck surely followed events surrounding the German art impresario, she still presented Cubist works at the summer exhibition in Domburg in 1913. It was not until she participated in Herwarth Walden's *Erster Deutscher Herbstsalon* in 1913 in Berlin that her work took another stylistic turn.

Herwarth Walden founded the magazine *Der Sturm* in March 1910 in Berlin. His ensuing extensive activities in publishing and exhibiting, his lectures, readings, theatricals and his European-wide network, all under the name of Der Sturm, were nothing less than a revolutionary movement, an 'upheaval in art'[14] which would introduce 'a new perspective of the world'[15] in the spirit of Expressionism. This idea was buoyed by the vision that abstract art would open up new experiences, in contrast to the fossilised structures of the Wilhelmine Empire and its cynical, imperialist, nationalist politics. Art should not, as it was taught in the academies, imitate nature or depict battles and wars to honour the empire, but rather address 'what is generally human' and the 'soul', and it should 'belong [...] to all of the people'.[16] The name 'Der Sturm' was programmatic as it was related to the idea of a revitalizing storm and expressing the sensation of being on the cusp of a sea change.[17]

Up until Der Sturm dissolved in 1932, the year Herwarth Walden emigrated, the movement retained its reputation across Europe as one of the avant-garde's most important centres for art, to which Van Heemskerck felt devoted until the end of her life. Van Heemskerck came to Walden's attention between 1912 and 1913, when he found himself visiting the Netherlands quite often.[18] He invited the artist to participate in the *Erster Deutscher Herbstsalon* which he was organising. That is probably where Van Heemskerck and Walden first met in person. The salon, which took place in Berlin from September to November 1913, was an ambitious project, and one of the most significant exhibitions during the pre-war years, bringing together around 370 works by nearly 90 artists from 12 different countries and providing an overview of Europe's avant-garde artists. Many of what are now the most famous paintings in modern art were first shown at Der Sturm's *Erster Deutscher Herbstsalon*.

A Lifelong Friendship

The exhibition marked the start of a loyal friendship and many years of collaboration involving Van Heemskerck, Herwarth Walden, and Nell Roslund-Walden, leading to the artist's agreeing to work exclusively with Der Sturm. Regular journeys to Berlin ensued and vice versa, as the Waldens travelled to The Hague and Domburg. Between 1914 and 1922 they undertook a lively exchange of letters. Most of the letters Van Heemskerck wrote in German to Herwarth and Nell Walden have survived and are maintained today in the Sturm-Archive, Staatsbibliothek zu Berlin. They are the most important historical source concerning the artist's life and work and have been partly available online in a newly revised edition since 2018.[19]

Just six months after the *Erster Deutscher Herbstsalon*, Van Heemskerck had more than twenty pieces on display in the 23rd Sturm exhibition in Berlin and then a solo show in Hamburg from April to October of 1914.[20] She became part of the innermost circle

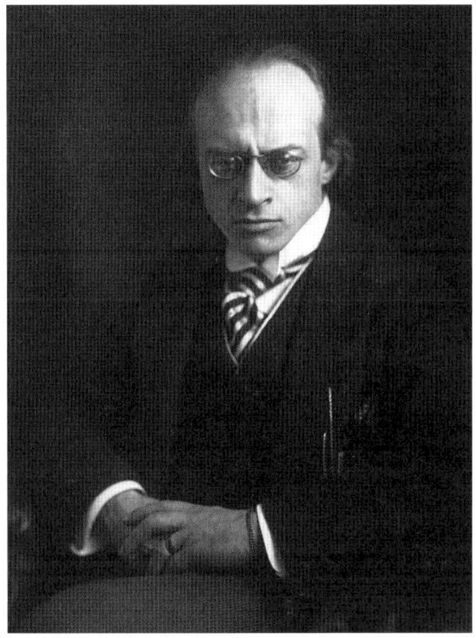

10 Herwarth Walden, 1918 (photo: Rudolf Dührkoop)

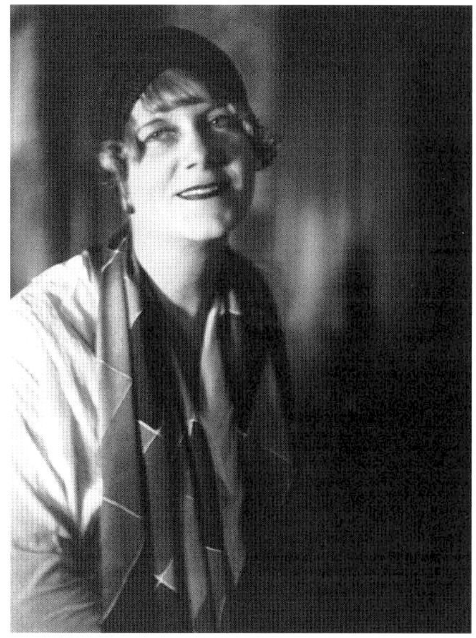

11 Nell Walden, c.1926

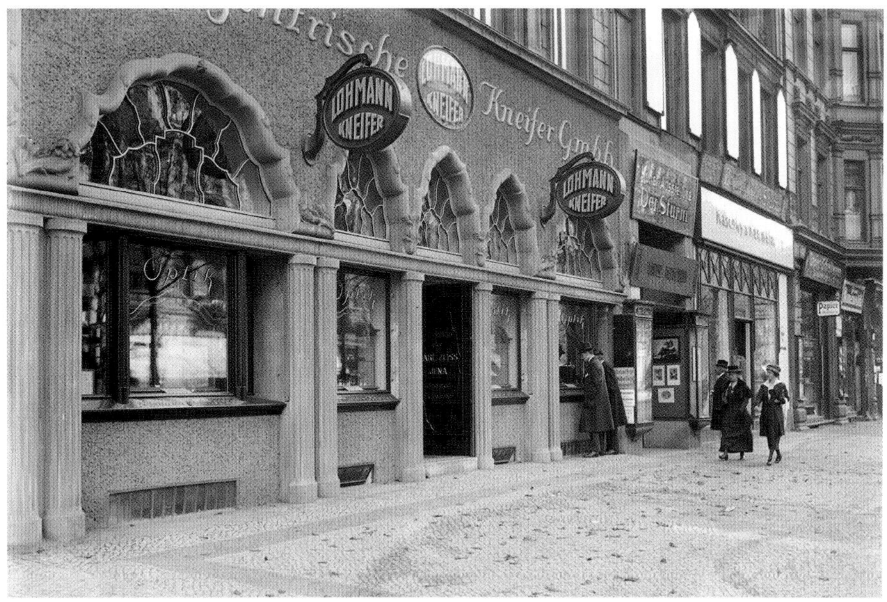

12 Sturm-Gallery, Potsdamer Straße 134a, Berlin, c.1914 (photo: Willy Römer)

of the Sturm artists in 1915, while her work was being seen all across Europe. Van Heemskerck is second only to Oskar Kokoschka as the artist whose work was most often on display, and the many woodcuts she produced for the covers of *Der Sturm* magazine had a strong influence on its image. Just a year later, she was engaged to teach 'Expressionist art' at Der Sturm's newly opened art school at Potsdamer Straße 134a in Berlin, where painting, poetry, music and acting were taught. Among her colleagues were Paul Klee and Gabriele Münter.[21]

The First World War: Sturm Activities in the Netherlands

Still entirely caught up in the spirit of the Wilhelmine empire, the *Erster Deutscher Herbstsalon* was received by the public as a vehement affront, and its critics went on the offensive. Newspapers even referred to the show as a 'gallery of loony paintings'.[22] It was not until the war ended in 1918 and Wilhelm II abdicated that Expressionism began appearing in German public museum collections. During the war years Van Heemskerck lived in The Hague and in Domburg—the Netherlands managed to remain politically and militarily neutral throughout the entire period of the war—and in her letters to the Waldens, she repeatedly emphasises that she stands by Germany, and that art matters far more than national interests.[23] During this period, she initiated and represented several Sturm activities in the Netherlands, such as a Sturm theatre under the direction of John Schikowski, a Sturm club, and a branch of Der Sturm's art school. She also contacted Lothar Schreyer, the dramaturge at the Deutsches Schauspielhaus in Hamburg and

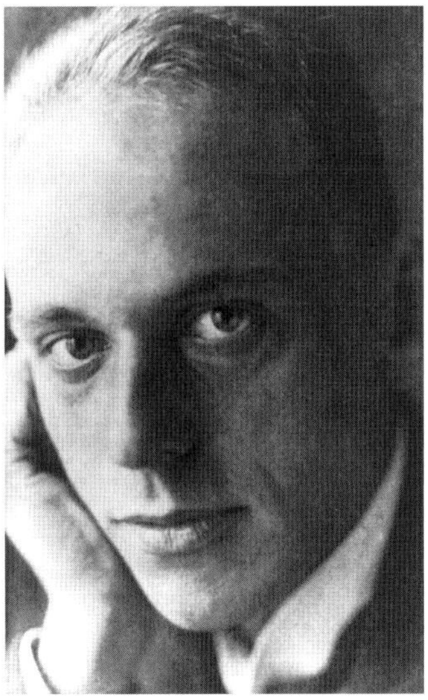

13 Willem Zeylmans van Emmichoven, *c.*1916

co-editor of *Der Sturm* from 1917 onwards, wanting to collaborate with him on a concept for an abstract, 'cosmic' puppet theatre.[24] Furthermore, she became an important contact for the existing international Sturm network, partly because she also regularly supplied Walden with clippings about the war from Dutch newspapers, which—unlike the nationalist, German propaganda news—provided him with an expanded view of the war's events, making it possible for him to run a news agency.[25]

As far as her style is concerned, Van Heemskerck altered it again during the war years. Her lines became stronger, and she used colours and black contours more extensively. Paintings from this period, such as *Bild no. 18* (*Image no. 18*, 1915) and *Bild no. 23 (Witte zeilschepen op een meer)* (*Image no. 23 (White Sailing Ships on the Sea)*, 1915), feature rhythmic gradations of the same motif (cat. pp. 89, 87). In both paintings she examines the sail, which often recurs in her art; in these works, they are oddly still and motionless. Marie Tak van Poortvliet described *Image no. 23* as showing the 'atmosphere of her native country: the sea, dunes, boats and sails' and a 'calm contemplation'.[26] The stillness communicated in the chain of mountains claustrophobically surrounding the boats, however, conveys a sense of oppression that might also mirror a perseverance and longing for the end of the war. The frequent recurrence of trees, waterscapes, sails and—from around 1916 onwards—the abstract compositions of forms that distinguish her as one of the major representatives of organic abstraction, are evidence of her intense study of form and colour. Her motifs became increasingly dynamic, some even resembling colourful streams of lava running across the canvas (cat. pp. 104, 105, 107). A vital understanding of nature and the universe resonates, in the same way that Henri Bergson's ideas on the concept of élan vital were often received as a breath of fresh air amid the technological rationalisation of life that was going on at the time.[27] Striving for the unity of humankind, nature and the universe was one of the utopian ideals Van Heemskerck embraced in company with many of Der Sturm's artists—ideals that were especially significant in the period of time around the First World War.

Friendship with Willem Zeylmans van Emmichoven

During the Sturm exhibition *Expressionisten, Kubisten* in 1916 in The Hague, in which Van Heemskerck, Nell Walden and Gabriele Münter were prominently featured alongside Franz Marc, Wassily Kandinsky and others, the artist happened to meet the architecture student Jan Buijs among the public. As the two of them stood in front of a Marc painting, Van Heemskerck said to him, 'Wonderful, isn't it?' 'Yes', Buijs is said to have replied, 'but I think the paintings hanging next to it are also grand.' 'They're mine,' said the little lady. 'I am Jacoba van Heemskerck.'[28] The conversation ended with an invitation to Domburg, which also included Buijs's friend Willem Zeylmans van Emmichoven. Zeylmans van Emmichoven was a medical student, albeit one interested in art, and just after his first meeting with Van Heemskerck, he wrote an essay about her work titled *The Spiritual Direction in New Painting: Jacoba van Heemskerck* (1917). We can assume that, after having spoken directly with the artist, many of her own thoughts were incorporated into his piece. Reflecting the zeitgeist, Zeylmans van Emmichoven writes that 'nature—not as landscape, but as spiritual truth' is 'in its lines and colours'. Viewers should approach the work with sensitivity in order to comprehend the 'smallest nuances of spiritual experience'.[29] It is, however, less about the artist's subjective feelings, as is often assumed when it comes to Expressionism. On the contrary, Van Heemskerck tries to avoid making any suggestions regarding the content, while at the same time using form and colour to open up a space for the viewer's sentiments and knowledge.[30]

It is remarkable how much the focus at that time shifted from the view of art created by geniuses to the question of observation. Van Heemskerck herself examined this theme in depth, as also her further exchanges with Zeylmans van Emmichoven make clear. The artist recommended Rudolf Steiner's anthroposophical writings to Zeylmans van Emmichoven—theories she herself had intensively explored ever since her meeting with Steiner in person in 1913, as shows her (now lost) lecture on modern art, given in The Hague at Steiner's invitation three years later. For Zeylmans van Emmichoven, Steiner's writings were a kind of awakening. Inspired by Van Heemskerck, he examined the psychological impact of colours in his dissertation for the medical school in Leipzig. He dedicated it to Van Heemskerck, partly because his studies had been preceded by experiments on the effects of colour on viewers, carried out in collaboration with her.[31] In Domburg in the summer of 1918 Van Heemskerck and Zeylmans van Emmichoven undertook empirical analyses on the impact of colours. It is likely that the methods were similar to those that Zeylmans van Emmichoven would use as the foundation for his dissertation. He incorporated the so-called 'tapping method' invented by William Stern, which assumes that the rhythmic tapping of the test subjects is a reaction to colours, corresponding to a state of excitement and something he called a 'psychic tempo'.

Works in Glass: Coloured Light

In 1919, besides continuing to paint and make woodcuts, Van Heemskerck began creating many works in glass, as well as mosaics (cat. pp. 114, 115, 123, 126-129). For some of these she produced preliminary studies in pencil or watercolour (cat. pp. 118, 119, 122). Glass was a new medium for her, but something she had already been contemplating for years, as is documented in a 1914 letter to Herwarth Walden.[32] According to Marie Tak van Poortvliet, Van Heemskerck bought a small kiln and soon learned how to use it, although she also commissioned some work based on her designs from the Heinersdorff factory in Berlin or from the studio J. W. Gips in The Hague. Van Heemskerck chose abstract, crystalline forms, most of which consist exclusively of triangles and squares, such as *Compositie naar Glasfensterentwurf no. 17* (*Composition for a Design for a Glass Window no. 17*, c.1920) and elaborate, often intertwined, flowing forms that evoke an amoeba-filled world seen under a microscope (cat. pp. 128, 114). Considering the heightened role that colours played in Van Heemskerck's work and ideas, her use of glass makes particular sense. The immanent connection of light and colour creates effects that reflect Van Heemskerck's long-term exploration of the theme.

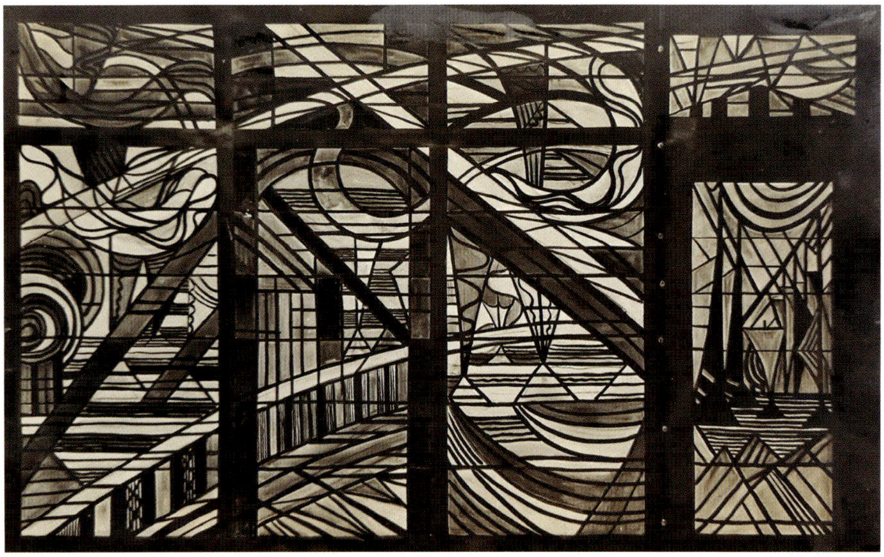

14 Design for a Glass Window, Villa Wulffraat, 1920, 135 × 70 cm (whereabouts unknown)

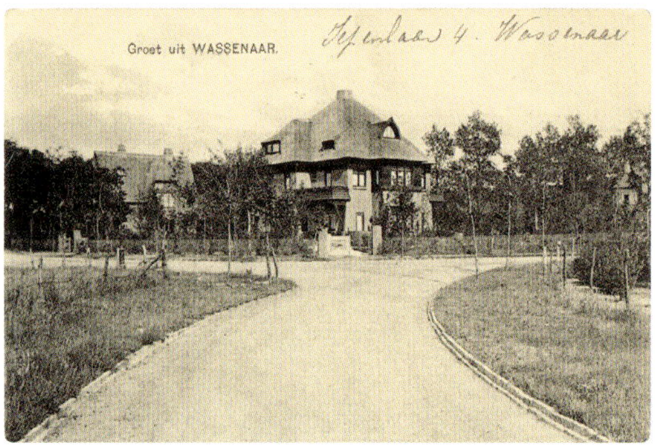

15 Villa Wulffraat, Wassenaar, 1922

From 1920 onwards the tone of Van Heemskerck's letters to Herwarth Walden gradually became less personal—partly because he reacted rather coolly to her artistic interest in working with glass—up to the point where she terminated his exclusive right to sell her work.[33] In making this decision, Van Heemskerck joined several other artists who distanced themselves from Der Sturm and increasingly went their own way or became more involved with other groups, such as the Novembergruppe; new artists such as Otto Nebel and Kurt Schwitters joined Der Sturm. In 1919, when Rosa Luxemburg and Karl Liebknecht were murdered in Berlin, Walden became a member of the Communist Party. Not everyone who belonged to Der Sturm's circle in the pre-war years shared this position, which was another reason why the movement's activities continued to splinter.[34] Van Heemskerck, who had previously kept largely apart from Dutch contacts in the Netherlands and orientated herself towards Germany, increasingly filled her last letters with descriptions of initiatives that were independent of Der Sturm and also enjoyed success in the Netherlands with her works in glass. She took part in an exhibition in Domburg (1920), planned solo shows in Amsterdam, Brussels and Paris (1921) and provided both public and private buildings with stained-glass windows. Van Heemskerck's windows for several houses—including the Wulffraat family's villa in Wassenaar, which Jan Buijs (with whom the artist remained in contact, as she did with Zeylmans van Emmichoven) designed to be a light-filled architecture—are notable works of glass art that still survive. In 1921 Van Heemskerck received a commission to equip the navy barracks in Amsterdam

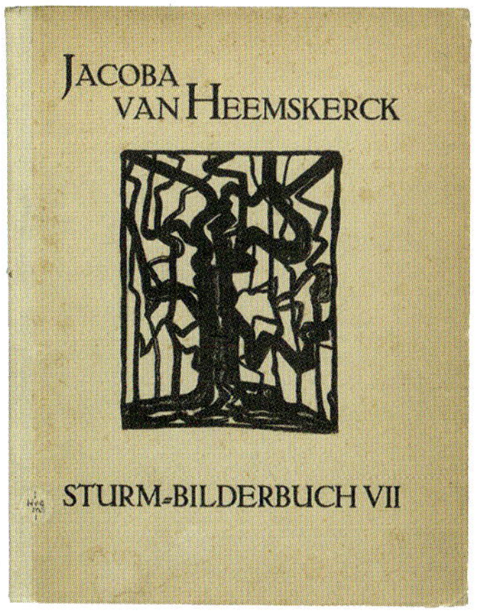

16 Jacoba van Heemskerck.
Sturm-Bilderbuch VII |
Sturm Illustrated Book VII
(Berlin: Verlag Der Sturm, 1924)

with large, stained-glass windows, a task that took her back to her father's profession and her own artistic beginnings.

Late Reputation and Reception

Despite her new artistic orientation, which was increasingly tied to the Netherlands and gave her new autonomy as an artist, Van Heemskerck remained loyal to the Waldens to the last, mainly due to their shared understanding of art. The esteem remained mutual, as the memorial exhibition in Berlin in 1924 that Herwarth Walden organised made clear; it was an honour accorded to no other female Sturm artist.[35]

During her lifetime, Van Heemskerck was highly respected as an artist; she belonged to the group that made up the heart of Der Sturm, and her work sold regularly. Presumably, her reluctance to write down her personal theories of art outside of her letters and the fact that her life came to an early end allowed the artist to fall almost completely into obscurity in Germany.[36] Much more serious, however, were the massive setbacks during the National Socialist era, which sidelined many well-known artists of the pre-war years who were—or are only now being—slowly rediscovered. Furthermore, the art historian Maaike van Rijn explains that the connection between Expressionism and anthroposophical, spiritual theories caused problematic imputations to arise, especially concerning female artists such as Van Heemskerck, some of which continue to hinder them to this day. The author detects a different, gender determined reception precisely in regard to female artists of a theosophical and anthroposophical persuasion. While, for example, Piet Mondrian's spiritual focus was advantageous for him, the 'connection between the artistic work [of women] to esoteric spiritual movements [continued] to be a great challenge for art history'.[37] In the study of art, it was not until the 1980s that scholars really began to examine the topic of how women are systematically excluded from history through structural mechanisms, which Herwarth and Nell Walden subverted with their Sturm activities, for they were exemplary in their promotion and exhibition of female artists. The last exhibition devoted to Van Heemskerck's work in Germany took place in 1983/84; in the Netherlands her work was seen in solo shows in 1924, 1933/34 and 1960. In 2005 the Kunstmuseum Den Haag (formerly Gemeentemuseum) gave new status to the artist with its presentation *Jacoba van Heemskerck: A Rediscovery*. Most recently, the group exhibition *Storm Women: Women Artists of the Avant-Garde in Berlin 1910–1932* at the Schirn Kunsthalle Frankfurt again drew attention to the artist in Germany. Today, the view of Jacoba van Heemskerck's body of work shows that her perceptions of nature, technology and the universe were not only progressive for her time, but that she remains a visionary to the present day.

1 Jacoba van Heemskerck to Herwarth Walden, letter dated 3 March 1915, quoted in Marjam Trautmann and Torsten Schrade, eds., *DER STURM: Digitale Quellenedition zur Geschichte der internationalen Avantgarde* (Digital Source Edition of the History of the International Avant-Garde) (Mainz, 2018), online: https://sturm-edition.de (accessed 2 August 2020). Van Heemskerck wrote her letters to Herwarth and Nell Walden in German.

2 Jacoba van Heemskerck always referred to the 'movement' in front of Herwarth Walden. See Van Heemskerck to Walden, 3 March 1915, as well as letters dated 8 March 1915, 21 March 1915 and 29 March 2015.

3 The most extensive biography to date remains the Van Heemskerck catalogue raisonné; see A. H. Huussen Jr and J. F. A. van Paaschen-Louwerse, *Jacoba van Heemskerck van Beest 1876–1923: Schilderes uit roeping* (Zwolle, 2005).

4 Marie Tak van Poortvliet, 'Jacoba van Heemskerck', in *Jacoba van Heemskerck: Sturm-Bilderbuch VII* (Berlin, 1924), 12.

5 D. v. d. K. Jr., 'Den tentoonstelling van werken van "l. Société des XX" in het panoramagebouw', *Nieuws van den Dag*, June 1889, quoted in Gerda Wendermann, 'Der Neo-Impressionismus und der Aufbruch der Moderne in den Niederlanden', in Burkhard Leismann, ed., *Aufbruch zur Farbe: Luministische Malerei in Holland und Deutschland*, exh. cat. Kunstmuseum Ahlen and elsewhere (Ahlen, 1996), 13–38, here 18–19.

6 See Wendermann, 'Der Neo-Impressionismus und der Aufbruch der Moderne in den Niederlanden'; and Ina Ewers-Schultz, 'Der holländische Luminismus', in Leismann, *Aufbruch zur Farbe*, 57–73.

7 Piet Mondrian to Israël Querido, *De Controleur* 20/1004, 23 October 1909, quoted in Marty Bax, 'Theosophie und Kunst in den Niederlanden 1880–1915', in Veit Loers, *Okkultismus und Avantgarde: Von Munch bis Mondrian 1900–1915*, exh. cat. Schirn Kunsthalle Frankfurt (Ostfildern, 1995), 282–94, here 292.

8 See Bax, 'Theosophie und Kunst', 282.

9 Charley Toorop, quoted in Bax, 'Theosophie und Kunst', 292.

10 Aleida B. Loosjes-Terpstra, *Moderne Kunst in Nederland 1900–1914* (Utrecht, 1959), 73.

11 L. van Ginneken, 'Documentatie: kunstenaarsbrieven Kees Spoor', *Museumjournaal*, 15 (1970), 264, quoted in Carel Blotkamp, 'Mondrian und der Luminismus: Kunst als "Übergang zu höheren Sphären"', in Leismann, *Aufbruch zur Farbe*, 75–94, here 83.

12 Herwarth Walden's real name was actually Georg Lewin (1878–1941). His first wife, Else Lasker-Schüler (1869–1945), came up with the pseudonym Herwarth Walden, as well as the name Der Sturm, which Walden used to start a publishing company in 1910. The gallery opened two years later.

13 See Arend H. Huussen Jr, 'Jacoba van Heemskerck and Herwarth Waldens "Der Sturm" in Berlin, 1913–1923', in Herbert Henkels and Arend H. Huussen Jr, eds, *Jacoba van Heemskerck, 1876–1923: Eine expressionistische Künstlerin*, exh. cat. Haus am Waldsee Berlin, Württembergischer Kunstverein Stuttgart, Rheinisches Landesmuseum (Bonn), Saarlandmuseum Saarbrücken, Städtische Galerie Erlangen (The Hague, 1983), 5-20 here 6; see also Huussen Jr and Van Paaschen-Louwerse, *Jacoba van Heemskerck van Beest*, 51.

14 See Herwarth Walden, *Expressionismus: Die Kunstwende* (Berlin, 1918; reprinted Nendeln, Liechtenstein, 1973).

15 L. H. Neitzel, 'Was ist der Sturm?', in *Der Sturm*, June exhibition 1920, 87, quoted in Antje Birthälmer, 'Der Sturm: Zentrum der Avantgarde', in Antje Birthälmer and Gerhard Finckh, eds., *Der Sturm: Zentrum der Avantgarde*, exh. cat. Von der Heydt Museum Wuppertal, 2 vols. (Bönen, 2012), 1:12-49, here 14.

16 Herwarth Walden, 'Zur Formulierung der Neuen Kunst', in Walden, *Expressionismus*, 104.

17 Lothar Schreyer also mentions a 'Weltwende', or 'global upheaval': 'This opening of spiritual reality within natural reality was the signal of the global upheaval, pointing to the future, albeit still distant, domination of the creative spirit over material, unhindered by human egoism.' Lothar Schreyer, 'Herwarth Waldens Werk', in Nell Walden and Lothar Schreyer, eds., *Der Sturm: Ein Erinnerungsbuch an Herwarth Walden und die Künstler aus dem Sturmkreis* (Baden-Baden, 1954), 114.

18 See Maaike van Rijn, '"Ich arbeite viel und denke viel über die Portraits nach": Jacoba van Heemskerck und andere Künstlerinnen beim Sturm', in Birthälmer and Finckh, *Der Sturm*, 2:348-358, here 348.

19 For more on this, see note 1. Currently, the letters from the years 1914–15 and 1919–22 are available in a newly revised digital edition.

20 The publication is based on remarkable research into the relationship between Hamburg and Der Sturm. See Volker Pirsich, *Der 'Sturm' und seine Beziehungen zu Hamburg und zu Hamburger Künstlern* (Göttingen, 1981).

21 An announcement from the art school, in *Jährliche Informationsborschüre Der Sturm* (Berlin, 1916), n.p., in *DER STURM: Digitale Quellenedition*.

22 For more on the public reviews of the *Erster Deutscher Herbstsalon*, see Mario-Andreas von Lüttichau, '"Uns ist nicht das Leben die Kunst. Aber die Kunst das Leben." (Herwarth Walden) Der Erste Deutsche Herbstsalon im Spiegel der zeitgenössischen Kritik', in Birthälmer and Finckh, *Der Sturm*, 2:243–250.

23 See Jacoba van Heemskerck to Herwarth Walden, 25 September 1914, in *DER STURM: Digitale Quellenedition*: 'we must advance with and through Germany in our art, we have you to thank for everything. [...] It is too stupid, mixing a war with art.'

24 Van Heemskerck writes about her ideas in a letter to Herwarth Walden dated 10 June 1917: 'I want to have the whole thing as non-figurative as possible. [...] Do you think that it is entirely impossible to use lines and colours instead of characters in a puppet show? With real puppets things are so material. Please write with your ideas. I want it to have a cosmic appearance', quoted in Arend H. Huussen Jr, 'Briefe von Jacoba van Heemskerck an Herwarth Walden, 1914–1922: Eine Auswahl, mit Anmerkungen und Register', in Henkels and Huussen Jr, *Jacoba van Heemskerck*, 89–121, here 107. A complete performance of the puppet show, which Van Heemskerck conceived of as a kind of tableaux vivant, never occurred, because she had to cancel her planned visit to Lothar Schreyer in Berlin. See Huussen Jr, 'Jacoba van Heemskerck and Herwarth Waldens "Der Sturm"', 16.

25 See Petra Jenny Vock, *'Der Sturm muß brausen in dieser toten Welt': Herwarth Waldens Sturm und die Lyriker des Sturm-Kreises in der Zeit des Ersten Weltkriegs: Kunstprogrammatik und Kunstlyrik einer expressionistischen Zeitschrift im Kontext* (Trier, 2006).

26 Tak van Poortvliet, 'Jacoba van Heemskerck', 11–12.

27 See Henri Bergson, *L'évolution créatrice* (Paris, 1907). The German translation, by Gertrud Kantorowicz, was published under the title *Schöpferische Entwicklung* (*Creative Evolution*) in Jena in 1912; the Dutch translation was not published until 1925. The author Anita Beloubek-Hammer describes Bergson's influence on Der Sturm as follows: 'This tendency to lean towards the "universal", so typical of the postwar years […] which manifested in rhythmical, vibrant curves, cosmic gyrations made of intertwining circles, can primarily be traced back to the influence of the vitalist philosophy of Henri Bergson. Even though Der Sturm came relatively late to the explicit exploration of this new philosophy, […] Der Sturm can be considered a kind of trade centre for Bergson's ideas about artistic life in Germany during the years around the First World War.' Anita Beloubek-Hammer, *Die schönen Gestalten der besseren Zukunft: Die Bildhauerkunst und ihr geistiges Umfeld* (Cologne, 2007), 518.

28 Willem Zeylmans van Emmichoven, 'Mein Weg zu Rudolf Steiner: Ein autobiographisches Fragment', in Emanuel Zeylmans, ed., *Willem Zeylmans van Emmichoven: Ein Pionier der Anthroposophie* (Arlesheim, 1979), 63.

29 Willem Zeylmans van Emmichoven, 'Die geistige Richtung in der neuen Malerei: Jacoba van Heemskerck' (1917), quoted in Herbert Henkels, 'Jacoba van Heemskerck: Ihr Werk', in Henkels and Huussen Jr, *Jacoba van Heemskerck*, 24–25. See also the text in this book 140 and 143.

30 On 16 October 1914 van Heemskerck wrote to Walden that she was planning on simply numbering her paintings and prints in sequence, a plan she persevered in carrying out to the last, partly to avoid fixed interpretations of her pictures. Lothar Schreyer examined this aspect with reference to Walden's understanding of art in a comparable manner: 'One hindrance is that the conceptual idea behind the image is what makes up a painting. It is an error to believe that the task of painting is to communicate intellectual or psychological content to a viewer. Only the form is essential, meaning the rhythmic, harmonious relationship between colour and form. The impact comes from the form, which moves people both in thought and in emotions, regardless of the content.' Schreyer, 'Herwarth Waldens Werk', 132.

31 Willem Zeylmans van Emmichoven became one of the leading anthroposophists in the Netherlands, and he has Van Heemskerck and her exploration of anthroposophy to thank for inspiring him to embark upon this path. See Zeylmans van Emmichoven, 'Mein Weg zu Rudolf Steiner', 62ff.

32 On 11 November 1914 Van Heemskerck wrote to Walden: 'I am working a great deal and thinking a great deal, I would so like to try painting on glass. […] If one wants to have the colours luminesce in a spiritual way then a time will come when oil paints and canvas are no longer suitable for that. You and your wife, who know my work so well, will understand what I mean and feel.' See *DER STURM: Digitale Quellenedition*.

33 In a letter on 7 August 1919 Van Heemskerck wrote that she would go her own way if Walden did not want to exhibit the glass window designs. At the 79th Sturm exhibition in Berlin (October 1919) her glass window designs were on display, but still, Van Heemskerck distanced herself a few months later from Der Sturm and at the same time reported upon her activities in the Netherlands, as can be seen in a letter to Herwarth Walden from 28 April 1920: 'I would prefer not to remain a member of the society of Sturm friends, since I am in Berlin so little I find that it is too expensive to pay 60 marks for it. […] I am quite busy with a very large order for three enormous glass windows and a door panel for a large, entirely new villa near The Hague. My designs were immediately accepted, and everything will be finished in two months. I have the whole management of the glass firing, etc.' See *DER STURM: Digitale Quellenedition.*

34 Exhibitions followed until around 1929; in 1932 Herwarth Walden gave up all of his Sturm activities and emigrated to Moscow. He was arrested in 1941 and died that same year in a prison in Saratov.

35 Walden also dedicated the *Sturm-Bilderbuch VII* (1924) to her. Rudolf Blümner and Lothar Schreyer, among others, were contributors.

36 In a letter to Walden dated 24 July 1916 on didactics at the Sturm art school, Van Heemskerck writes that she believes that the formation of theories, as Wassily Kandinsky dogmatically does, is problematic. She considered it 'dangerous to write about it as an artist [oneself]'. Quoted in Huussen Jr, 'Briefe von Jacoba van Heemskerck an Herwarth Walden', 102.

37 Maaike van Rijn, 'Bildende Künstlerinnen im Berliner "Sturm" der 1910er Jahre', dissertation, Tübingen, 2011, 223. See especially the chapters 'Aspekte einer weiblichen Identität in Selbst- und Fremddarstellung' (117–18) and 'Inszenierung und Konstruktion von Weiblichkeit in der kunsthistorischen Rezeption' (219–20). See also Ingrid Pfeiffer and Max Hollein, eds., *Sturm-Frauen: Künstlerinnen der Avantgarde in Berlin 1910–1932 / Storm Women: Women Artists of the Avant-Garde in Berlin 1910–1932*, exh. cat. Schirn Kunsthalle Frankfurt (Cologne, 2015).

Jacoba van Heemskerck

Laura Stamps

Becoming an Artist

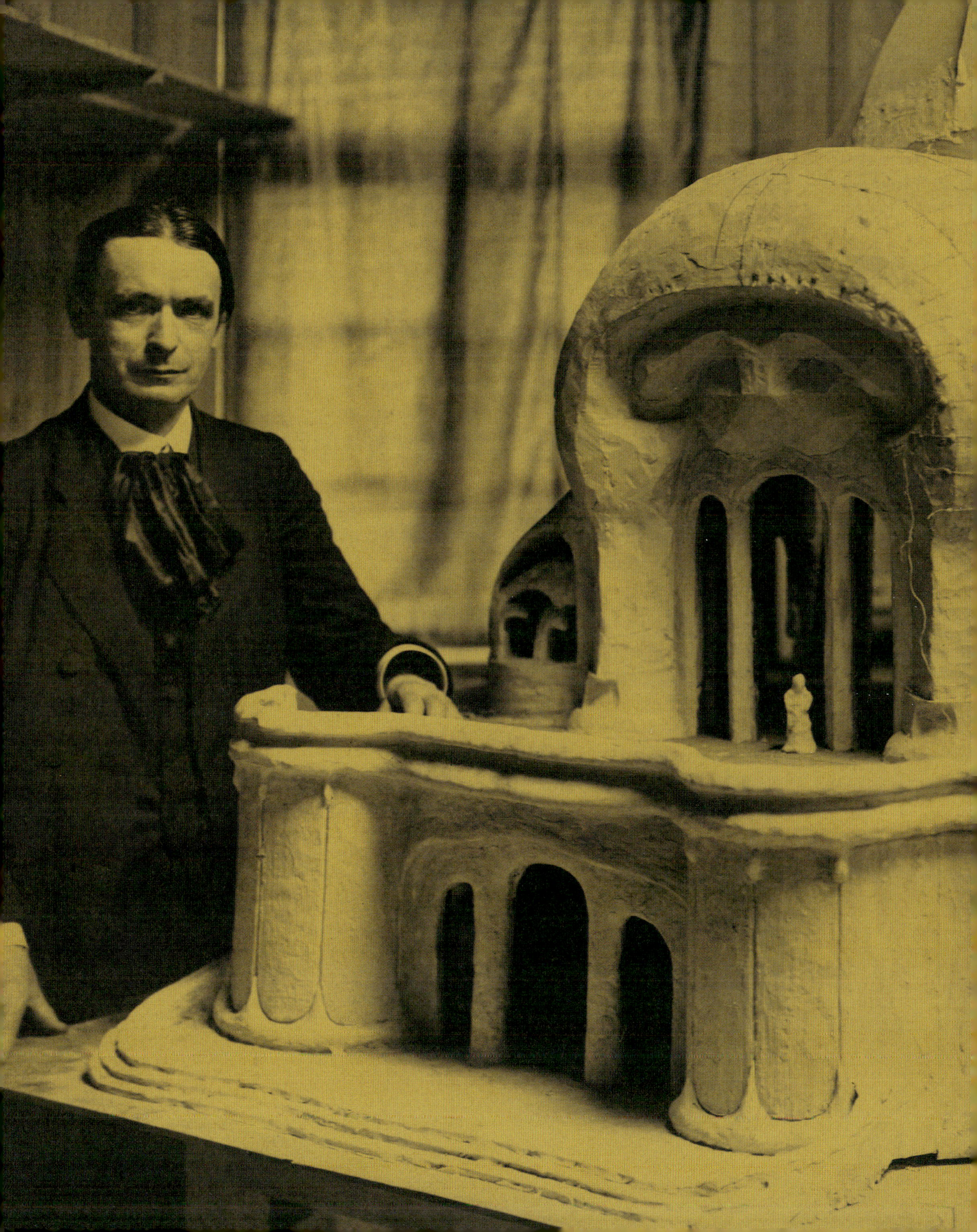

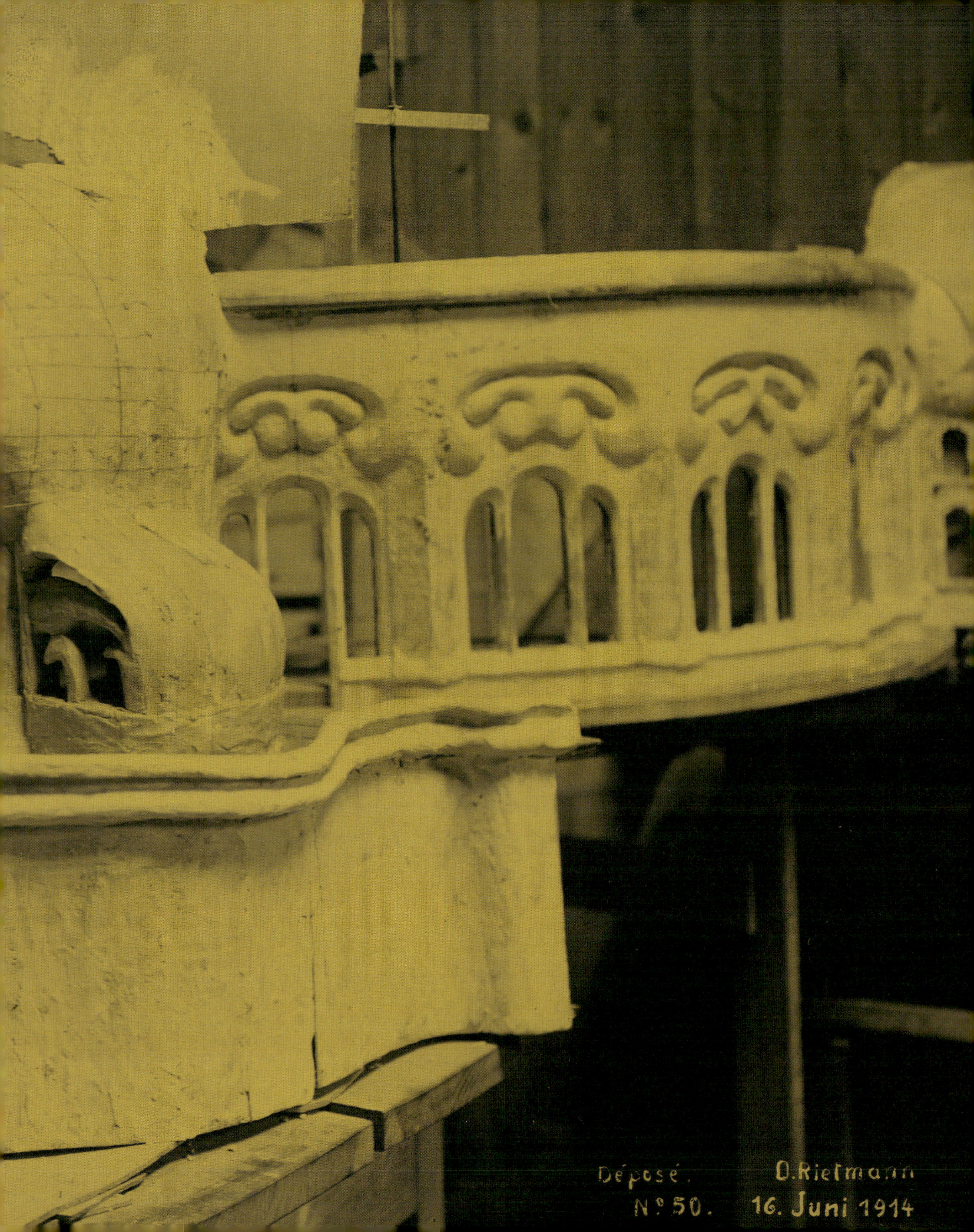
Déposé.
N° 50.
O. Rietmann
16. Juni 1914

17 Rudolf Steiner with the model of the first Goetheanum, 1914 (photo: Otto Rietmann)

18 Villa Loverendale, Domburg, c.1920

19 Jan Toorop, c.1910

20 Piet Mondrian, c.1908

21 Lodewijk Schelfhout in his studio in Paris, 1912; on the easel his painting *Les Angles*

It was 1908 when Jacoba van Heemskerck moved into Villa Loverendale, the home in Domburg that her friend Marie Tak van Poortvliet had specially built so they could spend their summers together by the sea, and Van Heemskerck could work in the studio in the garden. When she worked there on the island of Walcheren in Zeeland 'boldness came into her work'.[1] It was there that she was able to develop into a truly modern artist, something that was at the very least unusual for a woman at that time.

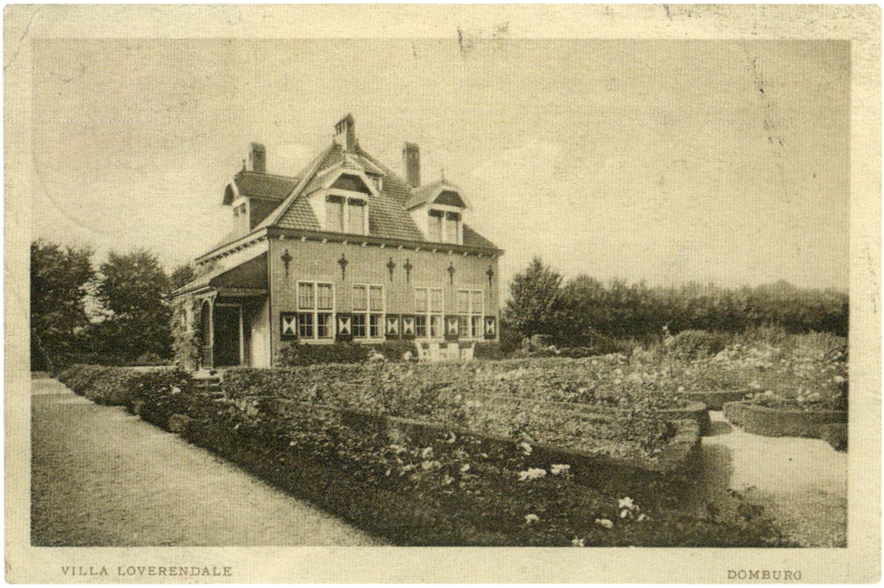

By 1908 Domburg had evolved into a vibrant artists' village, through the dedicated influence of artist Jan Toorop.[2] Contact and collaboration with the other artists Van Heemskerck met there—who, besides Toorop, also included Piet Mondrian and Lodewijk Schelfhout—was very important to her own artistic development. Another crucial factor was her membership in Herwarth Walden's gallery and art movement Der Sturm. To become 'yourself' as an artist, to develop your own visual idiom, you need others, after all. But it was not only artists who shaped Jacoba: theosophy and anthroposophy were also hugely important influences.

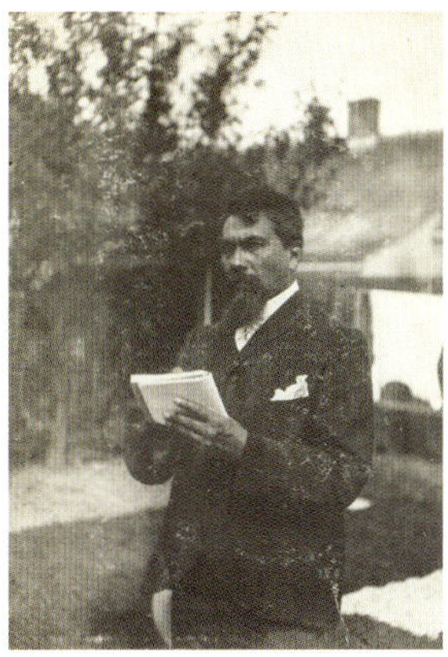

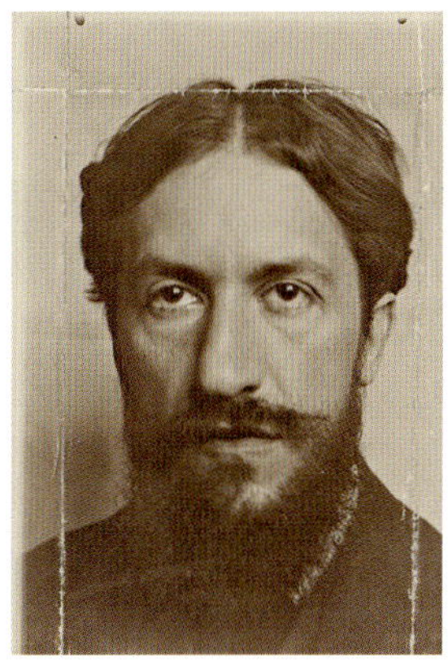

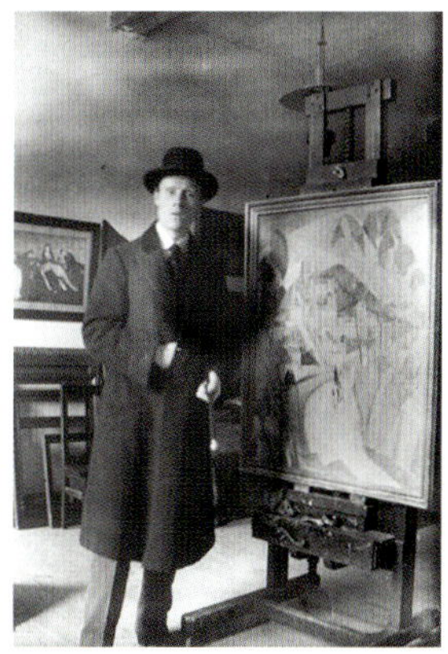

In the early twentieth century the tree was a popular motif for artists who were dealing with the spiritual in their paintings. The tree of life, as axis mundi, has been an important symbol in belief systems in various times and cultures. It symbolises the connection between the visible and the invisible, the material world and the cosmos. The tree's roots represent the underworld, the base and trunk the world around us, and the leaves and branches the infinite sky. In the Bible the tree of the knowledge of good and evil not

22 Jan Toorop
Zee en duinen te Domburg |
Sea and Dunes at Domburg 1908
Oil over a prepatory drawing in black crayon
on cardboard, 26,5 × 31,5 cm
Kunstmuseum Den Haag

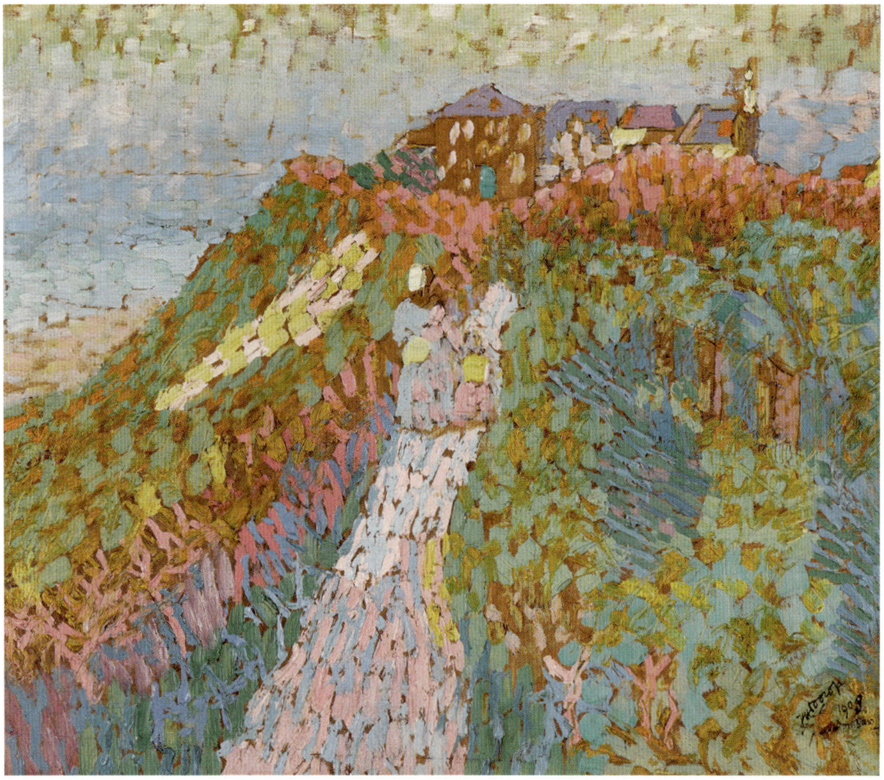

only represents man's fall from grace, but also the opposites that are an intrinsic part of life as good and evil, male and female, young and old, body and soul.[3] Trees also play a vital role in the work of Jacoba van Heemskerck. Indeed it is possible to reconstruct her making as an artist on the basis of a number of her trees which, together with sailboats, are the most common motif in her work.

Jan Toorop as an Inspiring Example

While in Domburg, Jacoba van Heemskerck regularly received advice from Toorop, who was almost twenty years older than her. He had already led a very full life. In 1882 he had moved to Brussels, whose art scene had close ties to that in Paris. A year later he became a member of Les XX (Les Vingt), a group of artists to which James Ensor and Fernand Khnopff also belonged. They used symbols to refer to the non-visible world, producing paintings that seem to depict a dream world, in which imagination, spirituality and intuition are the key ingredients. In Paris, Toorop also encountered the work of Georges Seurat and Paul Signac who, using theories of colour, applied paint in dabs of pure colour beside one another on the canvas which would then mix in the eye, creating all kinds of nuances. Toorop immediately adopted this pointillist technique, only to abandon it again a few years later in order to focus on Symbolism. But he returned to it around 1900. Toorop's pointillism was fairly precise at first, but his brushwork gradually became looser. He shifted from dots to strokes of paint in adjacent contrasting colours. Shapes appear to dissolve into colours, perfectly emulating the effect of shimmering sunlight, as in *Zee en duinen te Domburg* (*Sea and Dunes*

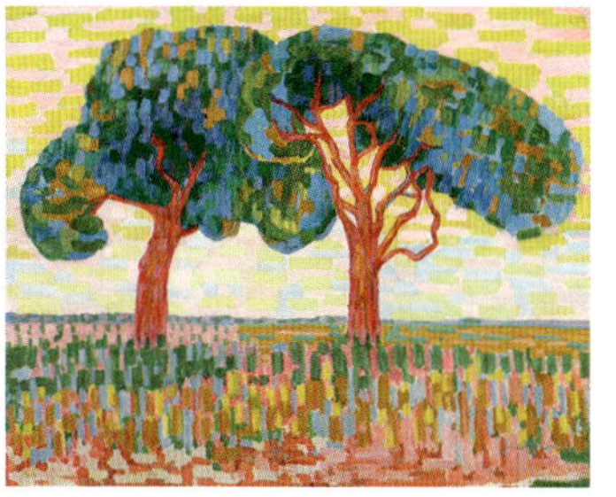

23 Jacoba van Heemskerck
Twee bomen |
Two Trees 1910
Oil on canvas, 70,5 × 88,2 cm
Kunstmuseum Den Haag

in Domburg, 1908). His work was vibrant and full of life, and it appealed to many young artists like Jacoba van Heemskerck and Piet Mondrian, and also Jan Sluijters and Leo Gestel. Together with Toorop, they developed the style known in the Netherlands as Luminism.[4]

Van Heemskerck's best-known Luminist work is *Twee bomen* (*Two Trees*, 1910). The trunks and leaves of the trees and the soil are rendered in yellows, greens, blues and reds applied with tight, short brushstrokes, while the background is made up of pink, light blue and yellow. As the brushwork appears somewhat forced, the Luminist technique seemed not to come naturally to her, but the contrast between the pastel and brighter colours nevertheless causes the trees to burst from the canvas, making this a powerful image. It was an experiment in the modern style of the time, and two aspects of it would become permanent features of her work: the urge to depict not the visible as such, but rather an experience of that reality, and the power and importance of colour in that endeavour.

In Step with Piet Mondrian

'And yet art can take us to more refined realms. I am perhaps wrong to call them spiritual realms, for anything that has form is not spiritual, I have read. Yet it is the path of ascension, away from matter.'[5] (Piet Mondrian)

Piet Mondrian first visited Jacoba van Heemskerck and Marie Tak van Poortvliet at Villa Loverendale in summer 1908. He stayed for about a week and gave Van Heemskerck some painting lessons. He did not paint anything himself while there, though he did make a few sketches of a distinctive apple tree in the garden, preliminary studies for a Luminist-influenced painting, *Avond; De rode boom* (*Evening: The Red Tree*), which he completed in 1910 (fig. 24). This painting reflects Mondrian's interest in Johann Wolfgang von Goethe's theory of colour, and his view 'that darkness seen through a perfectly transparent medium evokes a deep, dark saturated blue, whereas fading light (reflected on a tree) summons ruby red', as Hans Janssen puts it.[6] 1910 was also the year when Mondrian and Van Heemskerck became equals in their working relationship. That summer, they worked together and exchanged ideas.[7]

At the start of that year Mondrian wrote in a letter to his friend Aletta de Iongh, 'I studied the dunes and the churches most. If one does not concentrate on just a few things, one would not be able to do anything with all the beauty that exists, eh?'[8] It was in the towers and seascapes, like *Vuurtoren bij Westkapelle* (*Lighthouse at Westkapelle with Clouds*, 1908) and *Zeegezicht* (*Seascape*, 1909), that he discovered the expressive power of the horizontal and the vertical line (figs. 25, 26). He continually refined these motifs during the summers spent in Domburg (1908–14) until he managed to dematerialise them completely. He later linked 'the vertical with the male principle and the horizontal with the female principle —not in a narrow sexual sense but in the much broader sense in which Western and Eastern cultures and also theosophy understand these concepts and see them symbolised in various forms.'[9] In his understanding, the vertical, the male, denoted the spiritual and the horizontal, the female, was the material.

24 Piet Mondrian
Avond; De rode boom |
Evening: The Red Tree 1908-10
Oil on canvas, 70 × 99 cm
Kunstmuseum Den Haag

25 Piet Mondrian
Zeegezicht |
Seascape 1909
Oil on cardboard, 34,5 × 50,5 cm
Kunstmuseum Den Haag

26 Piet Mondrian
Vuurtoren bij Westkapelle |
Lighthouse at Westkapelle with Clouds 1908
Oil on canvas, 71 × 52 cm
Kunstmuseum Den Haag

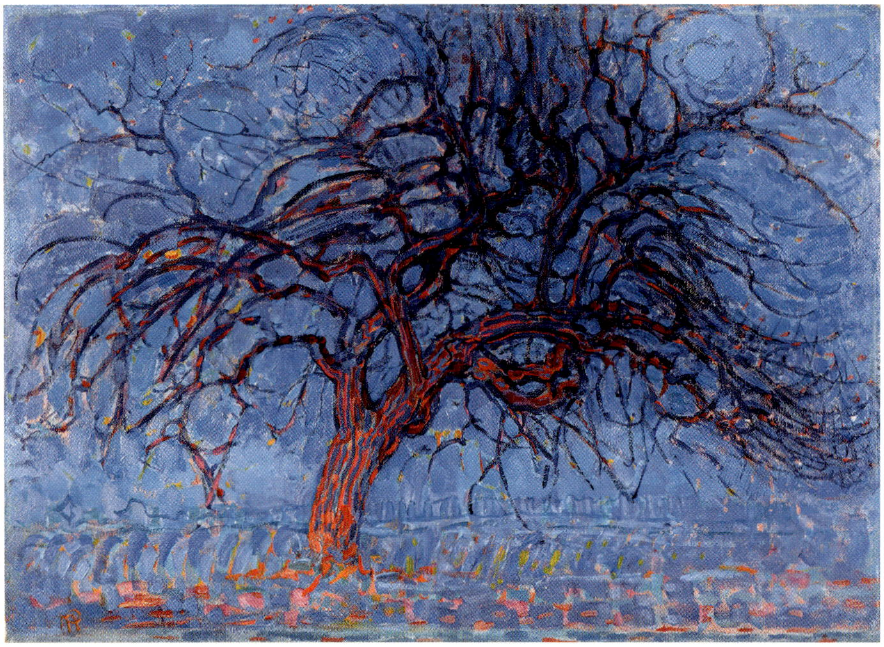

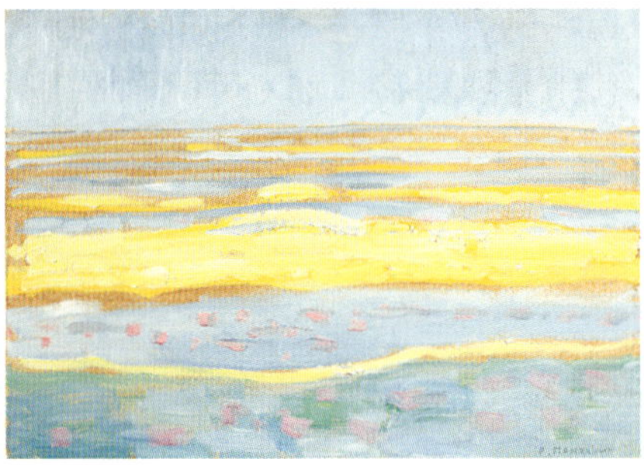

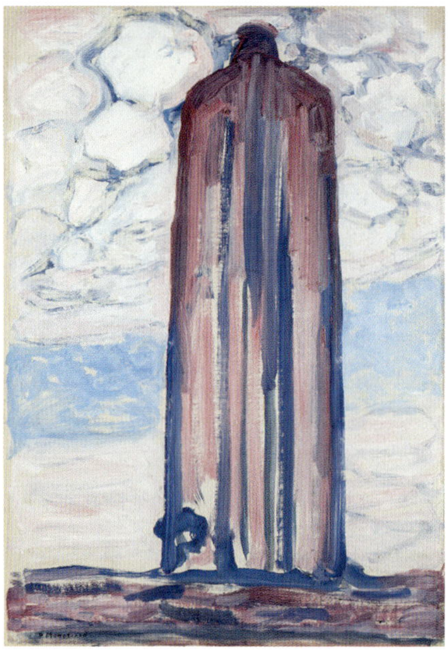

A drawing like *Pier en oceaan 4* (*Pier and Ocean 4*, 1914), consisting only of horizontal and vertical lines, some of which cross, was a vital step towards his ultimate goal to create a universal harmony through pure relationships. 'Short horizontal and vertical lines, many of them truncated [...], fill the picture plane in apparent symmetry. Yet nowhere does the image repeat; it appears the same, but is different every time. Same and different, light and dark, open and closed, flat and not flat, everything arriving at once.'[10] Mondrian took this breakthrough to its conclusion in *Compositie 10 in zwart wit* (*Composition 10 in Black and White*, 1915), where any reference to the natural world has disappeared, both from the title and from the image itself. In a review, the artist Theo van Doesburg, Mondrian's contemporary, wrote of this painting: 'Spiritually this work outweighs all the others. The impression it gives is one of Peace; the impassiveness of the soul.'[11] According to this, the male and the female are in balance in this work.

Until around 1913 Van Heemskerck and Mondrian would use each other to hone their ideas. About one year before, they both ventured into experiments with Cubism. Van Heemskerck also increasingly restricted herself to just a few motifs: trees, boats on the sea, landscapes and, later, fish. Like Mondrian, during this period she made important strides towards developing her own means of expression. And she too was endeavouring to depict the universal. In his quest, Mondrian moved increasingly 'away from matter', as he himself put it. Van Heemskerck, on the other hand, was looking for a way of visually linking the spiritual with the material, the observable,

27 Piet Mondrian
Pier en oceaan 4 |
Pier and Ocean 4 1914
Charcoal on paper, 51 × 63 cm
Kunstmuseum Den Haag

28 Piet Mondrian
Compositie 10 in zwart wit |
Composition 10 in Black and White 1915
Oil on canvas, 85,8 × 108,4 cm
Kröller-Müller Museum, Otterlo

using 'archetypes' from the visible world, like the tree, with all its symbolic meanings.

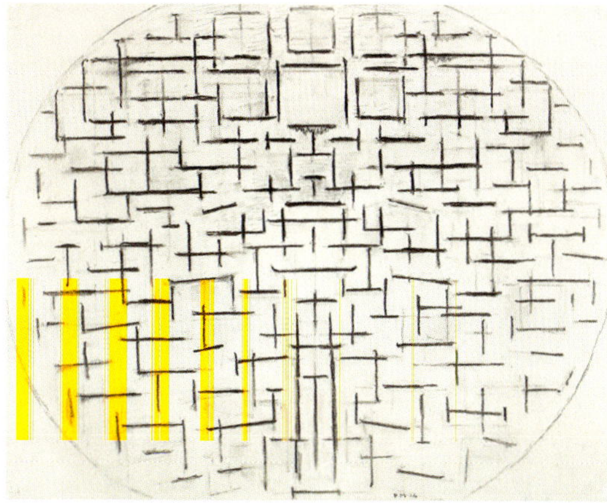

Helena Blavatsky's and Henry Steel Olcott's Theosophy

In the early twentieth century there was an international trend among artists to seek the spiritual and attempt to capture it in their work. This was prompted by a number of developments. Much of what scientists had long held to be true was drawn into question around the turn of the twentieth century. In 1886, for example, it was discovered that the atom could be split; in 1897 the electron was discovered, in 1889 radio waves, in 1895 X-rays and, in 1900, radioactivity. In that same year scientists took the first steps in the development of quantum theory, and in 1905 Albert Einstein published his special theory of relativity. Artists had always portrayed the world visible to the naked eye. But it was rapidly becoming clear that reality went far beyond the visible. What we can observe is only a fraction of what exists.[12] The Christian church had been concerned with the non-visible spiritual world for centuries. But, as in the world of science, a crisis was developing in the church, too—the Victorian crisis of faith. One of the factors behind this was the publication of Charles Darwin's *On the Origin of Species* in 1859. This study of the evolution of animals, including humans, through natural selection shook the Christian church to its foundations. If Darwin were right, the Creation story in the Bible could no longer be taken literally.[13]

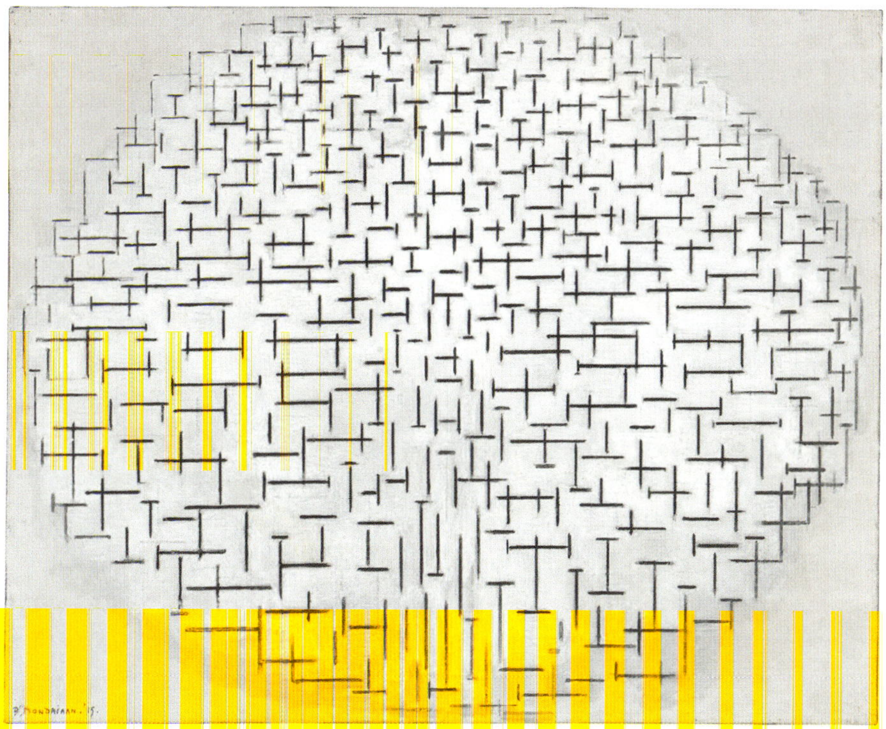

The Theosophical Society was founded by Helena Blavatsky and Henry Steel Olcott in New York on 7 September 1875. In a response to these crises, Blavatsky and

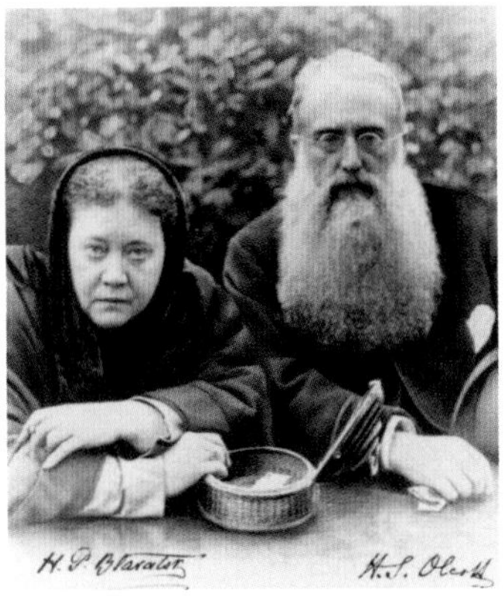

29 Helena Petrovna Blavatsky and Henry Steel Olcott, 1888

Olcott united the fundamental tenets of several religions and philosophies with new insights from science and psychology. Theosophy also held that Eastern religions such as Hinduism and Buddhism were not inferior to Western religions like Judaism and Christianity—different from a very common mindset in these times—but were in fact older and therefore closer to basic spiritual truths. The Theosophical Society thus not only attempted to unite religion and science but also to build a bridge between Eastern and Western cultures.[14]

The first objective of the Society was to form a nucleus of the universal society of humanity without distinction of origin, creed, sex, caste or colour. It offered women plenty of opportunity to hold prominent positions and develop as individuals, things that were still difficult for a woman in the world at large. After the deaths of Blavatsky and Olcott, sociologist Annie Besant became the Society's international president in 1907. The Dutch branch of the Theosophical Society opened in Amsterdam in 1891, and in 1896 a special art lodge was established, known as the Vâhana Lodge. 'Since church and science had failed with their soulless materialism, artists felt they had a special role to play in a revival of the spiritual in society.'[15] Many artists who visited the artists' village of Domburg were interested in the spiritual side of painting, and they became members of the society. Mondrian joined on 25 May 1909, and Van Heemskerck joined on 1 November 1910.[16]

Lodewijk Schelfhout and Cubism

'Heemskerck is currently Mondrianing and Picassoing. Whom will she imitate next year?'[17] (Jan Toorop)

In 1910 Mondrian produced a sketch which most probably features the same two trees seen in Van Heemskerck's painting *Two Trees*. He developed them into the Cubist painting *Paysage (Landschap)* (*Landscape*) in 1912. Van Heemskerck also began exploring the potential of Cubism that year. Both artists had seen the work of Pablo Picasso in Paris, which prompted them to start experimenting with the new style. That summer, Van Heemskerck invited the Netherlands 'first' Cubist Lodewijk Schelfhout to stay with her and Marie Tak at Villa Loverendale, where he gave her lessons. Schelfhout lived in Paris from 1903 to 1913 and was a friend of Henri Le Fauconnier, leader of the Montparnasse Cubists. Unlike the Cubists of Montmartre, Pablo Picasso and Georges Braque, the Montparnasse Cubists created a totality of prismatic surroundings and they preferred to remain closer to visible reality. They also sought to show the connection between humans and their surroundings, whether they be natural or metropolitan. This is perfectly illustrated by Le Fauconnier's *L'Abondance* (*Abundance*, 1910), in which mother and child visually merge with the surrounding landscape. Many of the Montparnasse Cubists used a restrained, earthy palette, with lots of browns, greens and greys. Although Schelfhout's work from around 1911–13 is less rhythmic and dynamic than that of the Montparnasse Cubists, it is nevertheless clearly influenced by their ideas.[18]

30 Piet Mondrian
Paysage (Landschap) |
Landscape 1912
Oil on canvas, 63 × 78 cm
Kunstmuseum Den Haag

31 Henri Le Fauconnier
L'Abondance |
Abundance 1910
Oil on canvas, 191,5 × 123 cm
Kunstmuseum Den Haag

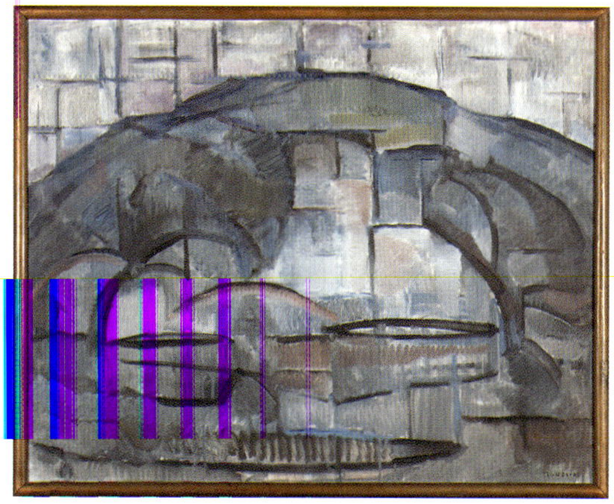

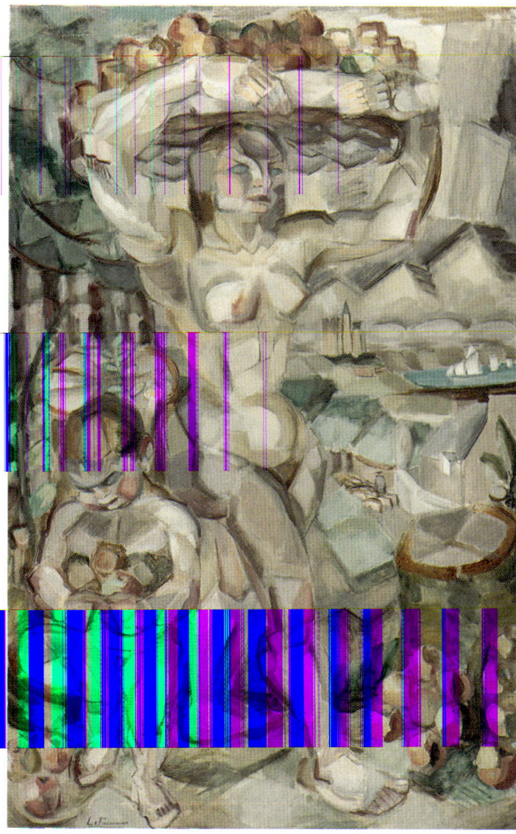

Schelfhout's influence can be seen first and foremost in the earthy colours of Van Heemskerck's *Bos I* and *II* (*Woodland I* and *II*, 1913, figs. 32, 33). In *Woodland I* she still applied the paint with loose, coarse brush-strokes reminiscent of the Luminist technique. But the choice of colours creates a diffuse light in this painting. Van Heemskerck positioned two trees in the foreground of *Woodland II* to enhance the illusion of depth, as Schelfhout often did, in *Huis tussen bomen* (*House among Trees*, 1913), for example (fig. 34). Here, Van Heemskerck fills the gaps created by the firm lines with strokes of dark green, blue and red-brown, making this painting darker than *Woodland I*. In the middle the colours have been mixed with white, so that light appears to emerge from between the trunks and underneath the leaves. Both Schelfhout and Van Heemskerck 'explained their linework as a search for peace and their juxtaposing of fields of colour as an attempt to enhance the balance'.[19] Van Heemskerck thus succeeded in her striving to present the trees and their surroundings as a single unit.

Mondrian abandoned the tree motif entirely in 1913, though he had painted his Cubist *The grijze boom* (*The Grey Tree*) in 1911 and *Bloeiende appelboom* (*Flowering Apple Tree*) in 1912, developing on the motif in *Avond; De rode boom* (*Evening: The Red Tree*) (figs. 35, 36). The paintings appear to show two stages (winter and spring) of a natural cycle.[20] Van Heemskerck's *Woodland I* and *II* could be interpreted as spring and autumn impressions of a patch of woodland. Day and night are also brought into balance. They are at any rate each other's counterpart; seen together, they emphasise her view that life features many pairs of opposites.

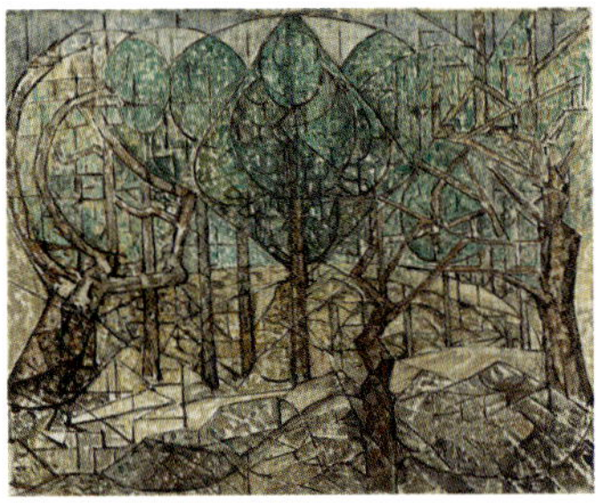

32 Jacoba van Heemskerck
Bos I | Woodland I 1913
Oil on canvas, 81 × 102 cm
Kunstmuseum Den Haag

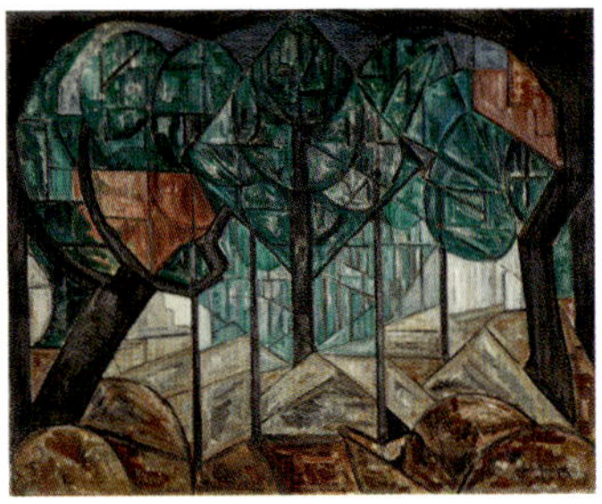

33 Jacoba van Heemskerck
Bos II | Woodland II 1913
Oil on canvas, 80,5 × 100,4 cm
Kunstmuseum Den Haag

Like the Luminist painting *Two Trees* (1910), the Cubist works *Woodland I* and *II* are deliberate experiments in a highly modern style—experiments in which Van Heemskerck not only explored the potential of line, plane and composition, but also sought ways to express the fact that everything under the sun is part of a greater cosmic whole, whether it be a tree, an animal or a human being.

Der Sturm and Wassily Kandinsky

The early years of the twentieth century saw the publication of a number of books which, for the first time, examined the work of female artists on a broader scale. They included *Women Visual Artists of the Modern Era* (1905) by Anton Hirsch and *Women and Art* (1908) by Karl Scheffler. These books were much less progressive than their titles might suggest, however, discussing female artists mainly as imitators, lacking any creativity, genius or originality of their own.[21] Jacoba van Heemskerck was keenly aware of these prejudices. Though she seldom spoke of her sex, she insisted that she be judged on the same criteria as her male colleagues.[22]

The years 1913 and 1914 were important for Jacoba, as she abandoned Cubism and came even closer to finding her own form of expression. She joined Der Sturm in 1913, Herwarth Walden's gallery and art movement that also included artists like Wassily Kandinsky. Rudolf Steiner's *Theosophy* (1904) was vital to Kandinsky. In the book Steiner described the division of the human being into three parts: body, mind and soul. He explained that a clairvoyant could see a person's mind as an aura, in colours that reflected their ideas and emotions. Steiner used Goethe's theory of colours to devise his own that would later become the basis of a separate branch of theosophy known as anthroposophy.[23]

Van Heemskerck was probably aware of the spiritual significance Steiner attributed to colours around 1908.[24] But it was not until she became a member of Der Sturm in 1913 that she started to use expressive colours and stopped using descriptive titles because, as she explained a few years later, 'colour and lines speak a different language to us all, which should not be specified in the title.'[25] Although she sometimes chose the Dutch word 'compositie' followed by a number as her title, she mainly used the German word 'Bild'.[26] In *Bild no. 10* (*Image no. 10*, 1914) a red tree fills the image against a dark blue background with green highlights (fig. 37). Both the use of colour and the form language are expressive, and immediately evoke a sense of energy. Any symbolic interpretation of the work is also in keeping with this sensation. The colour red could express the female, while blue could symbolise the male and green harmony. It is tempting to think that Van Heemskerck was trying here to allude to the fact that she had managed to balance the influence of her male fellow artists with her own inner voice. At the top of the tree trunk there is a yellow patch with small dots of black paint that resembles the pistil at the heart of a flower, a possible symbol of fertility and new life. The work is full of black lines, but Van Heemskerck painted white, angular patches between the branches, which appear to grow out of the trunk like the new emerging from the old.[27]

Van Heemskerck began to reject the artists who had been so important to her development, even calling Mondrian 'ossified'.[28]

34 Lodewijk Schelfhout
Huis tussen bomen |
House among Trees 1913
Oil on canvas, 197 × 158 cm
Private collection

35 Piet Mondrian
De grijze boom |
The Grey Tree 1911
Oil on canvas, 79,7 × 109,1 cm
Kunstmuseum Den Haag

36 Piet Mondrian
Bloeiende appelboom |
Flowering Apple Tree 1912
Oil on canvas, 78,5 × 107,5 cm
Kunstmuseum Den Haag

Der Sturm, which encompassed a huge stylistic diversity, gave Van Heemskerck scope to develop her own form of expression. The movement was, after all, about the expression of the artist's inner life. This also gave women—in a world that regarded them at best as imitators—the opportunity to articulate their own visions. One might conclude that this was why Der Sturm represented no fewer than thirty female artists, from Sonia Delaunay to Gabriele Münter, which was unique at the time.[29]

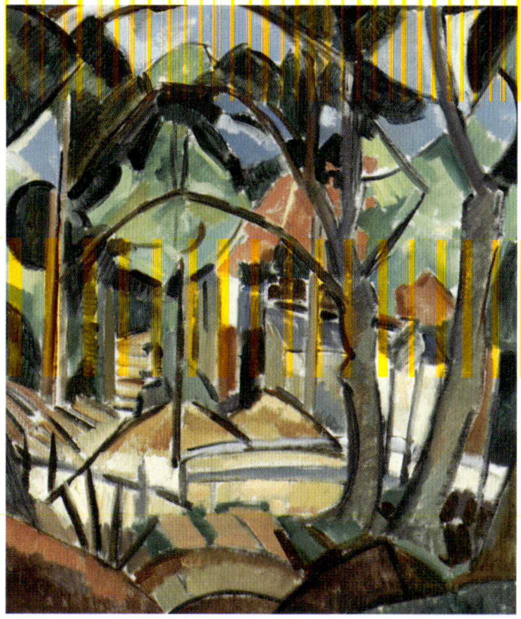

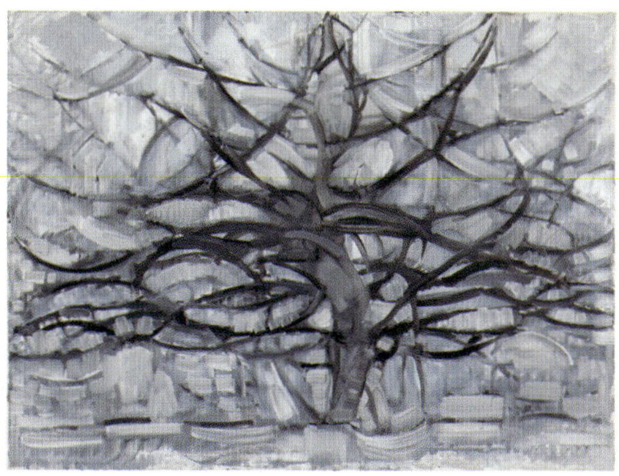

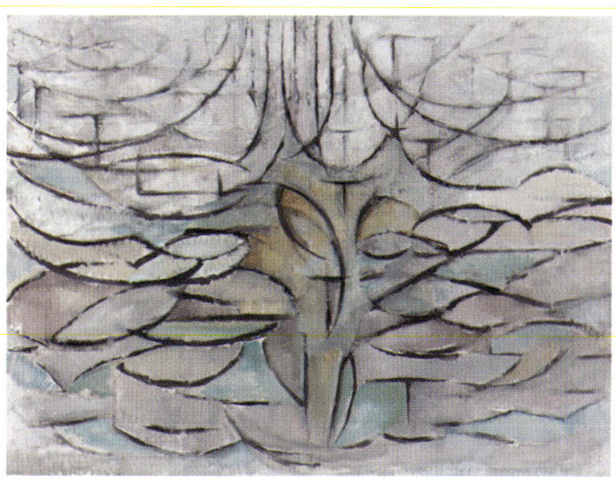

Jacoba van Heemskerck was Walden's favourite. She had ten solo shows at his gallery, and her woodcuts were published on the cover of *Der Sturm* magazine more frequently than any other artist's. Many are strictly modern compositions. On the cover of *Der Sturm* volume 5, no. 23/24 of March 1915, for example, we see a number of trees consisting of planes and lines in black and white (fig. 38). The large tree in the foreground spreads its branches, providing a base for the small trees in the background. Van Heemskerck thus combined all the visual elements: the tree and the wood, the large and the small, and the close and the distant. Here, she conforms to another expressionist ideal, which was to give a sense of totality—something we already encountered in the work of the Montparnasse Cubists.[30]

For a long time, the opinion of Herwarth and Nell Walden mattered greatly to Jacoba van Heemskerck.[31] The couple regularly visited Domburg in summer, and they also went to The Hague, where Van Heemskerck and Tak van Poortvliet spent the rest of the year living in separate homes. From 1916 onwards Van Heemskerck went to Berlin

37 Jacoba van Heemskerck
Bild no. 10 | **Image no. 10** 1914
Oil on canvas, 56,1 × 48,3 cm
Kunstmuseum Den Haag

38 *Der Sturm*, vol. 5, No. 23/24 (1915), cover

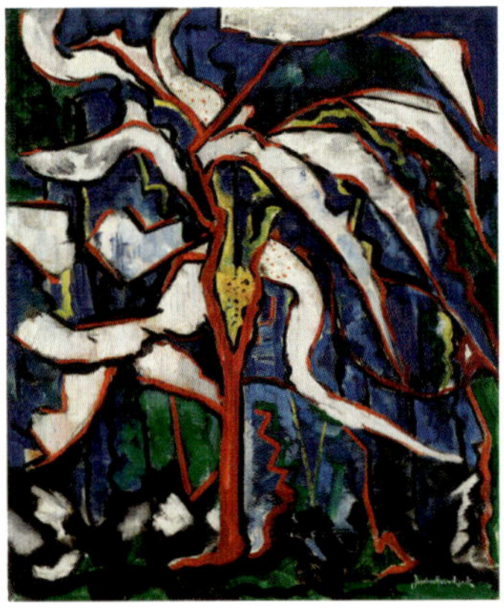

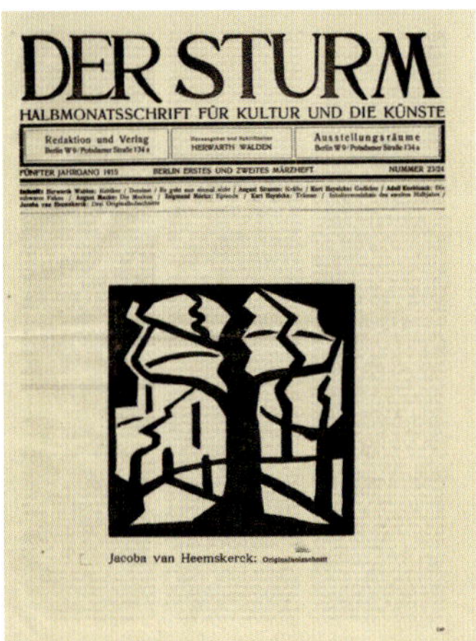

every year to teach at Walden's Der Sturm Kunstschule, giving painting lessons at first, and later teaching glass painting and theory of colour. She delved into Wassily Kandinsky's theory of art for her teaching. In his *Concerning the Spiritual in Art* (1912) he illustrated the process leading to the 'age of great spirituality' with a triangle. According to him at the top were the few people who had attained full spiritual development, and at the bottom were those who still had a long way to go. There were artists at every level of the triangle because —he was convinced—they had a particular feel for spiritual development.[32] Just like the meandering line we often see in Kandinsky's work, the triangle or pyramid also appeared regularly in Van Heemskerck's work in 1916 and 1917, at the height of the First World War. One example is *Bild no. 65* (*Image no. 65,* 1917), featuring in the foreground the black trunk of a tree from which a purple meandering path emerges, dominating the landscape: an 'apocalyptic landscape' in dark greens and blues and an ominous red, in which three narrow white, elongated triangles appear to reflect the hope of better, more spiritual times. Kandinsky regarded total abstraction as a reflection of this new spiritual world order. Van Heemskerck, on the other hand, would always continue to refer to the natural world in her work, however minimally, offering her viewers a small element of familiarity.

Having closely explored Kandinsky's ideas, Van Heemskerck informed Walden that she largely agreed with him, but that she found him too dogmatic.[33] She developed a teaching method that allowed choice of colour and composition to come from the purely personal. In 1917 Van Heemskerck and Tak van Poortvliet opened a Dutch branch of Der Sturm Kunstschule in The Hague, where only three students were taught one day a week, so that she could give them individual attention. In 1919 Walden became a Communist. This, combined with the fact that Van Heemskerck was concerned about the quality of the work of some new Der Sturm members, caused her to distance herself from him, though she continued to show at Der Sturm exhibitions.[34]

Rudolf Steiner's Anthroposophy

Steiner was expelled from the Theosophical Society in 1913 because he disapproved of the fact that Annie Besant had declared the Indian philosopher and theosophist Jiddu Krishnamurti to be the Maitreya, the messiah who—according to theosophical teaching—would guide humanity to a 'New Age'.[35] That same year, Steiner became the spiritual leader of the Anthroposophical Society. 'Anthroposophy is a path to insight that seeks to connect the spiritual in humans to the spiritual in the cosmos. It reveals itself in human beings as a craving of the heart and of feeling,' Steiner explained.[36] He was convinced that he could best convey his ideas to his followers through the arts. In Dornach, close to the Swiss city of Basel, he had built the Goetheanum, the School of Spiritual Science. It was a Gesamtkunstwerk combining architecture, painting and sculpture in a space for theatre and eurythmy.[37]

Jacoba van Heemskerck and Marie Tak van Poortvliet joined the Anthroposophical Society in 1915. Anthroposophy became a powerful force in Van Heemskerck's life. She even set up an altar to Steiner in a cupboard in her studio. His ideas about colour

39 Herwarth and Nell Walden in the dining room of their house, Potsdamer Straße, Berlin (on the wall two paintings by Marc Chagall), 1916

40 Wassily Kandinsky, *c.*1913 (photo: Marta Wolff)

41 Wassily Kandinsky
Bild mit weisser Form | **Painting with White Form** 1913
Oil on canvas, 120,3 × 139,8 cm
Kunstmuseum Den Haag – on permanent loan by the Guggenheim Museum, New York

42 Jacoba van Heemskerck
Bild no. 65 | **Image no. 65** 1917
Oil on canvas, 111 × 130,5 cm
Kunstmuseum Den Haag

and the way he used it in the stained-glass windows in the Goetheanum inspired Van Heemskerck to make her own colours 'leuchtend geistlich' (radiantly spiritual).[38] This led her to start painting on glass in 1916, which she had considered already two years before.

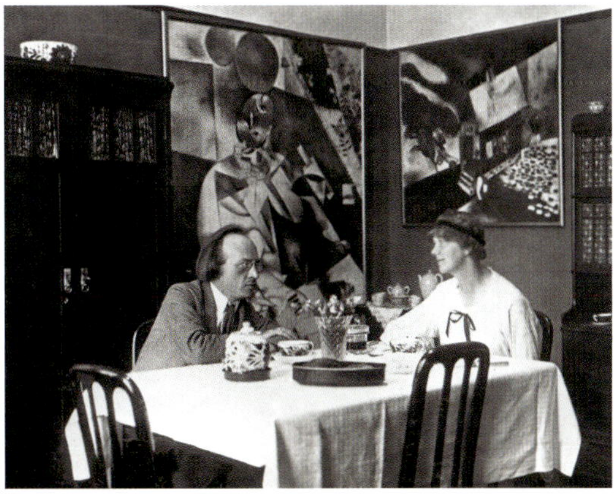

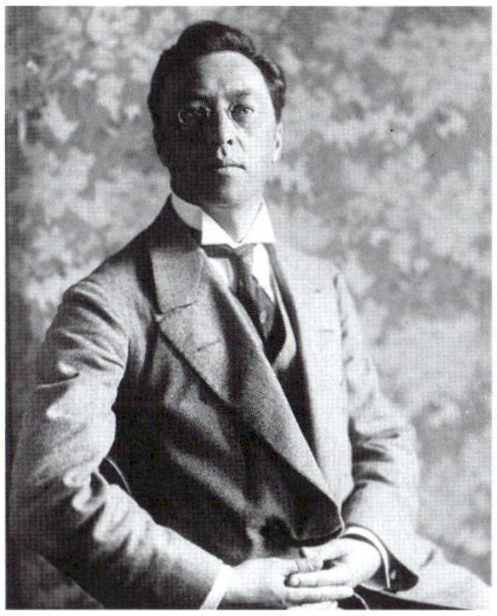

For Van Heemskerck, 1918 was a year of change. She painted a number of aura portraits based on Steiner's theory. According to Steiner only a clairvoyant could see auras, so it seems likely Van Heemskerck believed she possessed this gift. This was also the year in which she consolidated her own palette, almost always using black and white, green, red, blue, purple and yellow-orange to some extent. Her work was now 'more rhythmic and dynamic', the contours appear to dissolve, everything merges, everything becomes one.[39] Besides painting and glass painting she now also began to work with stained glass and glass mosaic, decorative art forms that were regarded as inferior to painting at the time. In Van Heemskerck's hands, however, they were all equal.

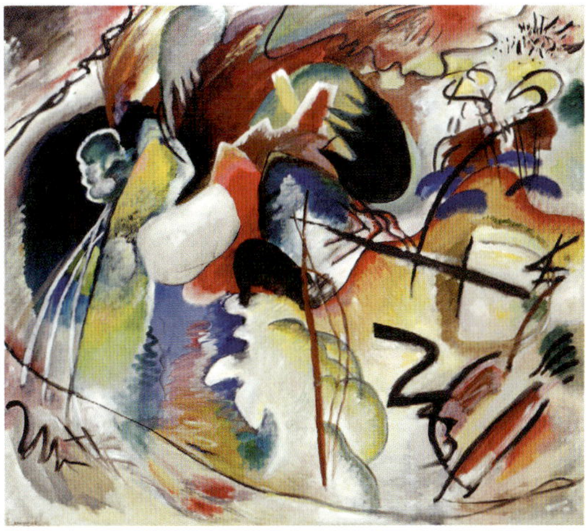

The painting *Bild no. 107 (Image no. 107)*, the stained-glass design *Compositie naar ontwerp no. 19 (Boom)* (*Composition after Design no. 19 (Tree))* and the glass mosaic *Compositie (Boom)* (*Composition (Tree))*, all from 1920, depict more or less the same motif (figs. 43-45). Although the painting features a tree and the colours can be interpreted symbolically, the immediate experience of colours and their impact on the viewer's mood are the key factors in this work. The meandering play of lines suggests movement, a dynamic involving all the colours, which might evoke a strong

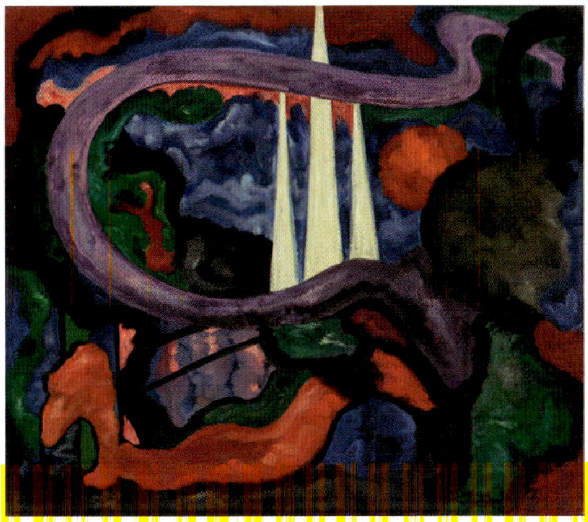

43 Jacoba van Heemskerck
Bild no. 107 |
Image no. 107 1920
Oil on canvas
95 × 75,5 cm
Kunstmuseum Den Haag

44 Jacoba van Heemskerck
Compositie naar ontwerp no. 19 (Boom) |
Composition after Design no. 19 (Tree) 1920
Stained glass
107,5 × 80,5 cm
Kunstmuseum Den Haag

45 Jacoba van Heemskerck
Compositie (Boom) |
Composition (Tree) 1920
Mosaic of coloured glass
107,5 × 93,5 cm
Kunstmuseum Den Haag

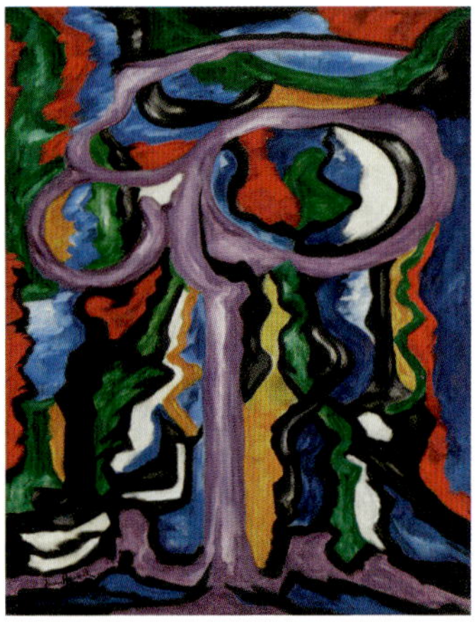

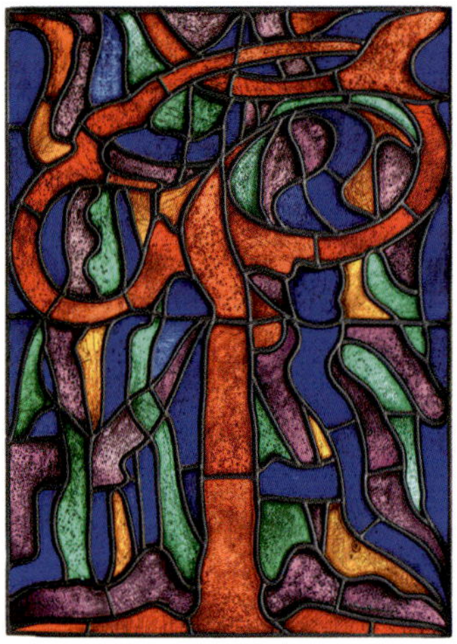

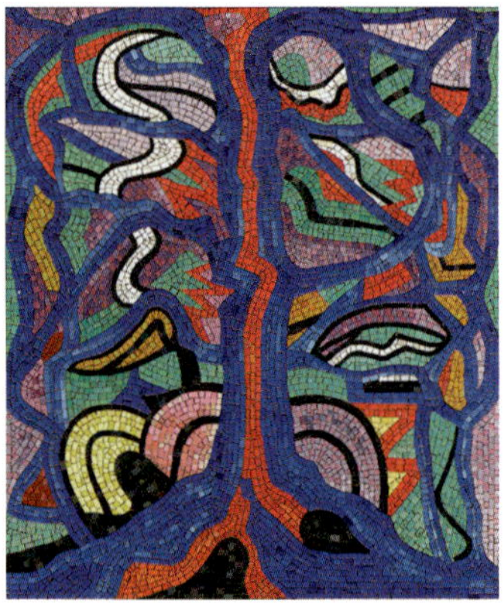

sense of vitality in the viewers. But it is in the stained-glass design that Van Heemskerck literally made her colours 'leuchtend geistlich'. In coloured glass the impact of the colour varies depending on the intensity and angle of the light. This originally decorative art form fitted Van Heemskerck like a glove. The sense of vitality that painting elicits is even more profound in this medium, where it is elevated to a spiritual experience. Although the painting and the stained-glass design depict a tree, without knowing this one can perceive them as purely abstract.

The glass mosaic *Composition (Tree)* (1920) appears to evolve from the painting and the stained-glass design, but here it is the symbolism that is the most prominent feature. A blue tree fills the entire picture plane. The trunk has a red core and divides the image vertically in two. The blue branches do not extend upwards, but turn down towards the earth, where they appear to take root—the tree as an eternal cycle linking heaven and earth, a closed circle that brings opposites into harmony. After an age of overwhelmingly male culture, Rudolf Steiner believed an age of cooperation between male and female forces was dawning, a union of the spiritual and the physical. Van Heemskerck seems to illustrate these ideas in this glass mosaic. Behind the tree are three semi-spheres, one pink, one light blue and one pale yellow: pink as a symbol of the female age, light blue for the male age and yellow for the coming age when both forces would come together.[40]

'Art is my life. It is so wonderful that I am able to express my ideas,' Van Heemskerck once wrote.[41] She celebrated her life as an artist in these three works, playing with the traditional hierarchy of art forms, using techniques from decorative art in her own autonomous fine art. She cared nothing for the prevailing conventions. Using this variety of techniques, she reveals both a symbolism that becomes abstract and an abstraction that turns out to be symbolic. She thus succeeded in connecting the spiritual and the material, thereby representing a new world order, just as Kandinsky aspired to do. Van Heemskerck became a truly modern artist by meeting the influence of male artists and thinkers with her own female voice. In her quest for harmony as an expression of the universal, she embodied in her attitude to life and in her work the age that Steiner believed was imminent, a future in which male and female forces would be in balance and sex would no longer determine one's fate. A future which now, a century later, is finally beginning to take shape.

1 See Jacqueline van Paaschen-Louwerse, 'In Domburg komt ief in werk Jacoba van Heemskerck', in Gemeentemuseum Den Haag, ed., *Aan Zee*, exhibition magazine (The Hague, 2018), 36–37, here 36.

2 According to new research results by Francisca van Vloten, Jan Toroop first went to Domburg in 1885; he spent every summer there from 1903 onwards.

3 See, among others, L. M. Almering-Strik, *Lodewijk Schelfhout: Nederlands eerste kubist* (Zwolle, 2018), 47.

4 See Laura Stamps, 'Jan Toorop: Spilfiguur van de kunstenaars-kolonie', in Gemeentemuseum Den Haag, *Aan Zee*, 10–13, here 10.

5 Piet Mondrian, quoted from Israël Querido, 'Van menschen en dingen', *De Controleur*, 23 October 1909.

6 Hans Janssen, *Piet Mondriaan in het Gemeentemuseum Den Haag* (Zwolle, 2008), 109.

7 Ibid., 107ff.; see also A. H. Huussen Jr and J. F. A. van Paaschen-Louwerse, *Jacoba van Heemskerck van Beest 1876–1923: Schilderes uit roeping* (Zwolle, 2005), 35–36.

8 Letter from Piet Mondrian to Aletta de Iongh, dated 'Sunday evening' [January–early February 1910], Kröller-Müller Museum archives, Otterlo.

9 Carel Blotkamp, *Mondriaan: Destructie als kunst* (Zwolle, 1994), 49.

10 Janssen, *Piet Mondriaan*, 199.

11 Theo van Doesburg, 'Kunstkritiek: Moderne Kunst, Stedelijk Museum Amsterdam: Expositie Mondriaan, Leo Gestel, Sluijters, Schelfhout, Le Fauconnier', *Eenheid*, 283 (6 November 1915).

12 This is explained by science historian Ernst Peter Fischer in Halina Dyrschka's documentary *Hilma af Klint: Beyond the Visible* (2019).

13 See Simon Heffer, *High Minds: Victorians and the Birth of Modern Britain* (London, 2013).

14 See Isaac Lubelsky, 'New York City, 1875: The Birth of Theosophy', in Kurt Almqvist and Louise Belfrage, eds., *Hilma af Klint: Visionary* (Stockholm, 2020), 59–69.

15 Huussen Jr and Van Paaschen-Louwerse, *Jacoba Heemskerck van Beest*, 25.

16 See Jacqueline van Paaschen, *Mondriaan en Steiner: Wegen naar nieuwe beelding* (The Hague, 2017), 47ff.; see also Huussen Jr and Van Paaschen-Louwerse, *Jacoba van Heemskerck van Beest*, 36.

17 Postcard from Jan Toorop to Lodewijk Schelfhout, dated 7 August 1913, Lodewijk Schelfhout Archive, RKD – Netherlands Institute for Art History, The Hague.

18 Schelfhout was also the one who introduced Mondrian to the art scene in Paris. *Landscape* (1912) shows that he had been influenced by Schelfhout's way of working. See also Mabel Hoogendonk and Arnold Ligthart, *Henri Le Fauconnier: Kubisme en Expressionisme in Europa* (Bussum, 1993), 16–25; and Almering-Strik, *Lodewijk Schelfhout*, 39–50.

19 Ibid., 59.

20 See Blotkamp, *Mondriaan*, 70.

21 See Ingrid Pfeiffer, 'Sturm-Frauen: Oder wie Herwarth Walden in grossem Stil die Künstlerinnen der Avantgarde gefördert hat', in Ingrid Pfeiffer and Max Hollein, eds., *Sturm-Frauen: Künstlerinnen der Avantgarde in Berlin 1910–1932*, exh.cat. Schirn Kunsthalle Frankfurt (Cologne, 2015), 12–23, here 12.

22 See Maaike van Rijn, '"Ich arbeite viel und denke viel über Portraits nach": Jacoba van Heemskerck und andere Künstlerinnen beim Sturm', in Antje Birthälmer and Gerhard Finck, eds., *Der Sturm: Zentrum der Avantgarde*, exh. cat. Von der Heydt-Museum, Wuppertal, 2 vols. (Bönen, 2012), 2:343–58, here 352.

23 Steiner also produced artistic works himself. He wrote four plays, which he called mystery plays. In the first, *The Portal of Initiation*, he explained how abstract art—the spiritualisation of art—had emerged, using the artistic career of painter Johannes Thomasius. Kandinsky is known to have seen performances of all four mystery plays. He produced his first abstract work in 1913, the year of the final performance; see Huussen Jr and Van Paaschen-Louwerse, *Jacoba van Heemskerck van Beest*, 69.

24 It is difficult to ascertain precisely when she first encountered the theory of colour, but Jacqueline van Paaschen suspects it was 1908 (possibly through Mondrian). This requires further investigation. She also made a number of aura portraits in 1918.

25 Letter from Jacoba van Heemskerck to Herwarth Walden, 14 January 1920, Staatsbibliothek zu Berlin, Sturm-Archive, Jacoba van Heemskerck (from here on referred to as Sturm-Archive, JvH). See also Marjam Trautmann and Torsten Schrade, eds., *DER STURM: Digitale Quellenedition zur Geschichte der internationalen Avantgarde* (Digital Source Edition of the History of the International Avant-Garde) (Mainz, 2018), online: https://sturm-edition.de (accessed 16 October 2020).

26 This will also be connected to the fact that, until 1922, her work was sold exclusively by Herwarth Walden, and therefore mainly to Germans.

27 Kandinsky regarded the trunk of a tree as the Old Testament and the branches that grew from it as the New, emerging out of it. Based in part on a description in Huussen Jr and Van Paaschen-Louwerse, *Jacoba van Heemskerck van Beest*, 73.

28 Letter from Jacoba van Heemskerck to Herwarth Walden, 9 February 1915, Sturm-Archive, JvH. See also *DER STURM: Digitale Quellenedition*.

29 See Pfeiffer, 'Sturm-Frauen', 12–23.

30 See Lea Schleiffenbaum, 'Jacoba van Heemskerck: "Man muss so ganz tief heraus immer Neues schaffen"', in Pfeiffer and Hollein, *Sturm-Frauen*, 138–41.

31 This is apparent from the 269 letters and postcards from van Heemskerck to the couple that are kept in the Sturm-Archive, Berlin.

32 See Huussen Jr and Van Paaschen-Louwerse, *Jacoba van Heemskerck van Beest*, 123.

33 She said as much in a letter to Walden of 24 July 1916, Sturm-Archive, JvH.

34 See Karla Bilang, *Frauen im Sturm: Künstlerinnen der Moderne* (Berlin, 2013), especially the chapter 'Moderne und Anthroposophie: Jacoba van Heemskerck, Den Haag', 69–80.

35 The coming of the Maitreya was a sensitive issue among theosophists. The theosophical liturgy regarded the Maitreya as an incarnation of the divine Supreme Being. His coming was so eagerly awaited that Blavatsky warned that he was unlikely to manifest himself in the near future. By contrast, Besant and Charles Webster Leadbeater, another prominent member, actively searched for the Maitreya.

36 Rudolf Steiner, *Kerngedachten van de antroposofie [Wat Michaël wil]*, 1924, Dutch translation (Zeist, 1997), 15.

37 Jacoba van Heemskerck and Marie Tak van Poortvliet did not actually visit the Goetheanum until it opened to the public in 1920, though they kept up-to-date with developments involving the building.

38 In a letter to Walden written on 11 November 1914 Van Heemskerck had already indicated that there would come a time when oils and canvas would no longer be suitable if one sought to make colours 'leuchtend geistlich'. Sturm-Archive, JvH. See also *DER STURM: Digitale Quellenedition*.

39 Bilang, *Frauen im Sturm*, 73.

40 See Huussen Jr and Van Paaschen-Louwerse, *Jacoba van Heemskerck van Beest*, 160.

41 Jacoba van Heemskerck in a letter to Herwarth Walden, 11 November 1914, Sturm-Archive, JvH. See also *DER STURM: Digitale Quellenedition*.

Jacoba van Heemskerck

Jacqueline van Paaschen

A Litany for the Dead: Sailing Boats

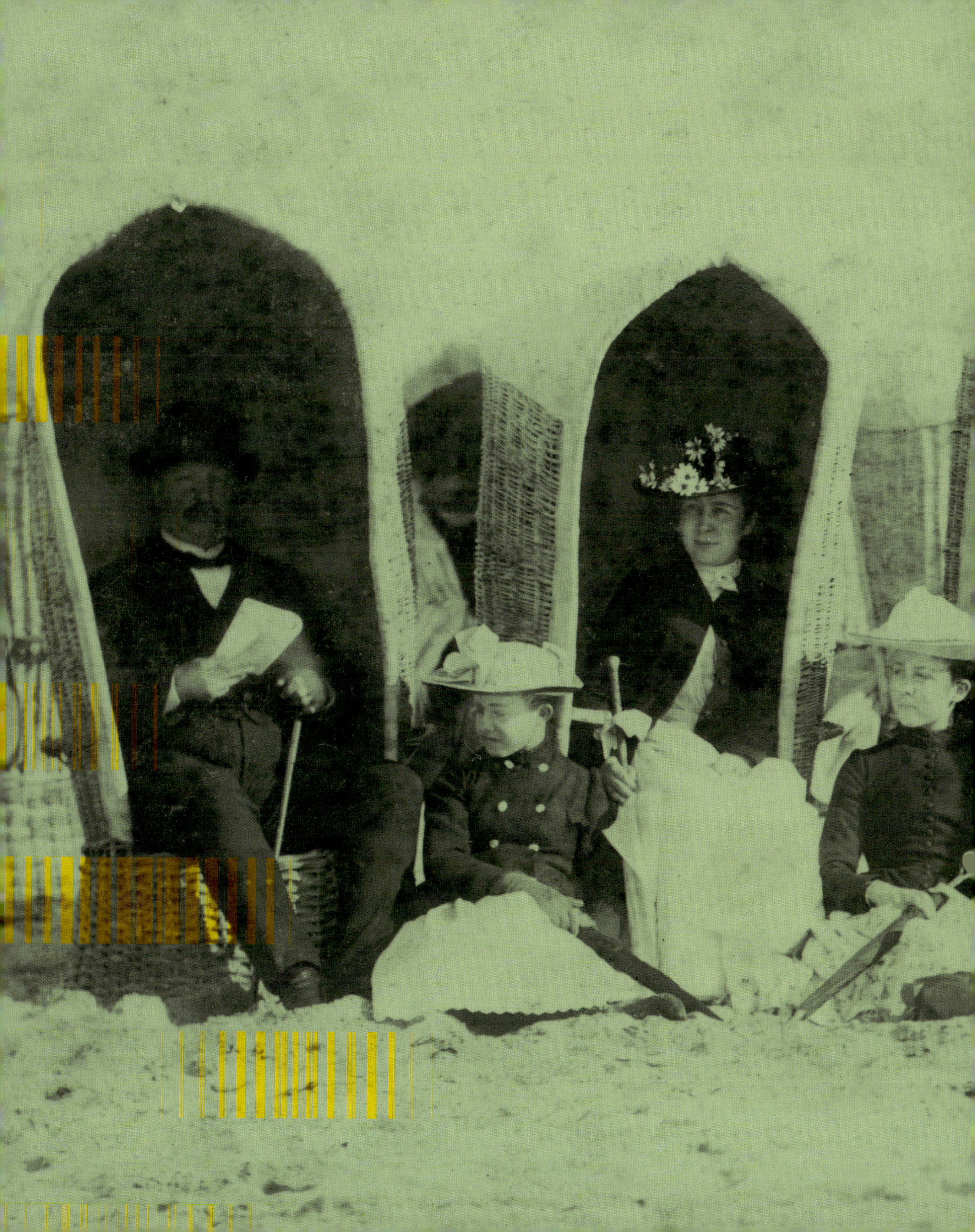

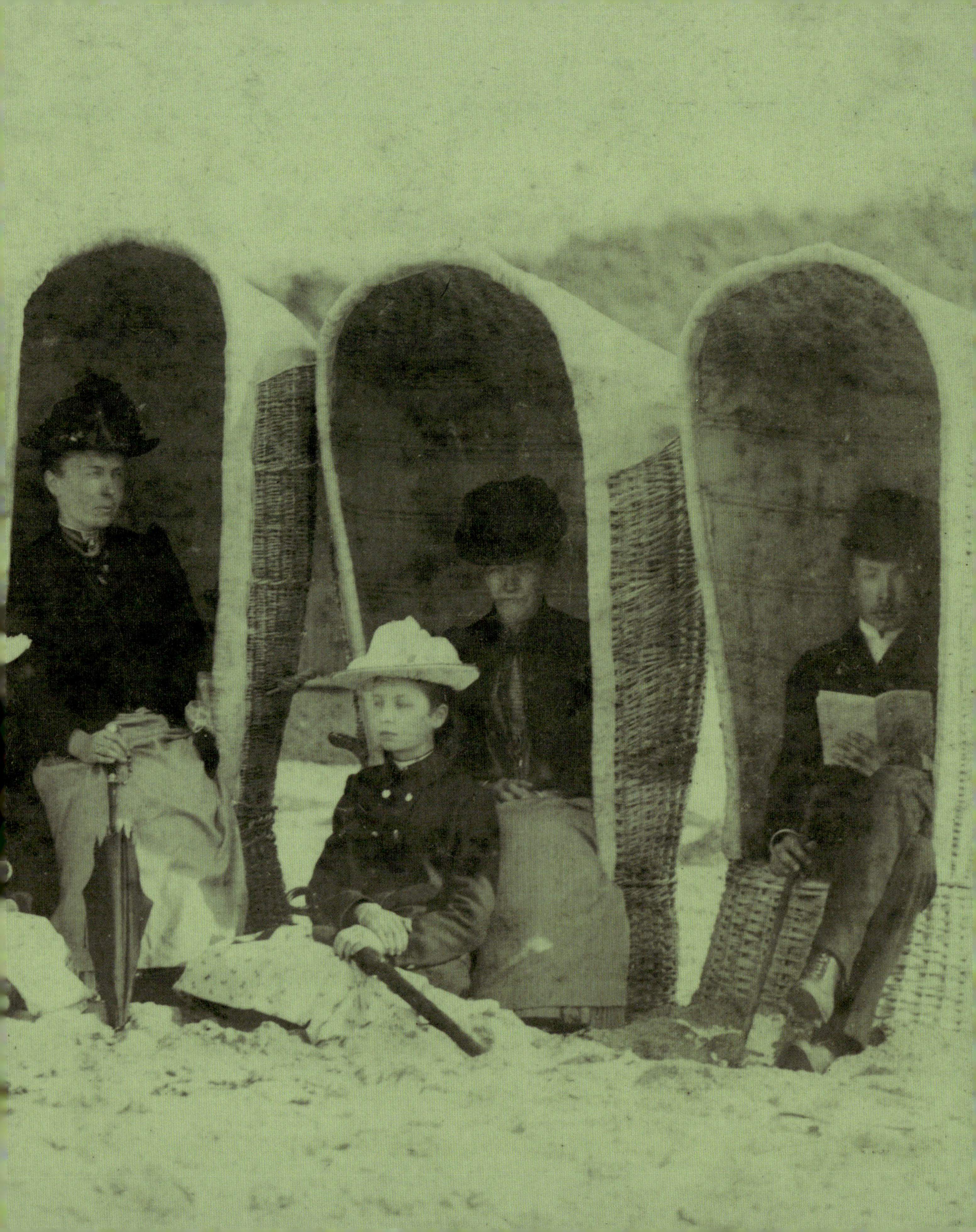

46 Family Tak van Poortvliet and Jacoba van Heemskerck (third from the left, wearing a hat with flowers) on the beach at Domburg, 1900 (photo: E. Helder)

47 Jacoba van Heemskerck
Bild no. 2 | **Image no. 2** 1914
Oil on canvas, 100 × 120 cm
Private collection

'When the double doors to the next room were open, Jacoba van Heemskerck's large, solemn painting *Bild 2* looked down upon the "house of the dead", its tight, grave rhythm revealing a litany for the dead.'[1] (Lothar Schreyer)

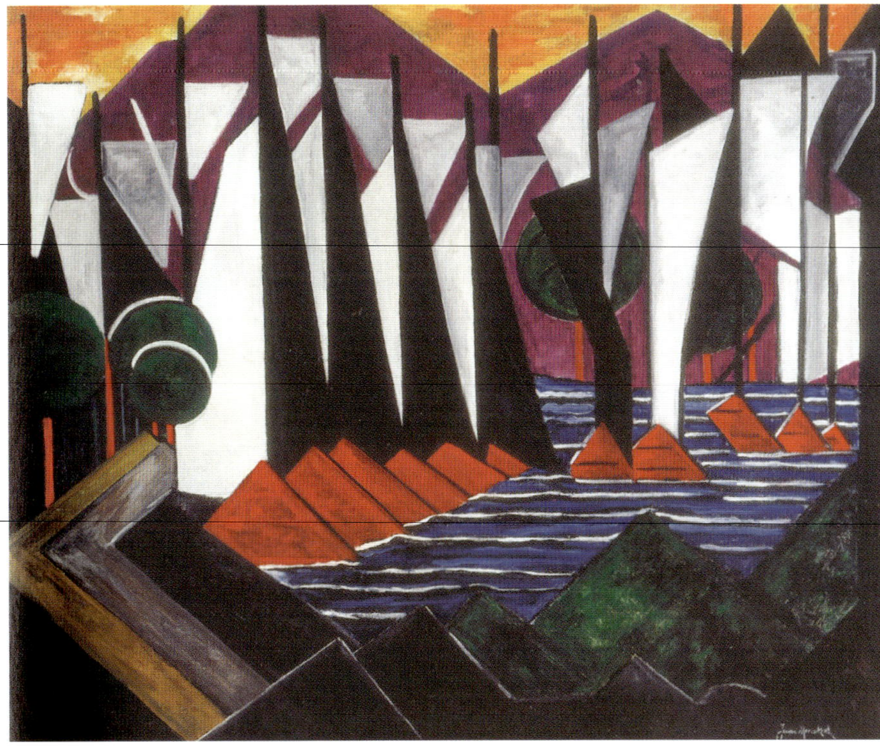

For dramaturge Lothar Schreyer the painting *Bild no. 2* (*Image no. 2*) by Jacoba van Heemskerck was an image that evoked a lamentation.[2] The repeating rhythm of triangles in black and white prompted in his imagination a litany for the dead —someone praying to God, and the faithful responding. The vividly coloured painting perfectly suited his fascination with the realm of the dead. Schreyer felt that his age needed a cult of the dead, as had existed among others in ancient Egypt. He decided to create one himself, painting two coffins —one for himself, and one for his wife. On the lid of one he painted an abstract female figure in bright blue, vermilion and gold on an ultramarine background. On the sides he depicted female figures and harp-like symbols. When the door to the room where the painted coffins stood was open, the painting *Image no. 2* 'looked down' on them, and so the lamentation began.

As a child, Jacoba van Heemskerck had always been fascinated by sailing boats, surrounded as she was by the seascapes painted by her father, naval officer Jacob Eduard van Heemskerck van Beest. She would not however follow in his footsteps as an artist. Endowed with the 'gift of clair-voyance', she tended more towards spiritual-isation in her art. She experienced the natural world 'not as a landscape but as a symbol of all expressions of life, as a spiritual truth'; art functioned there as a 'guide for

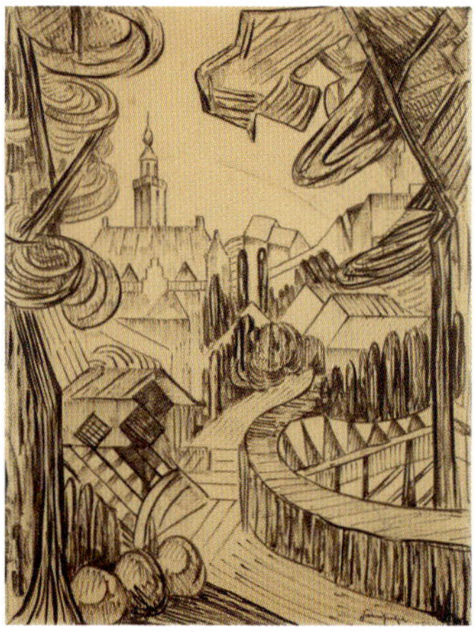

48 Jacoba van Heemskerck
Compositie (Veere) |
Composition (Veere) 1912
Indian ink, brush and pen on paper,
55 × 42,5 cm
Private collection

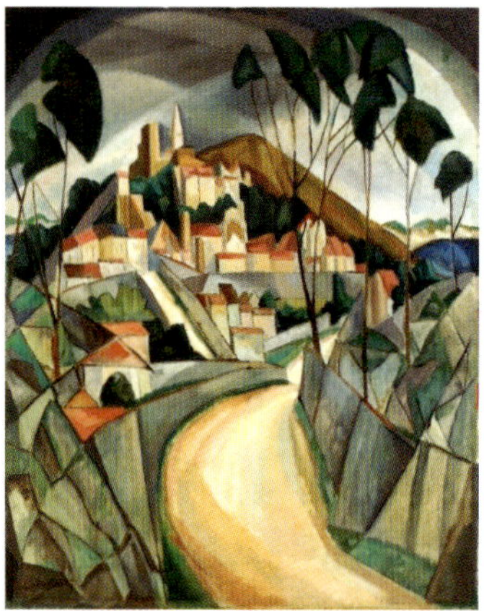

49 Lodewijk Schelfhout
Les Angles 1912
Oil on canvas,
98,3 × 79,3 cm
Private collection

humanity'.[3] At Der Sturm, the centre of Expressionist art, she was able to unleash her imagination as never before. She became close friends with founder Herwarth Walden, and in one of her early letters to him she revealed, 'I live alone with a sister many years older. […] My father was a painter around 1870–1890 and was very much against all modern movements; my family has precisely the same ideas. So you can see that I could not speak of my interests at home, either.'[4] Fortunately, by this time she had already developed a close friendship with Marie Tak van Poortvliet. The wealthy Tak van Poortvliet would come to play the same role in Jacoba van Heemskerck's artistic life as Theo van Gogh did for his brother Vincent. Van Heemskerck was thirteen when she met Tak van Poortvliet, who was three years her senior. The latter described her as 'always bright, full of humour and open [to] fun'.[5] She would support Van Heemskerck throughout her life in her lonely quest as a modern artist. There were very few women in modern art and, as Tak van Poortvliet noted, 'especially for a woman it is far from easy to be a pioneer'.[6]

In summer 1900 Jacoba van Heemskerck stayed with Tak van Poortvliet and her family at the Badhotel in Domburg. Tak van Poortvliet's father was a well-known liberal statesman, and he consulted the famous physician Johann Georg Mezger in Domburg.[7] The former was charmed by Van Heemskerck's aristocratic background, as she was one of the eminent people who was referred to as 'freule' (the equivalent of 'lady') in the best shops and salons in The Hague.[8] The two friends enjoyed themselves on the beach of the small seaside town, Van Heemskerck sitting in her wicker deckchair watching hoogaars, the traditional wooden fishing boats used in Zeeland, sail by. Sailing boats were to become an important motif in her paintings. Occasionally during their stay Van Heemskerck and Tak van Poortvliet were able to get away and walk together behind the Badhotel. There a path with stubby oaks deformed by the sea winds led to an area of woodland known as De Manteling. Inspired by the picturesque surroundings, they discussed their plans for the future.

In 1908 Tak van Poortvliet had Villa Loverendale built next to the hotel in Domburg. It would become a meeting place for artists and collectors. She and Van Heemskerck spent lovely long summers there, from June through to October. Domburg was not only good for her health, but also an inspiration for Van Heemskerck's paintings of the sea, the sailing boats, the dunes and the trees. From the very start, the two friends encouraged each other's interest in modern art. Van Heemskerck's boundless energy prompted Tak van Poortvliet to start collecting modern art. She was the first person in the Netherlands to build such a collection, which comprised mainly German art.[9] The first painting she bought was *Avond; De rode boom* (*Evening: The Red Tree*, 1908–10) by Piet Mondrian. By 1920 her collection included more than 150 works by Willi Baumeister, Georges Braque, Heinrich Campendonk, Henri Le Fauconnier, Lyonel Feininger, Emil Filla, Jacoba van Heemskerck, Wassily Kandinsky, Fernand Léger, Franz Marc, Piet Mondrian, Lodewijk Schelfhout and Georg Schrimpf.[10] Collecting contemporary art was not really regarded

50 Postcard of Jacoba van Heemskerck to Herwarth Walden, Trégastel, Brittany, 14 May 1914
Staatsbibliothek zu Berlin

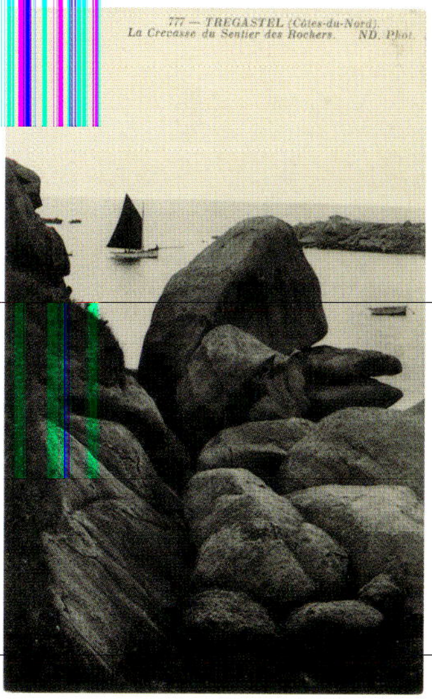

as the task of public museums at that time. Tak van Poortvliet felt the distinctive feature of her collection should be 'pure style and monumentality'.[11] With their interest in art movements like Luminism, Cubism and Expressionism, Van Heemskerck and Tak van Poortvliet were entirely in step with modernism. Van Heemskerck stuck to one key principle in this respect: 'Be true to your own conviction and render your vision in your own way.'[12]

Van Heemkerck's singular view of the world was informed by a mystical occultism, and in nature she found a spiritual world of lines and colours. In her search for universal truth, on 11 June 1910 she became a member of the Cazotte Co-Masonic lodge in Amsterdam. Women had been admitted to this occult lodge since 1904.[13] In 1910 she also became a member of the Theosophical Society, joining Helena Blavatsky's lodge in The Hague. Marie Tak van Poortvliet would follow in her footsteps two years later.[14] Together they became members of the Rakoczy Co-Masonic lodge in The Hague around 1911 and the rituals performed there introduced them to the transcendental power of symbols.[15] Freemasonry originated in sacred architecture and the symbolism of light. Over time, physical architecture came to symbolise a process of spiritual building. In the temple, which is regarded as representing the created universe, Freemasons work for the honour of God, the Supreme Architect of the universe. Using symbols and rituals, lodge members continually 'build' themselves so that they can help others and the world. Freemasonry gave Van Heemskerck the symbolism and theory of colour that laid the foundations for an abstract artistic idiom in her work. As a candidate she was inducted into the three basic degrees of entered apprentice, fellowcraft and master mason, and she and Tak van Poortvliet joined Lodge no. 43, Christian Rosenkreuz. This blue lodge was based in Hilversum and all seven members had already been inducted into the Cazotte lodge.[16] To Van Heemskerck and Tak van Poortvliet the temple meetings with other like-minded members, the Sisters from their own lodge, were like a refreshing spiritual bath. The members gave lectures in which they explored their ideas on symbolism, the theory of colour etc. They showed Jacoba van Heemskerck a path to awareness that helped her further develop her views on art and life. Another artist, the architect Karel de Bazel, developed his own theory of architecture at the lodges which—stripped of lodge terminology—he published and shared with his fellow architects. All kinds of groups, from the emancipation movement to vegetarians, also came to the lodges to give lectures and share new ideas.[17]

Van Heemskerck soon began using the symbols of Freemasonry in her Cubist work. This can clearly be seen in the reed pen drawing *Compositie* (*Composition*, 1912), in which she depicts the small town of Veere on the island of Walcheren in Zeeland. It features Masonic symbols like the chequered floor, the jagged edge, spheres and the spiral staircase.[18] The composition was originally inspired by the Cubist painting *Les Angles* (1912) by Lodewijk Schelfhout, which was in Marie Tak van Poortvliet's collection. Van Heemskerck was impressed by the three-dimensionality of the image, in which the forms of the landscape unfurl into the distance in a spiralling rhythm.[19] She added Masonic symbols to her composition,

51 Jacoba van Heemskerck
Bild no. 1 | **Image no. 1** 1914
Oil on canvas, 80 × 100 cm
Berlinische Galerie – Landesmuseum für Moderne Kunst, Fotografie und Architektur

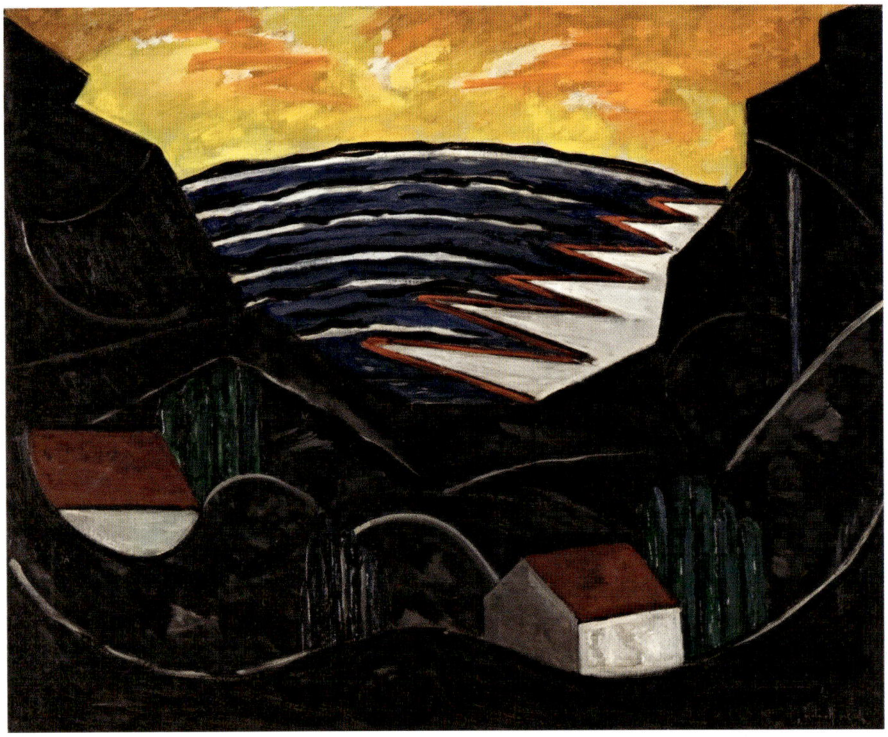

creating a kind of Masonic Cubism. The spiral staircase that Van Heemskerck included on the top left in her drawing symbolised the fact that she was ready, in her art, to leave the world of the senses and ascend to a transcendent world.[20] She regularly visited the picturesque town of Veere, which was not far from Domburg. Many artists had come to the harbour town to draw and paint its fishing fleet, and it was there that Van Heemskerck would draw her first sailing boats. The rituals and symbols of Freemasonry helped her to develop her abstract idiom. She would continue to employ the symbol of equilateral triangles that she used for her sailing boats throughout her life.[21] On 14 May 1914 she sent Herwarth Walden a picture postcard of a sailing boat off the rocky coast of Brittany, where she was on holiday in Trégastel (fig. 50), with the message: 'Yet the more abstract one works, the more one transforms the sketches into combinations.'[22]

In *Bild no. 1* (*Image no. 1*, 1914) Jacoba van Heemskerck painted the sea and dunes at Domburg. A path behind Villa Loverendale led to a beautiful, unspoilt area of dunes with a panoramic view of the sea. *Image no. 1* is dominated by a striking white jagged edge with a red outline over the sea. Van Heemskerck frequently used this symbol from Freemasonry.[23] The jagged edge refers to the planets in their orbits which form a border around the sun. Such a border or edging is used in Freemasonry around the black-and-white chequered floor in the temples for formal gatherings.[24] The chequered floor refers to the high and low points of human existence. By overcoming these one can become the high priest in one's own personal temple. The jagged

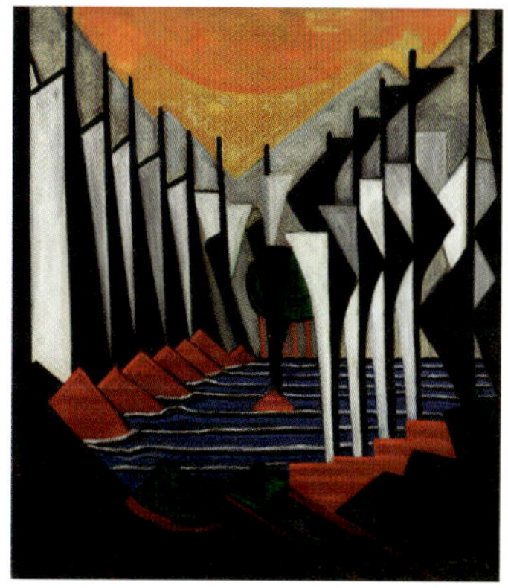

52 Jacoba van Heemskerck
Bild no. 18 | Image no. 18 1915
Oil on canvas
87 × 77,5 cm
Kunstmuseum Den Haag

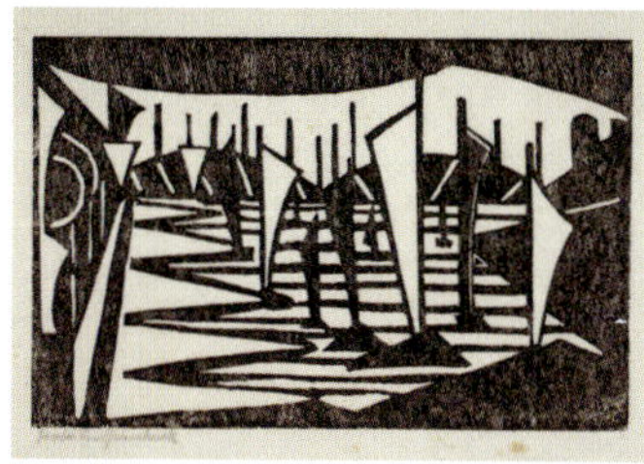

53 Jacoba van Heemskerck
Compositie (Boten in haven) |
Composition (Boats in Harbour) 1916
Woodcut on paper
37,8 × 36,1 cm (sheet)
Kunstmuseum Den Haag

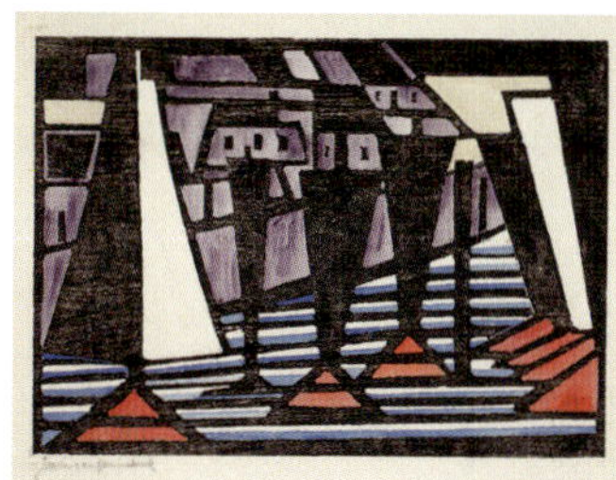

54 Jacoba van Heemskerck
Compositie VII (Zeilschepen voor de kust) |
Composition VII (Sailing Ships off the Coast) 1916
Woodcut and watercolour on Japanese paper
19,8 × 28 cm (sheet)
Kunstmuseum Den Haag

edge refers to the support of the community in this effort. In Van Heemskerck's seascapes the black-and-white chequered floor became the black-and-white sails of her boats. They first 'sail' into the picture, as it were, in *Image no. 2*. The boats are abstracted into red triangles with black-and-white sails, referencing a profound occult wisdom that manifests itself in various ways, including in the pyramids of Egypt. In Freemasonry the equilateral triangle symbolises the three elements of human nature: the senses, reason and spirituality. With her black-and-white sails, Van Heemskerck depicted the lot of humankind, and humanity's spiritual quest for perfection. In *Image no. 2* she also refers to the chequered floor that helped masons develop their spiritual power. In the bottom left of the painting are two brown L-shaped forms that represent the square—the first tool used in architecture to create right angles in a building. In Freemasonry the square is the symbol of the first degree, ensuring correct alignment with Masonic ideas and rules.[25] This symbol harmonises life, making it acceptable for the Supreme Being to whom Masons are accountable for their deeds. Van Heemskerck used the symbols of Freemasonry in many seascapes, not only in paintings but also woodcuts and drawings. In her finely balanced *Bild no. 18* (*Image no. 18*) she used not only the equilateral triangles of the sailing boats, but also the symbol of the cubical stone. This true square can only be constructed using a square and compasses.[26] It symbolises the balance between the four basic elements: fire, water, air and earth. Every person has either too much or too little of these. The goal of Masons is to bring them into balance.

It was in woodcuts that Jacoba Van Heemskerck achieved the ultimate expression of the rhythmic movement of the sailing boats. The linear repetition in the images has a meditative effect. Dramaturge Lothar Schreyer immediately saw this as a call to prayer. To him, it signified connection with the realm of the dead. In an alchemical process designed to extract the ultimate from the material, Van Heemskerck not only ground the pigment for her paints, she also cut her own blocks of wood for her woodcuts. Working in this traditional way connected her to the material.

In *Bild no. 23* (*Image no. 23*) the boats no longer sail rhythmically in line, but separately, as individual vessels with sails of different colours and shapes (fig. 55). Van Heemskerck added a new element to the image in the form of two black trees with winding roots. Her friend Willem Zeylmans van Emmichoven, who would become the first chairman of the Dutch Anthroposophical Society, wrote of *Image no. 23* in an essay: 'Eternal truth revealed to humanity. At the centre the motif of a ship gliding through the water, with a brilliant white sail, like a saint opening both arms to heaven to receive the wisdom of the divine. Beside this, and following the first, two others, also with spotless white sails, though their inner aspect is not fully developed. And so they proceed, silent and sure, over the rippling surface of the water, towards suffering humanity. For in the background are the mighty purple mountains on which a bright orange glows. [...] In the foreground, on either side, two powerful, heavy black tree figures, the branches twisted and reaching for each

55 Jacoba van Heemskerck
Bild no. 23 (Witte zeilschepen op een meer) | Image no. 23 (White Sailing Ships on a Lake) 1915
Oil on canvas, 111,1 × 130,9 cm
Kunstmuseum Den Haag

56 Jacoba van Heemskerck
Bild no. 77 | Image no. 77 1917
Oil on canvas
75,7 × 75,7 cm
Kunstmuseum Den Haag

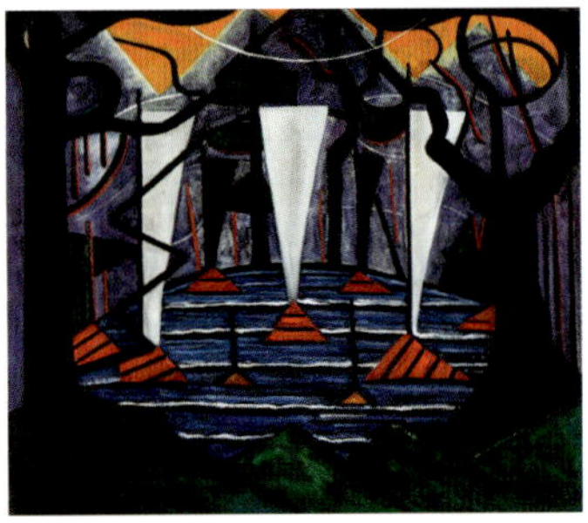

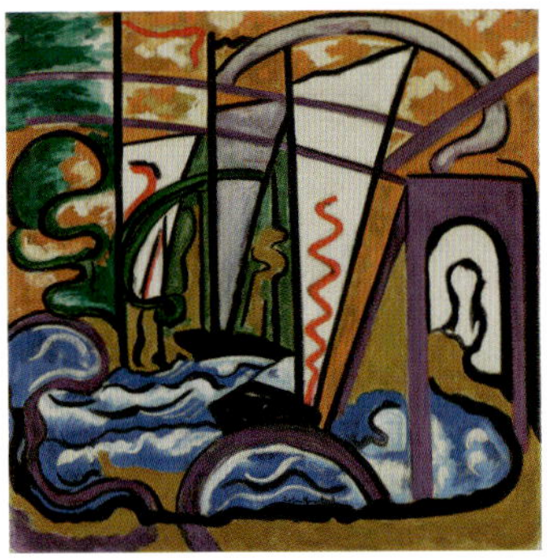

other, forming the gateway of misery and suffering through which must pass anyone who wishes to give to mankind something that might help. Beneath that, depicted in hefty angular blocks, is the earth from which the trees grow, the earth and its fertility.'[27] Van Heemskerck felt a great urge to metamorphose her seascapes into universal images. As in other Expressionist compositions, she used contrasting colours and lines, revealing her temperament.

Sailing boats on a calm or rough sea recur throughout her entire oeuvre. They symbolise humanity and its restless searching for all that is concealed in the cosmos. Some of Van Heemskerck's sailing boats reflect human tragedy, a result of their eternal struggle. They have only a black sail, and rather than exuding spiritual harmony, they reveal an endless longing. 'Jacoba van Heemskerck has grasped and deconstructed all the forms that fascinated her in the great game of nature. She studied the motif of boats on the water. The longing in the sails reaching up towards heaven, the calm they represent when, white and gleaming, they stand motionless against the distant sky. And then the endless firmament, as it arcs over the world, taut and all-sheltering.'[28]

Jacoba van Heemskerck and Marie Tak van Poortvliet joined the Anthroposophical Society in April 1915. Her membership meant a great deal to Van Heemskerck. The spiritual science of philosopher and writer Rudolf Steiner enabled her to deepen her spiritual life. Steiner believed that an invisible world lay at the basis of the outwardly perceptible world. It was of the utmost importance that humanity became aware of its spiritual origins, for after death its life experience would become the seed of its further development. This idea of human reincarnation was particularly appealing to Van Heemskerck. She wrote to Marie Steiner, 'Joining the Anthroposophical Society was a great event for me, and I hope later to persuade you personally of my sincere endeavour.'[29] From the very start of her artistic career she sought to abstract the material and, as we have seen, in this process she encountered the imagery and symbolism of Freemasonry. Gradually, as she developed, she began to discern transubstantiation in nature. Shapes and colours had their own laws and could evoke a dynamic, metaphysical world. These ideas were inspired by the anthroposophical teachings of Rudolf Steiner and his architectonic-plastic design for the first Goetheanum, which stood on a hill in Dornach, Switzerland. The two friends visited it many times. Van Heemskerck saw in the large domes of the Goetheanum how colours and shapes express the spiritual. She perceived in the painted windows a fluid world of colour and light. It took her to the boundary between the world of the senses and the transcendental world. Glass painting and the use of vegetable pigments were Steiner's way of ensuring that the domes of the Goetheanum became transparent, as it were, allowing the cosmic world to flood in. This inspired Van Heemskerck to such an extent that it would become her next challenge in art. From that point on, her sailing boats must become 'radiantly spiritual'.[30] That is why she spent so much time trying to make her colours as transparent as possible, mainly with the use of glass.

57 Jacoba van Heemskerck
Bild no. 109 | Image no. 109 1920
Oil on canvas
98,5 × 183,5 cm
Kunstmuseum Den Haag

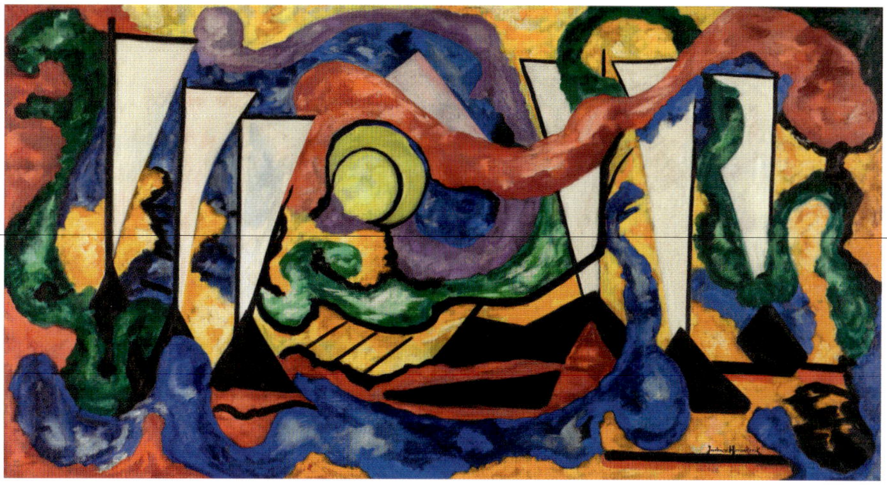

Towards the end of her short life Jacoba van Heemskerck designed some stained-glass windows for the Marinekazerne, the naval barracks in Amsterdam. The windows are a highlight of her oeuvre. Sailing boats are radically abstracted here, and are now simply a transparent interplay of lines; the lead cames define the diagonals, verticals and horizontals. She was commissioned to design nine windows for three floors of the building, which would let in plenty of light, as the spaces inside were rather dark. Van Heemskerck used yellow glass in several shades, with some blue for contrast. This created a cascade of warm golden light that flooded the interior. The commission for the Marinekazerne was an ideal opportunity for Van Heemskerck to honour her father, Jacob Eduard van Heemskerck van Beest, who had been a naval officer, with her abstract sea-scapes. A boat sails triumphantly through the centre of the middle window on the second floor, as the image culminates above it in three diamond shapes. This radiant trinity represents her aesthetic concept. Jacoba van Heemskerck wanted to show people their origins. The windows embody her quest for true spiritual knowledge. She found the tools for her search in Free-masonry and anthroposophy, organisations where she felt a sense of solidarity and affinity with people who looked further than the boundaries of rank, origin and creed.

After Jacoba van Heemskerck's death on 3 August 1923, Marie Tak van Poortvliet had inscribed on her gravestone the words of Christian Rosenkreuz: Ex Deo nascimur, In Christo morimur, Per spiritum sanctum reviviscimus (From God we are born, In Christ we die, Through the Holy Spirit we are reborn).[31] She was undoubtedly thinking

58 Design for a Glass Window, central part (ground, first, and second floors) of the Marinekazerne Amsterdam

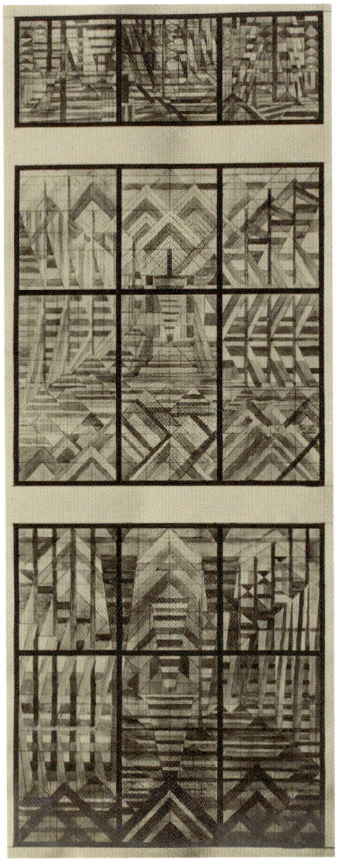

of the radiant central window on the second floor of the Marinekazerne. Lothar Schreyer wrote a meditative poem in memory of Van Heemskerck which features her sailing boats, and which can be read as a litany:[32]

Your barque sails away
    Your sail blows you home to Heaven
Now the storm is silent
    Now you rest
All your sails pass through the world
    Bringing your heaven to us
Then we humans shall rest
    And we humans shall return home

Woman of the sea
    In our darkness your star shines.

59 Jacoba van Heemskerck
Stained-glass windows of the Marinekazerne Amsterdam 1921
ca. 660 × 635 cm
Kunstmuseum Den Haag – long-term loan by the
Rijksdienst voor het Cultureel Erfgoed

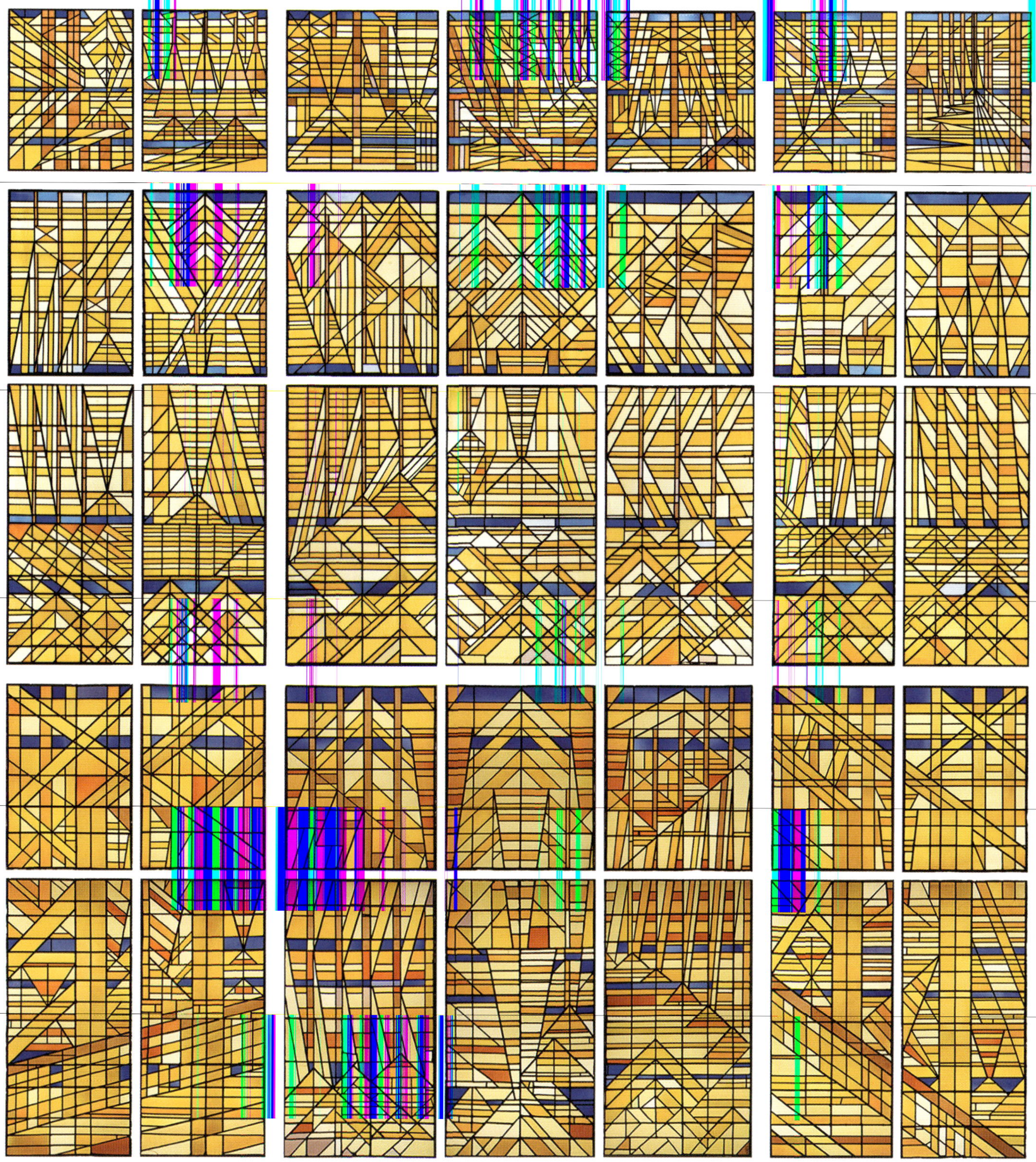

1 'Wenn die Flügeltür zum Nachbarzimmer geöffnet war, so blickte auf das Totenhaus das große feierliche *Bild 2* von Jacoba van Heemskerck herab, dessen strenger ernster Rhythmus eine Totenlitanei sichtbar macht.' Lothar Schreyer, *Erinnerungen an Sturm und Bauhaus* (Munich, 1956), 161.

2 Schreyer, a dramatist at the Deutsches Schauspielhaus in Hamburg and editor of *Der Sturm* magazine, bought *Bild no. 2* in 1916. See A. H. Huussen Jr and J. F. A. van Paaschen-Louwerse, *Jacoba van Heemskerck van Beest 1876–1923: Schilderes uit roeping* (Zwolle, 2005), 123 and 213 n. 440.

3 Paul Citroen, 'Jacoba van Heemskerck', *Museumjournaal*, 5 (1960), 143.

4 Jacoba van Heemskerck to Herwarth Walden, 22 March 1914, Staatsbibliothek zu Berlin, Handschriftenabteilung, Sturm-Archive I. See also Marjam Trautmann and Torsten Schrade, eds., *DER STURM: Digitale Quellenedition zur Geschichte der internationalen Avantgarde* (Digital Source Edition of the History of the International Avant-Garde) (Mainz, 2018), https://sturm-edition.de/index.html (accessed on 18 September 2020).

5 Marie Tak van Poortvliet, 'Jacoba van Heemskerck', in *Jacoba van Heemskerck. Sturm-Bilderbuch VII* (Berlin, 1924), 8. The first meeting between Jacoba van Heemskerck and Marie Tak van Poortvliet is described in an as yet unpublished dissertation on the biography of Marie Tak van Poortvliet by the present author.

6 Tak van Poortvliet, 'Jacoba van Heemskerck', 10.

7 See *Domburgsch Badnieuws*, 1 September 1900: report of the arrival of Mr J. P. R. Tak van Poortvliet, his family and servants, 7, The Hague.

8 See Jan Hein Furnée, *Plaatsen van beschaafd vertier: Standsbesef en stedelijke cultuur in Den Haag 1850–1890* (Amsterdam, 2012), 20. With their aristocratic roots, the Van Heemskerck family belonged to the same class of eminent citizens as the Tak van Poortvliet family.

9 See Gregor Langfeld, *Duitse kunst in Nederland: verzamelen tentoonstellen kritieken 1919–1964* (Zwolle, 2004), 26.

10 See Friedrich Markus Huebner, *Moderne Kunst in den Privatsammlungen Europas*. Part 1: Holland (Leipzig/Amsterdam, 1921); *Die neue Malerei in Holland*, Die Junge Kunst in Europa, I (Leipzig/Arnhem, 1921); 'Die Sammlung Tak van Poortvliet im Haag', *Der Ararat: Glossen, Skizzen und Notizen zur neuen Kunst*, 2/10 (October 1921), 262ff. Huebner concluded in his publication that Marie Tak van Poortvliet's collection was the most progressive in the Netherlands. He dedicated the publication to her.

11 Tak van Poortvliet, 'Jacoba van Heemskerck', 10.

12 Jacoba van Heemskerck, quoted in ibid.

13 The International Order of Mixed Freemasonry, known as the Grande Loge Symbolique Ecossaise de France Le Droit Humain, was founded by Marie Deraismes and Georges Martin in France in 1893. It later became known as the Orde Maçonnique Mixte International Le Droit Humain. This International Order currently has branches in 60 countries all over the world. In the Netherlands several lodges split off in 1919 to form the Dutch Association of Freemasons (Nederlandsch Verbond van Vrijmetselaren). Information provided by Andréa Kroon, art historian and chair of Stichting OVN, which promotes academic research into the history of Freemasonry and related movements in the Netherlands, on 10 August 2020.

14 See Marty Bax, *Het web der schepping: Theosofie en kunst in Nederland van Lauweriks tot Mondriaan* (Amsterdam, 2006), 542: 'lid loge Blavatsky (DH) 01.11.1910 te den Haag nr. 43022'.

15 See Andréa A. Kroon and Audrey Wagtberg Hansen, *Geheim Den Haag: Vrijmetselaarstempels en andere esoterische gebouwen in Den Haag rond 1900* (The Hague, 2011), 195. The authors indicate that art historians have not yet considered the influence of masonic geometric symbols on the work of Jacoba van Heemskerck. I have taken up the challenge in the present essay. In doing so I made grateful use of the publication Robert Lomas, *Symbolen van de Vrijmetselarij: De geheime kracht van maçonnieke symbolen en hun invloed op de geschiedenis* (Kerkdriel, 2013), originally published as *The Secret Power of Masonic Symbols* (Beverly, MA, 2011).

16 See Kroon and Wagtberg Hansen, *Geheim Den Haag*, 195–96.

17 Information provided by Andréa Kroon on 10 August 2020.

18 See Kroon and Wagtberg Hansen, *Geheim Den Haag*, 196.

19 See Aleida Betsy Loosjes-Terpstra, *Moderne Kunst in Nederland 1900–1914* (Utrecht, 1959), 165.

20 See Lomas, *Symbolen van de Vrijmetselarij*, 211.

21 Ibid., 240–41.

22 'Je mehr abstract man aber arbeitet je mehr man die Skizzen zu combinationen um arbeitet.' Jacoba van Heemskerck to Herwarth Walden, 14 May 1914, Staatsbibliothek zu Berlin, Handschriftenabteilung, Sturm-Archive I. See also Trautmann and Schrade, *DER STURM: Digitale Quellenedition*, https://sturm-edition.de.

23 See Lomas, *Symbolen van de Vrijmetselarij*, 184–85.

24 Ibid., 180–81.

25 Ibid., 134–35.

26 Ibid., 189.

27 See Willem Zeylmans van Emmichoven, 'De geestelijke richting in de nieuwe schilderkunst: Jacoba van Heemskerck' [1917], *Tableau: Tijdschrift voor beeldende kunst*, 4/6 (1982), 595. See also the translation in this book 145.

28 Zeylmans, 'De geestelijke richting in de nieuwe schilderkunst', 594. See also the translation in this book 143-44.

29 Jacoba van Heemskerck to Marie Steiner, The Hague, 21 April 1915, Rudolf Steiner Nachlassverwaltung, Dornach.

30 Jacoba van Heemskerck to Herwarth Walden, 11 November 1914, Staatsbibliothek zu Berlin, Handschriftenabteilung, Sturm-Archive I ('leuchtend geistlich'). See also Trautmann and Schrade, *DER STURM: Digitale Quellenedition*, https://sturm-edition.de/.

31 See Huussen Jr and Van Paaschen-Louwerse, *Jacoba van Heemskerck van Beest*, 196.

32 'Dein Nachen fährt dahin / Dein Segel weht Dich in den Himmel heim / Nun schweigt der Sturm / Nun ruhe Du / All Deine Segel fahren durch die Welt / Und bringen Deinen Himmel uns / Dann ruhn wir Menschen / Und wir Menschen kehren heim / Du Frau vom Meer / In unser Dunkel leuchte Dein Gestirn.' Lothar Schreyer, 'Für Jacoba van Heemskerck', in *Jacoba van Heemskerck: Sturm-Bilderbuch VII* (Berlin, 1924), 20.

Jacoba van Heemskerck

Anne Lorenz

Connections to Der Sturm

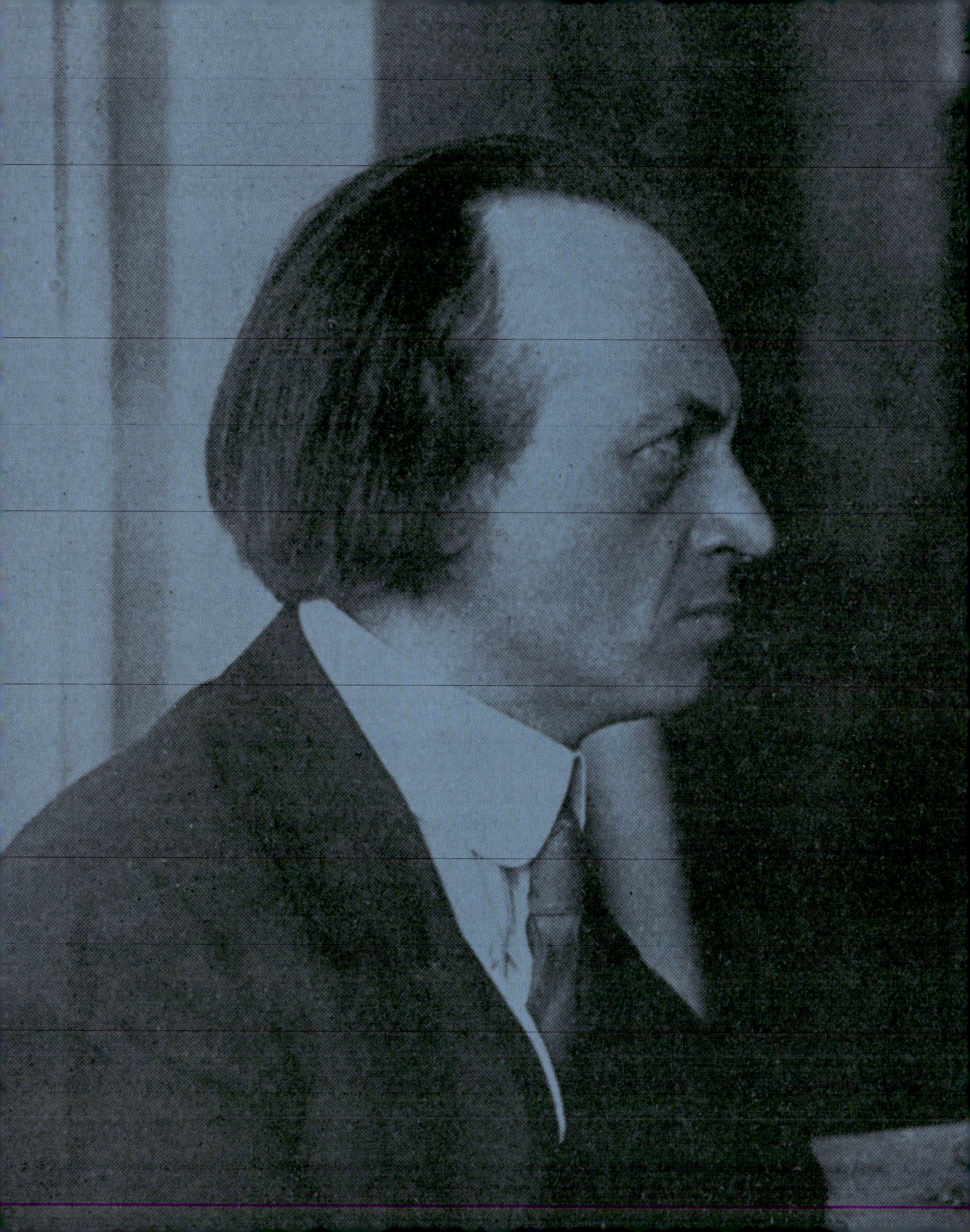

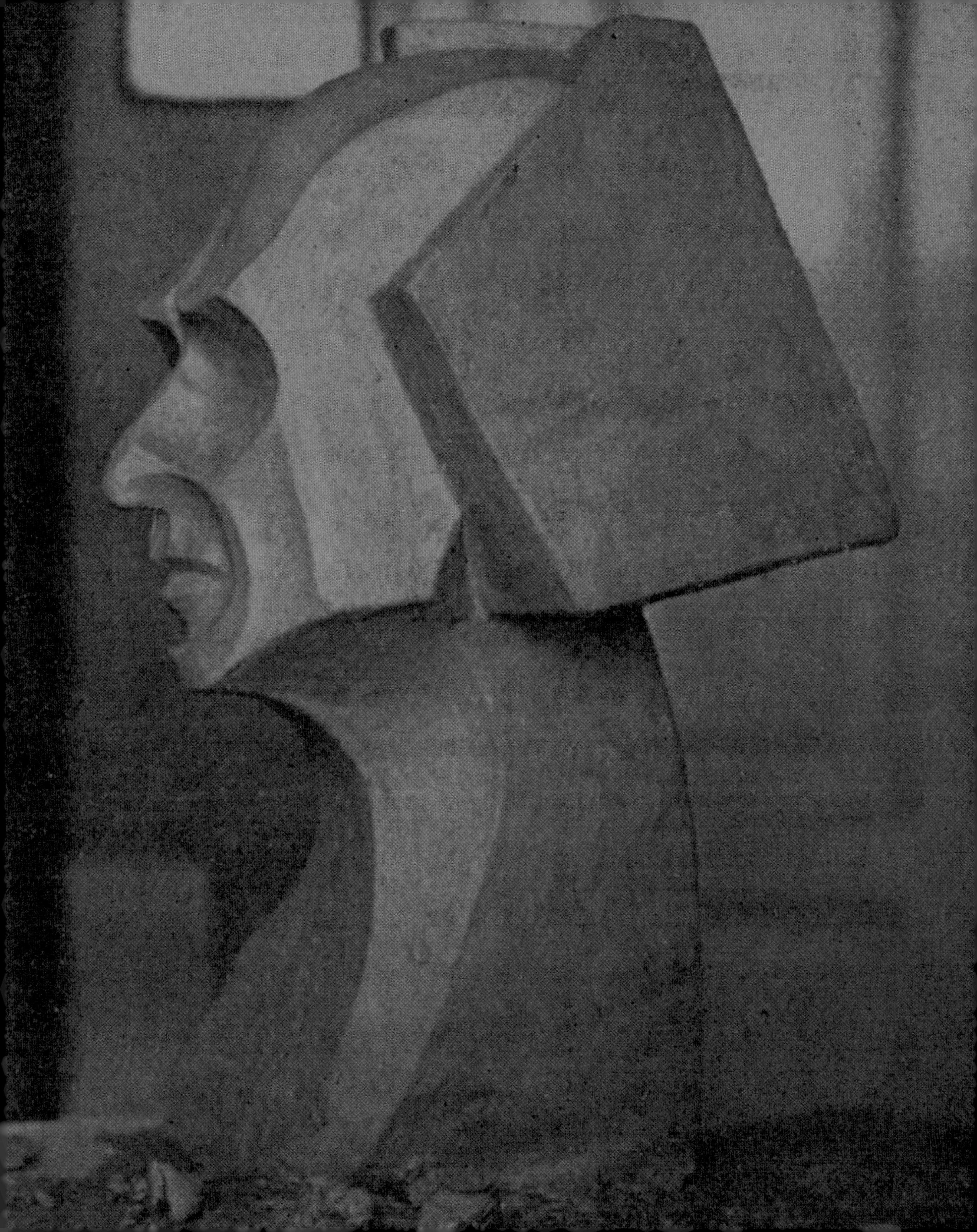

60 Herwarth Walden in front of his portrait bust by William Wauer, c.1918

61 World Press Office of Der Sturm, undated

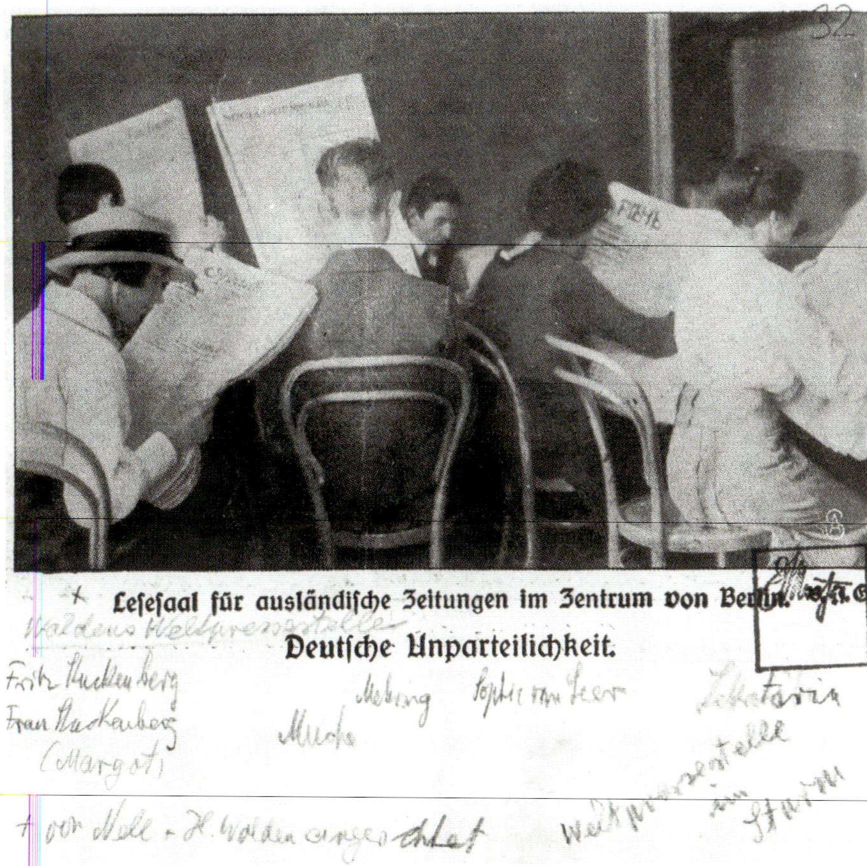

"We must, in any case, stick together." (Jacoba van Heemskerck)

From the moment that she joined Der Sturm, the Dutch painter Jacoba van Heemskerck avoided everything that might have distracted her from the special, powerful impact of Expressionism. She numbered her works instead of giving them titles; she rid herself of artistic role models and even in her painting class she came down on the side of individualised support for up-and-coming artists. Only in this way, she opined, could modern art help to express what moved people inside. Generally, Van Heemskerck did not think much of preformed concepts and attributions: Modern artists should paint, not write about painting.[1]

In contrast to her contemporaries Wassily Kandinsky and Franz Marc, Van Heemskerck never systematically elaborated upon her views of art. Her aversion to dogmatic viewpoints and establishment objectives was reflected in her aesthetic style, while her unique individualism also defined her social contacts to the avant-garde art scene. From the moment she became a member of Der Sturm, she kept her distance, particularly in her own country, from various art groups and their leaders.

There was only one person she trusted fully: Herwarth Walden. Years of close friendship—based on their shared avant-garde idea of living for and with art—connected her to the founder of the Berlin-based enterprise Der Sturm and his wife, Nell Walden-Roslund. Since her participation in Walden's *Erster Deutscher Herbstsalon* in Berlin in 1913, her regular exhibits at the Sturm gallery and the reproductions of her works printed in the magazine *Der Sturm* had assured her international recognition and an income as a professional painter.[2] Her exchanges with the Waldens had a fundamental influence on her artistic development. Their conversations during their visits to each other in Berlin, The Hague, and Domburg, where Van Heemskerck spent the summer with her friend Marie Tak van Poortvliet, were expanded upon and continued in intense correspondence. They provided significant ideas and were an inexhaustible source of inspiration for Van Heemskerck's creative work. In return, the presence of the Dutch painter in Der Sturm contributed to its image as an international centre for new art, and even kept it going during the First World War, when the transfer and exchange of art and culture came more or less to a standstill. The Netherlands' neutral stance during the war also made it possible for Van Heemskerck to support the Waldens in their secretive gathering of intelligence for German cultural propaganda.[3] From the Netherlands she supplied Dutch magazines and German-friendly contacts to the Nachrichtenbüro Der Sturm (The Storm Berlin News Agency), which garnered considerable income on its side during the war years.

Jacoba van Heemskerck's Letters

Between 1914 and 1922 Van Heemskerck wrote at least 269 still extant letters to Herwarth and Nell Walden, which tell of this useful and enriching relationship between the Sturm enterprise and the artist.[4] Although the return letters from the Waldens have not survived, the documents archived in the Staatsbibliothek zu Berlin ultimately form a valuable basic source for researchers, also because, of all of the Waldens' correspondence, these letters cover by far the longest period of time. Jacoba van Heemskerck's connection to Der Sturm is considered to be one of the most enduring of all its artistic relationships. Starting with 'mutual stimulation and sympathy'[5] and 'great fidelity and loyalty',[6] the relationship is described as being crucial to the establishment of her identity and characterised by the words 'exclusive',[7] 'unconditional'[8] and 'unreserved'.[9] Her strong sense of belonging eventually led Van Heemskerck to grant Herwarth Walden the sole right to sell her works and to present them exclusively in exhibitions he organised, which in turn must have reinforced the close personal connection.

Researchers agree that Van Heemskerck's exclusive position as a Sturm artist in Germany also had a negative effect on her reputation in her own country.[10] This discrepancy had already been verified by her contemporaries: 'She was never able to garner the kind of admiration in Holland that she rightfully earned in Germany,'[11] it says in a brief notice of her death on 3 August 1923, which appeared two months later in the art collectors' magazine *Der Cicerone*. Among the Sturm artists, she was second only to Oskar Kokoschka in having the most works on display,[12] but her position in contemporary Dutch painting was described as 'peripheral'[13] and 'isolated'.[14] Doubtless, the much-quoted passages from her letters prove that Van Heemskerck harboured a deep dislike for her Dutch colleagues and her compatriots' general understanding of art during her Sturm period, and she repeatedly sought to assure Walden of her status as an associate of Der Sturm.

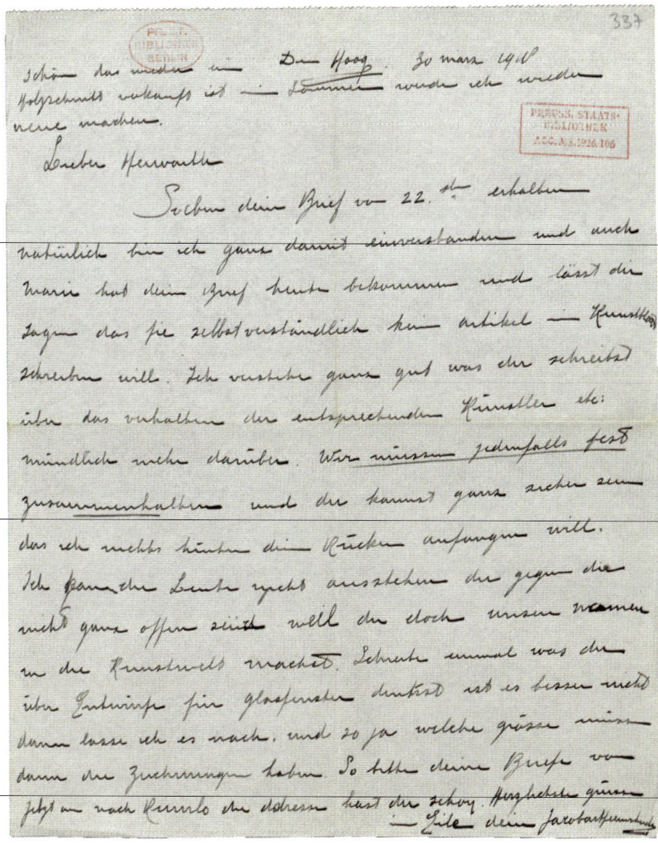

Den Haag. 30 maerz 1918

Schön das wieder ein Holzschnitt verkauft ist — im Sommer werde ich wieder neue machen.

Lieber Herwarth

Soeben dein Brief vom 22.ten erhalten natürlich bin ich ganz damit einverstanden und auch Marie hat dein Brief heute bekommen und lässt dir sagen das sie selbstverständlich kein artikel im [illegible] schreiben will. Ich verstehe ganz gut was du schreibst über das verhalten der entsprechenden Künstler etc: mündlich mehr darüber. Wir müssen jedenfalls fest zusammenhalten und du kannst ganz sicher sein das ich nichts hinter dein Rücken anfangen will. Ich kann die Leute nicht ausstehen die gegen dir nicht ganz offen sind weil du doch unsern namen in der Kunstwelt machst. Schreibe einmal was du über Entwürfe für glasfenster denkst ist es besser nicht dann lasse ich es nach. und so ja welche grösse müssen dann die Zeichnungen haben. So bitte deine Briefe von jetzt an nach [illegible] die adresse hast du schon. Herzlichste grüsse — Eile dein Jacobavanheemskerck

62 Letter of Jacoba van Heemskerck to Herwarth Walden, The Hague, 30 March 1918 Staatsbibliothek zu Berlin

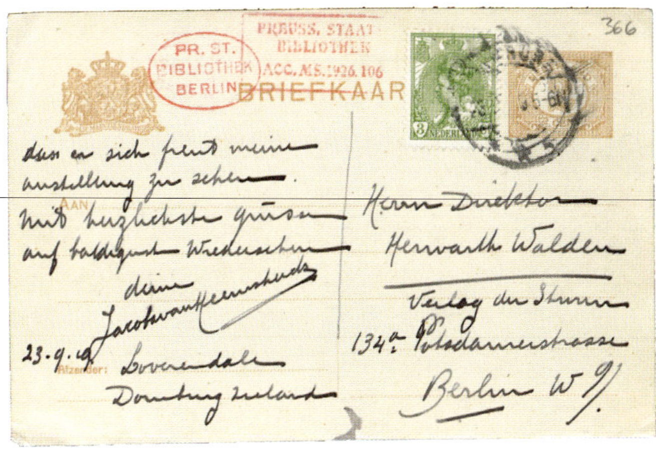

dass er sich freut meine ausstellung zu sehen. Mit herzlichsten grüssen auf baldiges Wiedersehen deine Jacobavanheemskerck

23.9.19 [illegible] Domburg Zeeland

Herrn Direktor Herwarth Walden Verlag der Sturm 134a Potsdamerstrasse Berlin W 9

63 Postcard of Jacoba van Heemskerck to Herwarth Walden, Domburg, 23 September 1919 Staatsbibliothek zu Berlin

Beyond this demarcation, however, arises the question of which artists she actually had personal contact with. Was there anyone besides the Waldens in the very heterogeneous Sturm circle whose concept of art and the art scene she unfailingly shared? Or were her points of contact limited to the innermost circle, in accordance with August Stramm's statement, 'Der Sturm is Herwarth Walden'?[15]

In the few relevant individual studies of Jacoba van Heemskerck, her letters have been evaluated in detail, mostly as evidence of the international nature of Der Sturm or of the significant female participation in the Expressionist movement.[16] An attempt at a somewhat different approach, of the kind that can be achieved with computer-supported analysis, has yet to be carried out. Currently, the DER STURM project at the Mainz Akademie der Wissenschaften und der Literatur, the *Digitale Quellenedition zur Geschichte der internationalen Avantgarde* (Der Sturm: Digital Source Edition of the History of the International Avant-Garde) is laying the foundation for it. The aim of this edition is to create a virtual compilation of the various Sturm sources, which are scattered around the world and have mostly been digitalised, and to work through their content and form according to established standards.[17] This sort of data-based digital evaluation of Van Heemskerck's letters, which takes into account and visualises developments over time, can also help to identify the most important artistic and social points of contact.

A Friendship with Herwarth and Nell Walden

As little as Van Heemskerck valued public statements about art made by creatives, she found in Herwarth and Nell Walden the indispensable, trusted conversation partners with whom she did not mince words. She frequently invoked her special friendship in order to speak frankly with them and even criticise Der Sturm. In return, she energetically urged them for their honest opinions—about her art, her work methods, and, above all, about her art market strategy. She was particularly concerned about specific decisions, such as whether or not she should participate in an exhibition, what the best time would be for her next presentation at Der Sturm, or which regional newspapers would be good to advertise her shows in.[18]

That she did not want to leave anything to chance, and that she was aware of her impact as a female artist in public can be seen in the matter she discusses in a letter dated 23 March 1915, in which she asks Herwarth Walden not to address her in the future with her aristocratic title: 'I hope that you understand my intention. Here in Holland many noblewomen are painters and musicians and they make sure never to neglect to mention it.'[19] As Maaike van Rijn has established, Van Heemskerck insisted upon being defined by her art in the same way that her male colleagues were and did not want to be equated with the amateur female painters of the Dutch nobility.[20] Strictly speaking, however, her remark does not refer to the situation of women artists in general. Rather, it conceals a critique of the gap she herself experienced between the 'backward' Dutch art scene—she also felt rejected and undervalued by her aristocratic family[21]—and the art milieu in Berlin, which was modern in every way. The subsequent flattering assurance, almost apologetically added, ultimately emphasises her sense of belonging to Der Sturm, sets the basic tone of her letter, and can be read as the maxim underlying her friendship with the Waldens: 'Please don't be angry at what I write, but among friends like you and your wife, I always state my honest opinion. If you find the time, please let me know if you think I am wrong.'[22]

At the same time, Van Heemskerck worried about the continued existence of Der Sturm and its image. Hardly a letter ends without an inquiry into how things are going with Der Sturm. Early on in the first year of their correspondence, which happened to coincide with the first year of the First World War, she even told Herwarth Walden that she would make woodcut prints at her own expense and donate the proceeds from the sales to him.[23] In relation to this Hubert van den Berg points out that, although Van Heemskerck and her friend Marie Tak van Poortvliet were doubtless actively and knowingly involved in Der Sturm's intelligence gathering, they were probably not really aware of its financial dimension and magnitude.[24] A further indication of this is that Van den Berg believes that although the Dutch artist continues to praise Walden's skill as an art dealer in her letters, she never connects Der Sturm's solid financial strength during the war years with its profitable intelligence-gathering business.[25] And, in fact, such a silence hardly corresponds to the emphatic passages in which Van Heemskerck invokes the honesty and openness of their friendly relationship.

64 Herwarth and Nell Walden's living room (on the walls paintings by Franz Marc and Oskar Kokoschka), after 1912

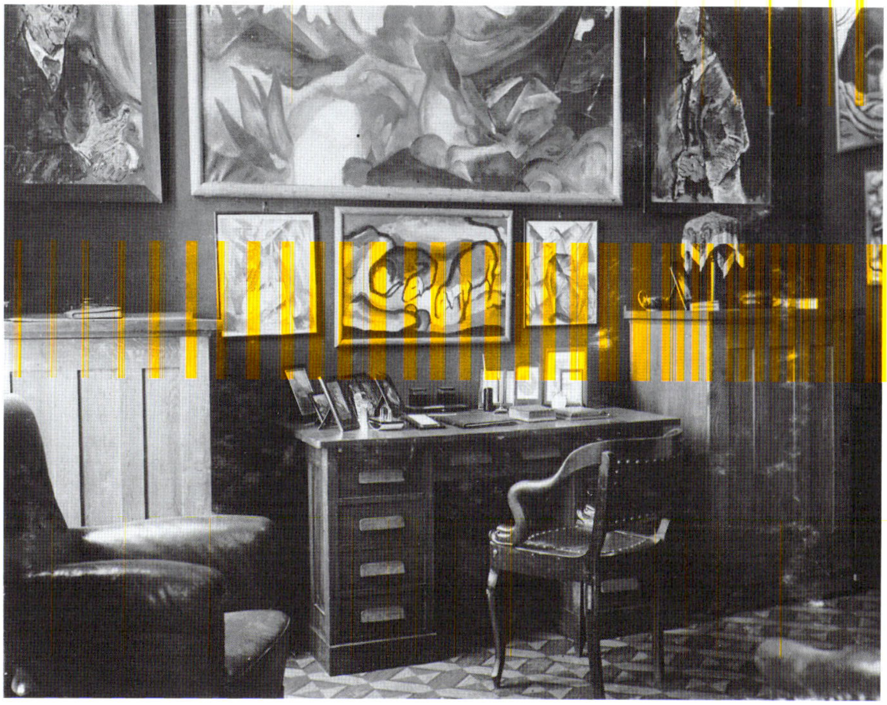

The bottom line of Van den Berg's in-depth study of the dovetailing of art and politics at Der Sturm is the picture of a friendship that was not entirely reciprocal, nor completely free of pragmatic calculation on Walden's side.

Contacts to the Sturm Artists

With the end of the war Herwarth Walden forfeited the advantage he had been able to secure for himself as a double agent —for both art and politics—and hence, Der Sturm soon lost its position as an avant-garde pioneer. Its figureheads, Franz Marc and August Stramm, had been killed in the war and their memories were only kept alive in shared remembrances at so-called Sturm art evenings. New galleries and art dealerships arrived, offering modern artists additional platforms that managed without Walden's mediation. Right around the same time, Van Heemskerck seems to have finished her intensive search for new expressive styles. Just two years prior she had enthusiastically announced her intention of designing a puppet theatre for the Sturm stage,[26] of planning illustrations for fairy tales for a Sturm children's book, and 'in our striving to bring the portrait',[27] but she now attempted to find suitable collaborators among architects to realize her window designs.

Researchers unanimously agree that her relationship to Walden cooled around the end of the war or at least by 1920, and in turning to stained glass, Van Heemskerck took a new artistic path that separated them in terms of business. Scholarly research on Van Heemskerck identifies roughly two tendencies based on opposing perspectives: on the one hand, the focus

Number of mentions of Sturm painters (black) and Sturm associates (blue) in Van Heemskerck's letters

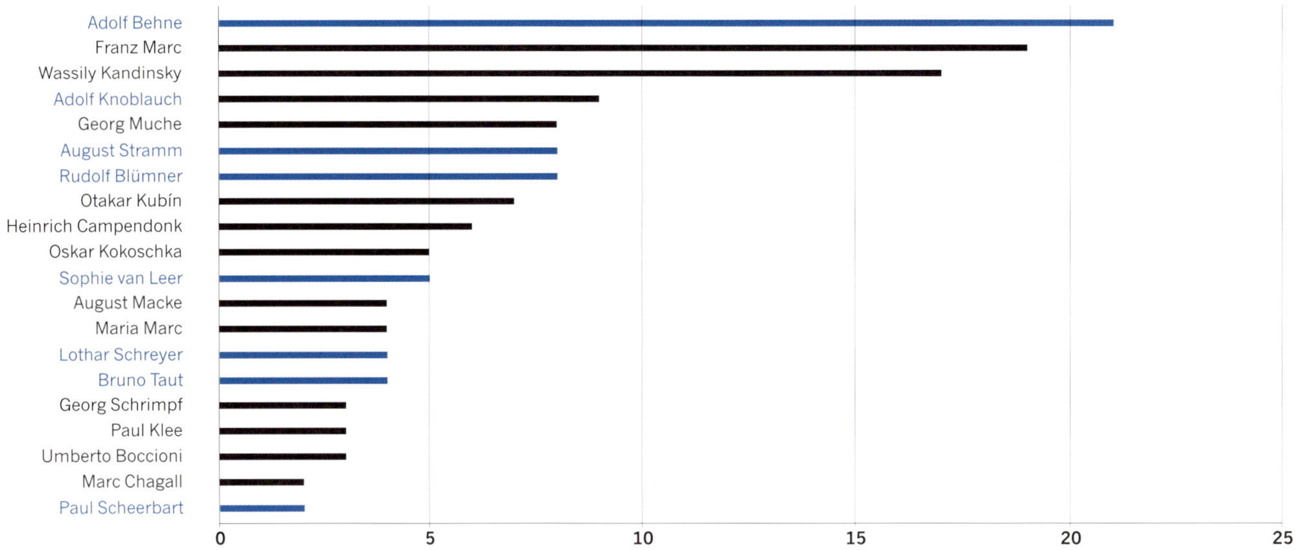

Groups of people mentioned in Van Heemskerck's letters, by percentage

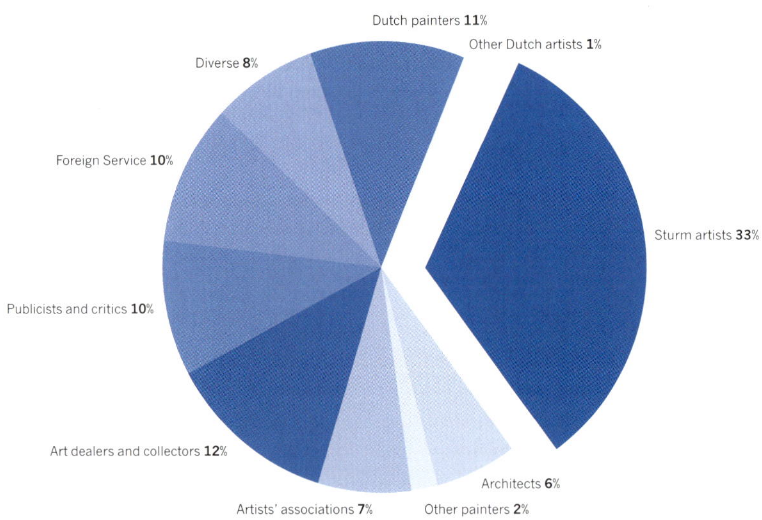

is on her relationship to Walden as an 'impresario',[28] 'road manager'[29] and the most important reference point in her life. On the other, the networking character of Der Sturm is emphasised specifically in reference to female role models. With a view to the increasingly fragile relationship between the Dutch painter and Walden, it would be revealing to find out to what extent she relied upon the Sturm network from around 1917 onwards. Thanks to her tendency to provide Walden with a running commentary on her opinions about certain people, it is possible to reconstruct her actual relationship to the people she mentions in her letters relatively well. Using computerised methods, we can identify the contexts in which the names arise and extrapolate from her statements her attitudes towards the people she mentions. This qualitative evaluation provides (albeit not comprehensively, due to the limited amount of data) a demonstrably positive example of the possibilities of semi-automated text analyses. Of course, we must also take into consideration that not all of her correspondence with Walden has survived. In tracking the number of letters exchanged per year, A. H. Huussen gives us a detailed view of the surviving documents.[30] The total for December 1919 shows, however, that we should assume that Van Heemskerck wrote many more letters to Walden. Even though only three letters from this month survive, Van Heemskerck summarises in mid-December: 'every day a letter'.[31]

Looking at all of the people Van Heemskerck names in the surviving letters at the Sturm Archive, a very heterogeneous picture emerges. In the attempt to discover which of her contacts in Der Sturm's network were important to Van Heemskerck and what her attitude was to the individual artists, the observation here will focus exclusively on the groups of Sturm artists who are mentioned by name in more than three letters. From this point of view, it is particularly noticeable that the names of the Sturm frontmen, Franz Marc and Wassily Kandinsky, are mentioned quite frequently throughout the first half of the correspondence, although a second glance shows that these mentions rarely occur in connection to their works. Except for Kandinsky, who is disparaged for his reference to his theory of art, their names are all mentioned in a positive context. This is mainly due to the worried and regularly sent inquiries about Franz Marc and others who were drafted or had gone into exile.[32] Her continued personal interest in Marc is especially surprising, given that she never met him personally.[33] The same is true of August Stramm, the model artist and major representative of the Sturm's 'theory of word-art'. In attendance at the first Sturm art evening on 1 September 1917, the so-called 'memorial celebration'[34] for the dead poet, Van Heemskerck expressed her regret at never having met him in person.[35]

Among the list of persons from the Sturm circle, however, a few names connected to critical statements made by Van Heemskerck appear. The main targets were Der Sturm 'renegades', such as Maria Marc, for example. Marc's widow allowed the Münchener Neue Secession but not Walden to publicise itself for setting up the first Franz Marc memorial exhibition.[36] That Maria Marc did not leave the posthumous sales of her husband's works to Der Sturm alone clashed with the forthright sense of gratitude Van Heemskerck had towards

Walden, even after four years of collaboration.[37] Even more devastating, though, is Van Heemskerck's criticism of the surviving Sturm artists who were looking about for more distribution channels behind Walden's back. Indicative of this is Van Heemskerck's reaction in the matter of Otakar Kubín, who several times turned to her, and not to Walden, out of financial need.[38] When the former Sturm painter asked for her help in finding distribution for his pictures in the Netherlands, Van Heemskerck was indignant mainly over his lack of consideration for Der Sturm: 'Today received an odd letter from Kubín, don't you also find it ridiculous that he asked through me not you to do the shows in Christiania and Stockholm. He doesn't talk at all about Der Sturm. Such a stupid fellow can't make it on his own, I can't sell his pictures here.'[39] The same went for the Czech Sturm painter Emil Filla, who fled to Amsterdam in 1914 and sought an opportunity to exhibit his works in the Netherlands three years later.[40] Again, in 1918 Van Heemskerck accused the former Sturm painters Albert Bloch, Carlo Mense and Georg Schrimpf of betraying their original common identity, when they permitted the Galerie Hans Goltz in Munich to represent them.[41] In comparison to Van Heemskerck, Walden was far more ready to compromise in such matters, and certainly more business-orientated, as well. As he did in the cases of Paul Klee and Oskar Kokoschka, he continued to show individual works by these artists, even after they were no longer under exclusive contracts with him.

Van Heemskerck's unconditional loyalty to Walden appeared to have an impact, not only on her position in the Dutch art world, but also on her position in Der Sturm's circle. Although in her letters she often asked about artists like Kandinsky or the deceased Marc, it is obvious that she had little direct contact to painters in Der Sturm's milieu. Huussen identifies Lothar Schreyer, Rudolf Blümner, Adolf Behne and Adolf Knoblauch as her sympathisers among the Sturm circle; they were authors, critics, and performing artists, but none were painters.[42] All four were among Walden's closest colleagues, without being artistically outstanding representatives of Der Sturm. It is no wonder, therefore, that the names of Behne and Knoblauch cease to appear in Van Heemskerck's letters after both had distanced themselves from Der Sturm, each in his own way. Van Heemskerck's straightforward manner and her absolutism about the art of Der Sturm were hardly compatible with the notion of continuing to stay in touch with someone who had turned his back on Walden. In 1916, when the rather solitary poet Knoblauch began to distance himself gradually from Walden, probably to avoid being swallowed up by Der Sturm, she must have been disappointed, because Walden had promoted him in particular and had asked his circle of acquaintances for financial support for the impoverished artist.[43] Her friend Marie Tak van Poortvliet had also regularly donated money to Walden, and for Van Heemskerck, this interpersonal gesture was a logical sign of the socio-normative function of art: 'the morality of art must illuminate everything', as she put it in 1916.[44]

In contrast to Knoblauch, she had already decided that Adolf Behne, the art theorist and critic, was suspect even before he broke with Der Sturm and Walden. In her eyes, artists and critics who allowed that any other art outside of Der Sturm's art might be valid committed sacrilege. She only grudgingly made an exception for Behne, even though his admiration and words of praise for her works expressed in his speech at the opening of the 29th Sturm exhibition flattered her. She forgave him as little for the fact that he mentioned her and her work in the same breath as the painters Max Liebermann and Hans Thoma as she did his for equal admiration for the 'Realist' Heinrich Zille and the incomparable Franz Marc in the same article.[45] What she found especially disconcerting, however, was the fact that Behne discussed his views on art theory and asked for her judgement in a letter, even though he had already spoken to her in person in Berlin.[46] This would hardly have conformed to her concept of a sincere friendship.

Considering that Van Heemskerck categorically rejected anyone from the Sturm milieu who did not identify with Der Sturm as she did, her explicit reference to her loyalty in the spring of 1918 reads like a warning: 'we must, in any case, stick together and [ensure] that I don't start anything behind your back'.[47] Initially, she did not take any step without Walden's full approval. As soon as she began playing with the idea of a marionette show, wanting to stage Lothar Schreyer's piece *Nacht* (*Night*, 1918), she went to get Walden's permission to contact the playwright. For the teaching concept at the Sturm art school and its branch in The Hague, which was set up specifically for her latest in fall of 1918, she also asserted their common theoretical foundations.[48] She openly confessed to Walden that she thought that Kandinsky's remarks in *Concerning the Spiritual in Art* (1912) were not suitable for the classroom because they were too dogmatic.[49] She also believed that the teaching methods employed by the painter Georg Muche at the Sturm school in Berlin were too limiting, in her opinion, to the free development of the students, since Muche relied too much on imitating established artists.[50] Walden's position on the matter can only be guessed at from another of Van Heemskerck's letters, but it was with relief that she agreed with him, that for 'correction',[51] as classes were called, books were unnecessary and that they should rely more on supporting the new generation of artists.[52] When she took up the plan for stained glass again, she did not neglect to inform Walden of it, and to request an introduction to the architect Bruno Taut.[53] Ultimately, the Dutch architect Jan Buijs was the first to commission windows from her, after Van Heemskerck exhibited her designs in Amsterdam to a good reception —for the first time, all entirely without Walden's participation.

Up until then, Herwarth and Nell Walden had been practically her only direct access to the Sturm world in Berlin. Through them she learned the latest news about the whereabouts of the Sturm artists during the war, about Kandinsky and Münter or, very late, about the founding of Der Sturm Klub.[54] As if in an internal artistic exile, Van Heemskerck was isolated in two ways at home. Her dilemma—on the one hand, her desire to do justice to her notion of loyalty in her friendship with Walden, but on the other, her near inability to converse with other artists—is revealed in the moment in which she sets foot on new artistic terrain and seeks a broader connection to the Sturm network.

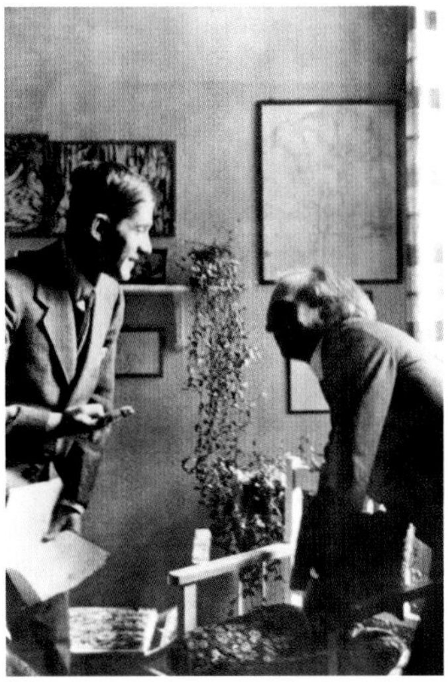

65 Oskar Kokoschka and Herwarth Walden in the design room of *Der Sturm* magazine, 1916

Breaking up with Der Sturm

The delicate crack in their common boundary between friendship and enmity probably appeared when Van Heemskerck encountered Kokoschka. The artist, known for his portraits full of nervous tension, that resemble psychograms, proceeded to dissolve the contract with Walden at that time so that he could switch to Paul Cassirer's art salon.[55] As was the case with so many of Der Sturm's representatives, the relationship between Walden and his early colleague was already strained when Van Heemskerck wrote to Walden in December of 1916 about how much she was looking forward to finally meeting Kokoschka at her Sturm exhibition. Perhaps the meeting with Kokochka did give her needed inspiration; at any rate, six months after her visit to Berlin, Van Heemskerck—so far known for her deserted compositions of sailboats and trees—eagerly turned to portrait painting. Enthusiastically, she described to Walden her intuitive, synaesthetically guided process, which is characteristic of what Rudolf Steiner's theosophists called 'aura portraits' (cat. pp. 109, 110).[56]

Whether due to Kokoschka's influence or the opening of the Sturm's theatre, Van Heemskerck spent the years of 1917/18 working intently on abstract images of people and exploring the boundaries of figural perception. In the process she allowed herself to be guided by the basic idea of how modern art could be better integrated into society. She fixated on the young, up-and-coming generation, planned the Sturm book of fairy tales and experimented with colours and their impact on children.[57] Furthermore, she set up a sort of branch of the Sturm gallery in her studio.[58] In her letters from this period her spirit of personal optimism is notable, but soon it was joined by her worry about the flagging progress of the Sturm movement.

As before, her and Walden's different perspectives converged in their shared ambition, the 'striving'[59] to renew society. So, from around 1918 onwards, she worried all the more about the possible loss of quality of the Sturm art. She felt that its prime position among the avant-garde was threatened and ultimately did not hesitate to share her thoughts with Walden vehemently: 'Really think about it, we say everything to each other openly as friends and new blood needs to be incorporated, not so much literature, we need important painters, it can't go on like this.'[60] Just three months later, when Walden inquired about a Dutch painter whom he considered a potential Sturm artist, she again warned him of too much artistic arbitrariness in the group and confronted him with the changed external perception of Der Sturm. According to her, a rumour was going around in the Netherlands that Walden was desperate to sign any artists to replenish the thinning ranks of his colleagues.[61] Her frankly expressed criticism of Der Sturm management clearly marks one of the turning points in her friendly relations with the Waldens, even though her letters after her visit to Berlin continued to be optimistic 'that Der Sturm would always remain at the top'.[62] But they say nothing about a new beginning or the intensive search and true struggle for a common path to new art. And yet, up to her untimely death in 1923, no one else took the position at her side that Walden had occupied as a well-meaning friend, an art expert, and business partner. For Van Heemskerck, Herwarth Walden was Der Sturm.

1 See Staatsbibliothek zu Berlin, Sturm-Archive, Jacoba van Heemskerck (from here on referred to as Sturm-Archive, JvH), 23 July 1915 and 14 October 1915.

2 See Herwarth Walden, *Erster Deutscher Herbstsalon*, exh. cat. Der Sturm (Berlin, 1913). For an overview of all of Der Sturm's verified exhibitions, see Volker Pirsich, 'Ausstellungen der Galerie DER STURM 1912–1919', in Barbara Alms and Wiebke Steinmetz, eds., *Der Sturm im Berlin der zehner Jahre*, exh. cat. Städtische Galerie Delmenhorst (Bremen, 2000), 257–70.

3 See Hubert van den Berg, '"... wir müssen mit und durch Deutschland in unserer Kunst weiterkommen": Jacoba van Heemskerck und das geheimdienstliche "Nachrichtenbüro Der Sturm"', in Petra Josting and Walter Fähnders, eds., *'Laboratorium Vielseitigkeit': Zur Literatur der Weimarer Republik: Festschrift für Helga Karrenbrock zum 60. Geburtstag* (Bielefeld, 2005), 67–87.

4 In 2011, as part of the project *Europeana Collections 1914–1918*, the Staatsbibliothek zu Berlin, which has had Herwarth Waldens' Sturm-Archive since 1926 (when it was still the Prussian State Library) and the papers of Nell Walden-Roslund since 1960, made the letters of Jacoba van Heemskerck, Franz Marc, and others available in its digitalised collections. See Bernhard Andergassen, *Bibliothek – Museum – Digital: Die Präsentation von Exponaten aus Bibliotheken in realen und digitalen Räumen am Beispiel des Sturm-Archives: Eine vergleichende Studie*, Berliner Handreichungen zur Bibliotheks- und Informationswissenschaft 367 (Berlin, 2014), online: https://doi.org/10.18452/2110. There is a detailed itemisation of the Sturm-Archive in Walther Gebhardt, 'Das "Sturm-Archive" Herwarth Waldens', in *Jahrbuch der deutschen Schillergesellschaft*, ii (Stuttgart, 1958), 348–65.

5 Arend H. Huussen Jr, 'Jacoba van Heemskerck und Herwarth Waldens "Der Sturm" in Berlin 1913–1923', in Herbert Henkels and Arend H. Huussen, eds, *Jacoba van Heemskerck, 1876–1923: Eine expressionistische Künstlerin*, exh. cat. Haus am Waldsee Berlin, Württembergischer Kunstverein Stuttgart, Rheinisches Landesmuseum (Bonn), Saarland-Museum Saarbrücken, Städtische Galerie Erlangen (The Hague, 1983), 5–20, here p. 10.

6 Maaike van Rijn, '"Ich arbeite viel und denke viel über Portraits nach": Jacoba van Heemskerck und andere Künstlerinnen beim Sturm', in Antje Birthälmer and Gerhard Finck, eds., *Der Sturm: Zentrum der Avantgarde*, exh. cat. Von der Heydt-Museum Wuppertal, 2 vols. (Bönen, 2012), 2:343–58, here 350.

7 Ibid., 349.

8 Lea Schleiffenbaum, 'Jacoba van Heemskerck', in Ingrid Pfeiffer and Max Hollein, eds., *Sturm-Frauen: Künstlerinnen der Avantgarde in Berlin 1910–1932*, exh. cat. Kunsthalle Schirn Frankfurt am Main (Cologne, 2015), 138–50, here 138.

9 Huussen Jr, 'Jacoba van Heemskerck und Herwarth Waldens "Der Sturm"', 10.

10 For more on this, see, among others, A. H. Huussen Jr and J. F. A. van Paaschen-Louwerse, *Jacoba van Heemskerck van Beest 1876–1923: Schilderes uit roeping* (Zwolle, 2005), 179, and Huussen, 'Jacoba van Heemskerck und Herwarth Waldens "Der Sturm"', 10.

11 *Der Cicerone*, 19 (1923), 891.

12 See Van den Berg, '"... wir müssen mit und durch Deutschland in unserer Kunst weiterkommen"', 67.

13 Hubert van den Berg, '"Der Sturm" und die niederländische literarische Avantgarde: Eine kleine Bestandsaufnahme', in Irene Chytraeus-Auerbach and Elke Uhl, eds., *Der Aufbruch in die Moderne: Herwarth Walden und die europäische Avantgarde* (Berlin, 2013), 79–113, here 80.

14 Huussen Jr, 'Jacoba van Heemskerck und Herwarth Waldens "Der Sturm"', 10.

15 The Sturm colleague Lothar Schreyer ascribed the words to the poet August Stramm. See Lothar Schreyer, *Erinnerungen an Sturm und Bauhaus: Was ist des Menschen Bild* (Munich, 1956), 7.

16 See letters from Jacoba van Heemskerck to Herwarth Walden, 1914–1922, in Huussen Jr, 'Jacoba van Heemskerck und Herwarth Waldens "Der Sturm"', 89–121; Huussen Jr and Van Paaschen-Louwerse, *Jacoba van Heemskerck van Beest*; Van Rijn, '"Ich arbeite viel und denke viel über Portraits nach"'; and Schleiffenbaum, 'Jacoba van Heemskerck'.

17 See Marjam Trautmann and Torsten Schrade, eds., *DER STURM: Digitale Quellenedition zur Geschichte der internationalen Avantgarde* (Digital Source Edition of the History of the International Avant-Garde) (Mainz, 2018), online: https://sturm-edition.de (accessed 3 September 2020).

18 For more on this, see, for example, her letter dated 19 December 1914: 'What do you think about my exhibition, is it better to wait until things are calmer? Just speak your mind. You always know what to do and I will gladly act according to your views.' Sturm-Archive, JvH, 19 December 1914.

19 Ibid., 23 March 1915.

20 See Van Rijn, '"Ich arbeite viel und denke viel über Portraits nach"', 352.

21 See Sturm-Archive, JvH, 3 March 1915.

22 Ibid., 23 March 1915.

23 Ibid., 23 December 1914.

24 See Van den Berg, '"... wir müssen mit und durch Deutschland in unserer Kunst weiterkommen"', p. 83.

25 Ibid.

26 See Sturm-Archive, JvH, 10 June 1917.

27 Ibid., 15 August 1917.

28 This description of Walden as an entrepreneur is often used to describe him, for instance, by Jan de Vries, 'Impresario's van de avant-garde', *Kunstschrift*, 54/2 (2001), 18–31. Quoted in Van den Berg, '"... wir müssen mit und durch Deutschland in unserer Kunst weiterkommen"', 81.

29 Ibid.

30 See Huussen Jr, 'Jacoba van Heemskerck und Herwarth Waldens "Der Sturm"', 9.

31 Sturm-Archive, JvH, 12 December 1919.

32 Ibid., 8 September 1914.

33 Ibid., 18 August 1915. This is also the case because he fell at the front.

34 See announcements for Der Sturm art evenings in *Der Sturm*, 7/5 (1917), 60.

35 See Sturm-Archive, JvH, 27 August 1916.

36 See *Franz Marc Gedächtnis-Ausstellung*, exh. cat. Münchener Neue Secession (Munich, 1916).

37 See Sturm-Archive, JvH, 4 April 1917.

38 Ibid., 7 February 1916.

39 Ibid., 24 March 1916.

40 Ibid., 11 November 1917.

41 Ibid., 8 October 1918.

42 See Huussen Jr, 'Jacoba van Heemskerck und Herwarth Waldens "Der Sturm"', 12ff.

43 For more on Knoblauch's process of separating from Der Sturm, see Volker Pirsich, 'Adolf Knoblauch zum 100. Geburtstag am 25. Mai 1982: Adolf Knoblauch und sein Verhältnis zum "Sturm" Herwarth Waldens', *Auskunft: Zeitschrift für Bibliothek, Archiv und Information in Norddeutschland*, 2 (1982), 83–107, esp. 88ff.

44 Sturm-Archive, JvH, 24 July 1916.

45 Ibid., 8 May 1916 and 19 February 1917.

46 Ibid.

47 Ibid., 30 March1918.

48 Ibid., 15 August1917. During her sojourn in Berlin in 1916 Van Heemskerck taught at Der Sturm art school. According to the official announcement in *Der Sturm* magazine, the branch in The Hague did exist latest in September 1918. See *Der Sturm*, 9/6 (1918), 88.

49 See Sturm-Archive, JvH, 24 July 1916.

50 Ibid., 15 August 1917.

51 Ibid., 27 August 1916.

52 Ibid., 15 August 1917.

53 Ibid., 8 April 1918.

54 Ibid., 18 August 1915. When Jacoba van Heemskerck finally heard about the founding of Der Sturm-Klub, it had been in existence for nearly a year. Ibid., 30 September 1918.

55 See Werner J. Schweiger, *Der junge Kokoschka: Leben und Werk 1904–1914* (Munich, 1983), 159, quoted in Andrea von Hülsen-Esch, 'Das Unternehmen "Der Sturm" und Herwarth Walden als Unternehmer', in Wuppertal, Der Sturm: Zentrum der Avantgarde, 2:201–25, here 210.

56 See Huussen Jr and Van Paaschen-Louwerse, *Jacoba van Heemskerck van Beest*, 127.

57 See Huussen Jr, 'Jacoba van Heemskerck und Herwarth Waldens "Der Sturm"', 16 and 17, n. 185. Here, Huussen refers to unpublished letters from F. W. Zeylmans van Emmichoven, who met Van Heemskerck and Tak van Poortvliet at the Sturm exhibition in the Kunstzalen d'Audretsch in March 1916 and had been friends with them ever since.

58 Sturm-Archive, JvH, 13 March 1917.

59 Ibid., 8 September 1914.

60 Ibid., 19 June 1919.

61 Ibid., 5 September 1919.

62 Ibid., 7 November 1919.

Catalogue

Kunstmuseum Den Haag

Vliegdennenbos |
Naturally Seeded Pine Wood 1910
Oil on canvas
93,6 × 71,3 cm

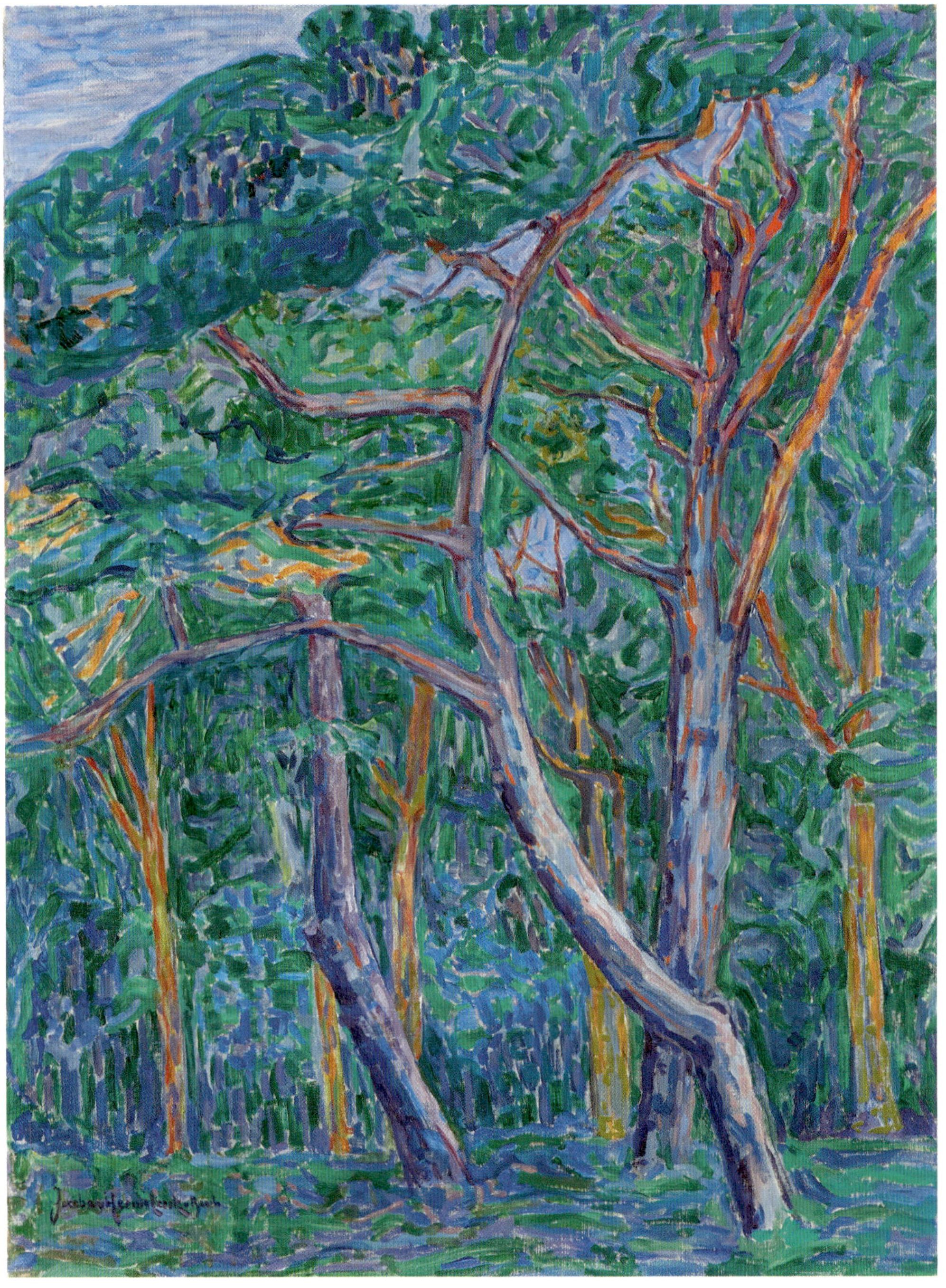

Twee bomen |
Two Trees 1910
Oil on canvas
70,5 × 88,2 cm

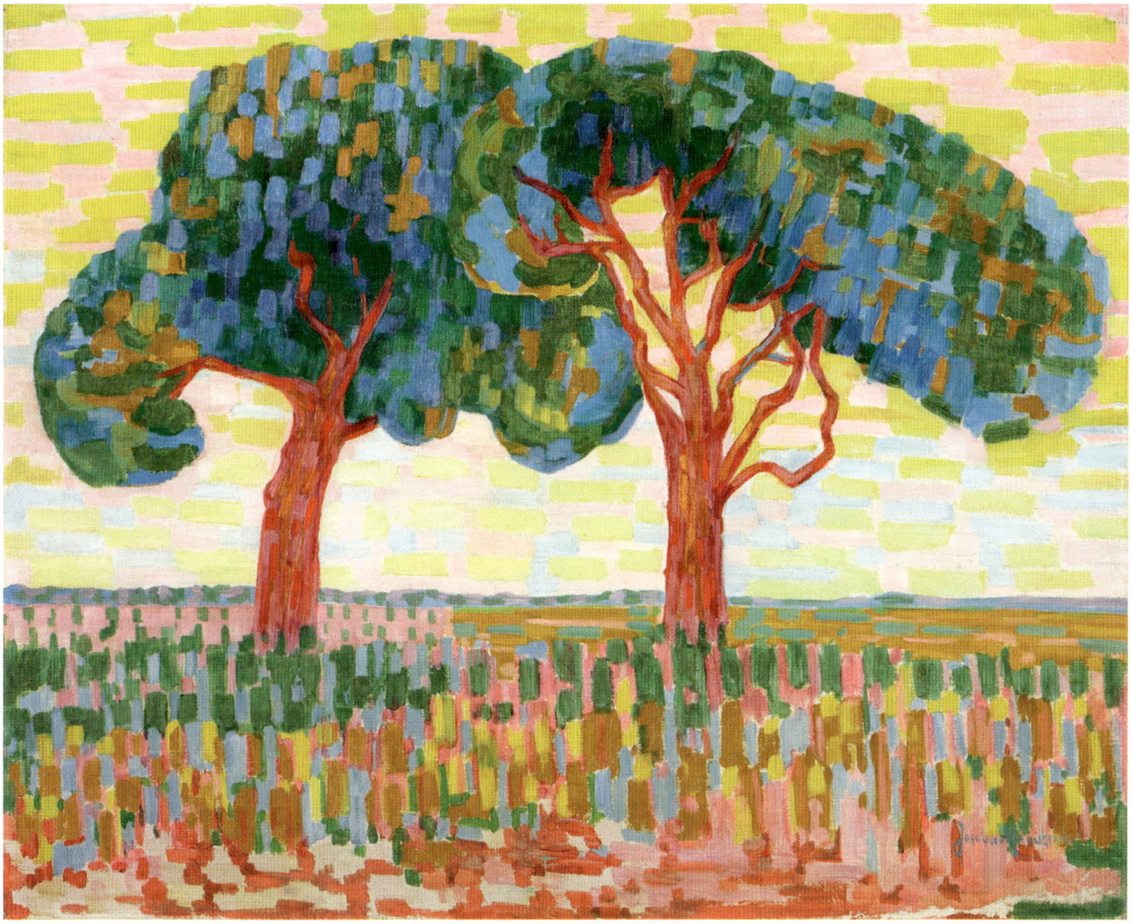

Compositie no. 1 |
Composition no. 1 1912/13
Oil on canvas
100,1 × 80,4 cm

Berglandschap met groene boompjes |
Mountain Landscape with Green Trees 1912/13
Oil on canvas
46 × 38,2 cm

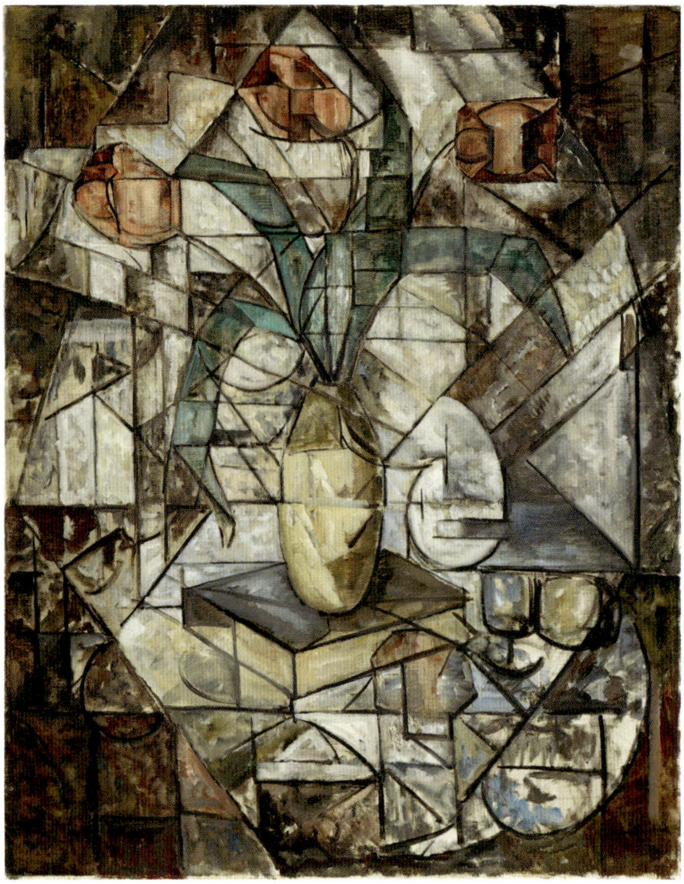

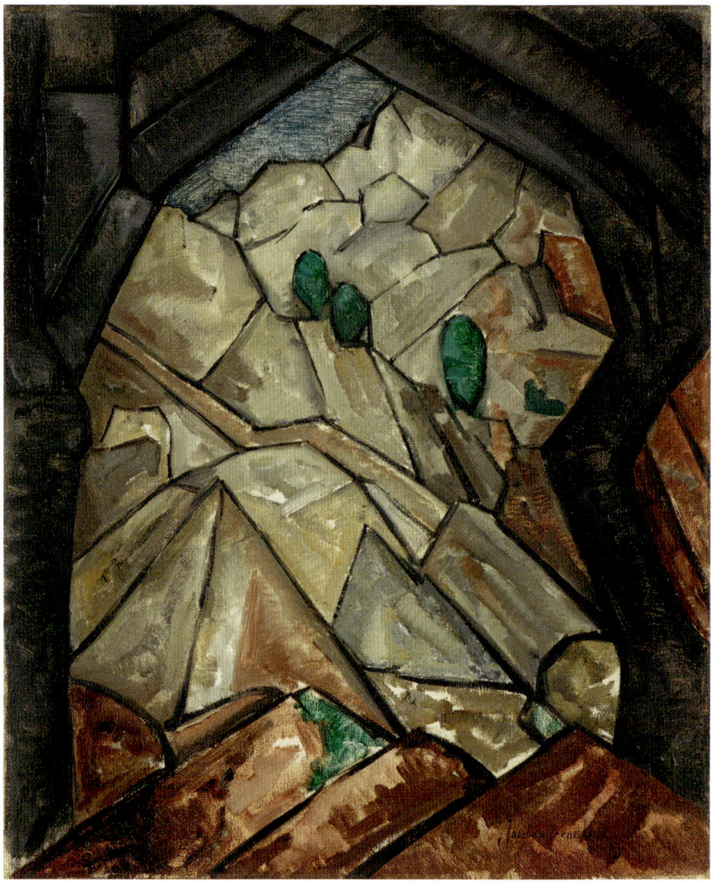

Compositie no. 2 |
Composition no. 2 1912/13
Oil on canvas
80 × 60,5 cm

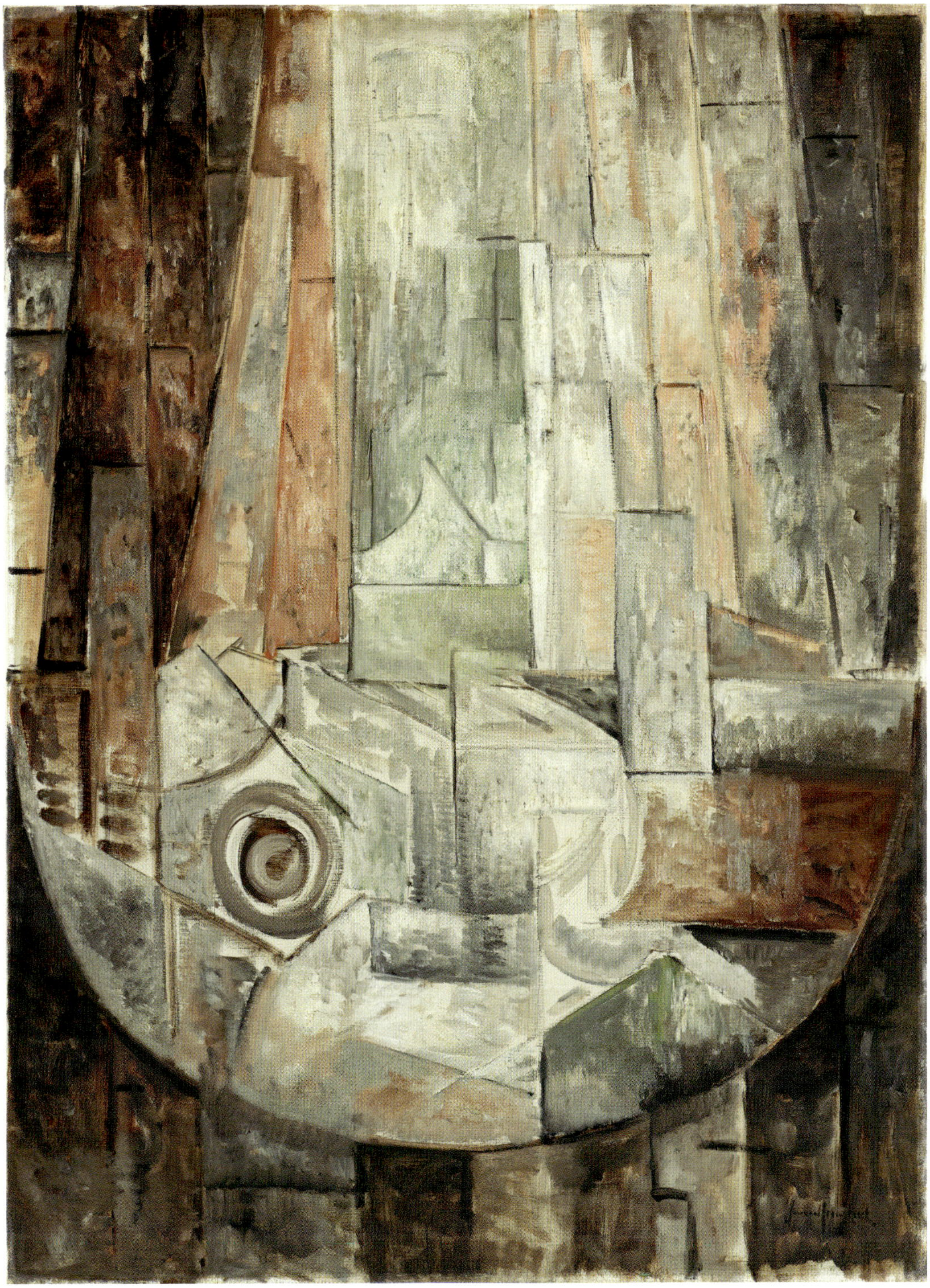

Bos I | **Woodland I** 1913
Oil on canvas
81 × 102 cm

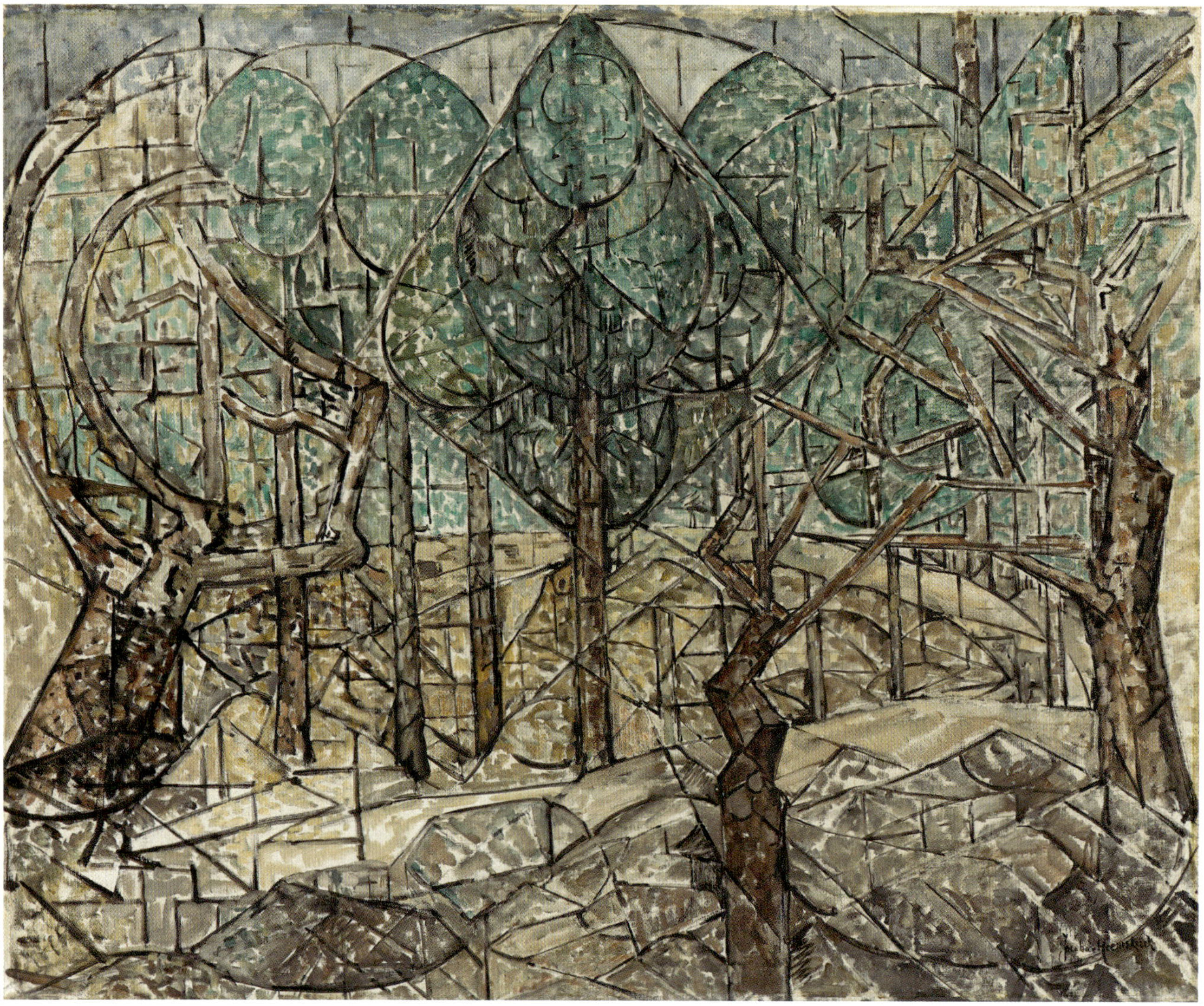

Bos II | Woodland II 1913
Oil on canvas
80,5 × 100,4 cm

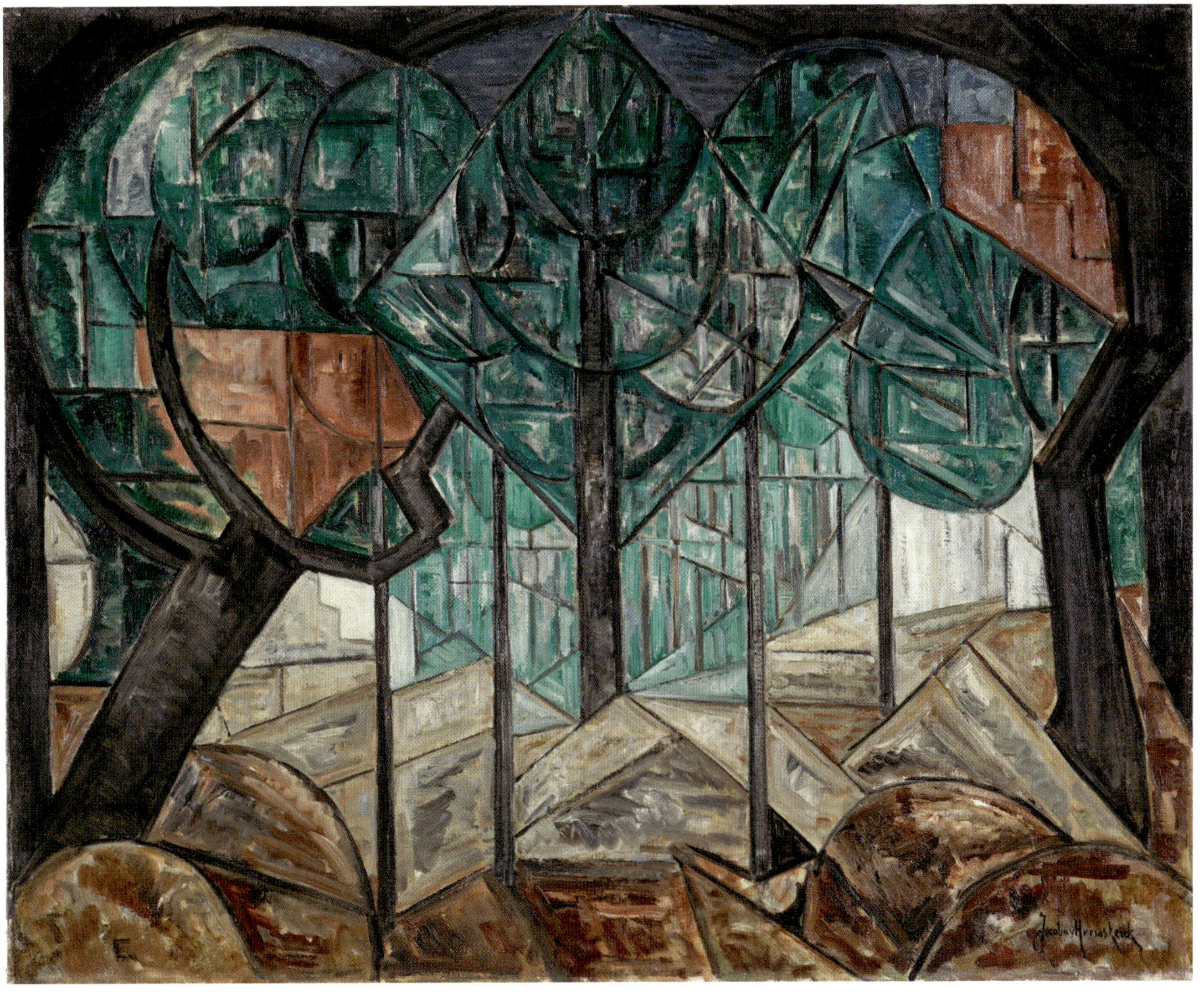

Landschap no. 6 |
Landscape no. 6 1913
Oil on canvas
100 × 80,6 cm

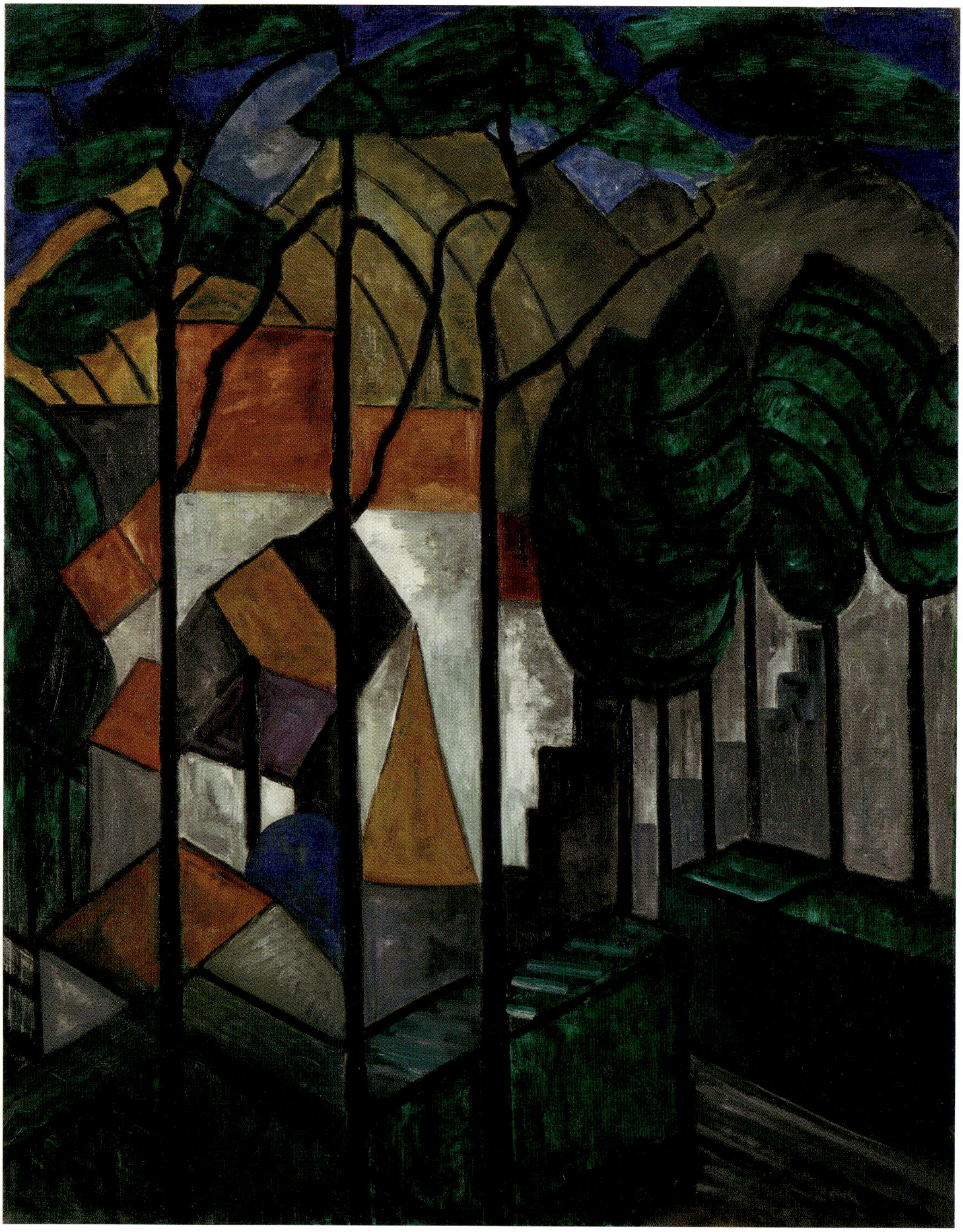

Landschap no. 15 (Dorpsgezicht) |
Landscape no. 15 (View of the Village) 1914
Oil on canvas
61 × 57 cm

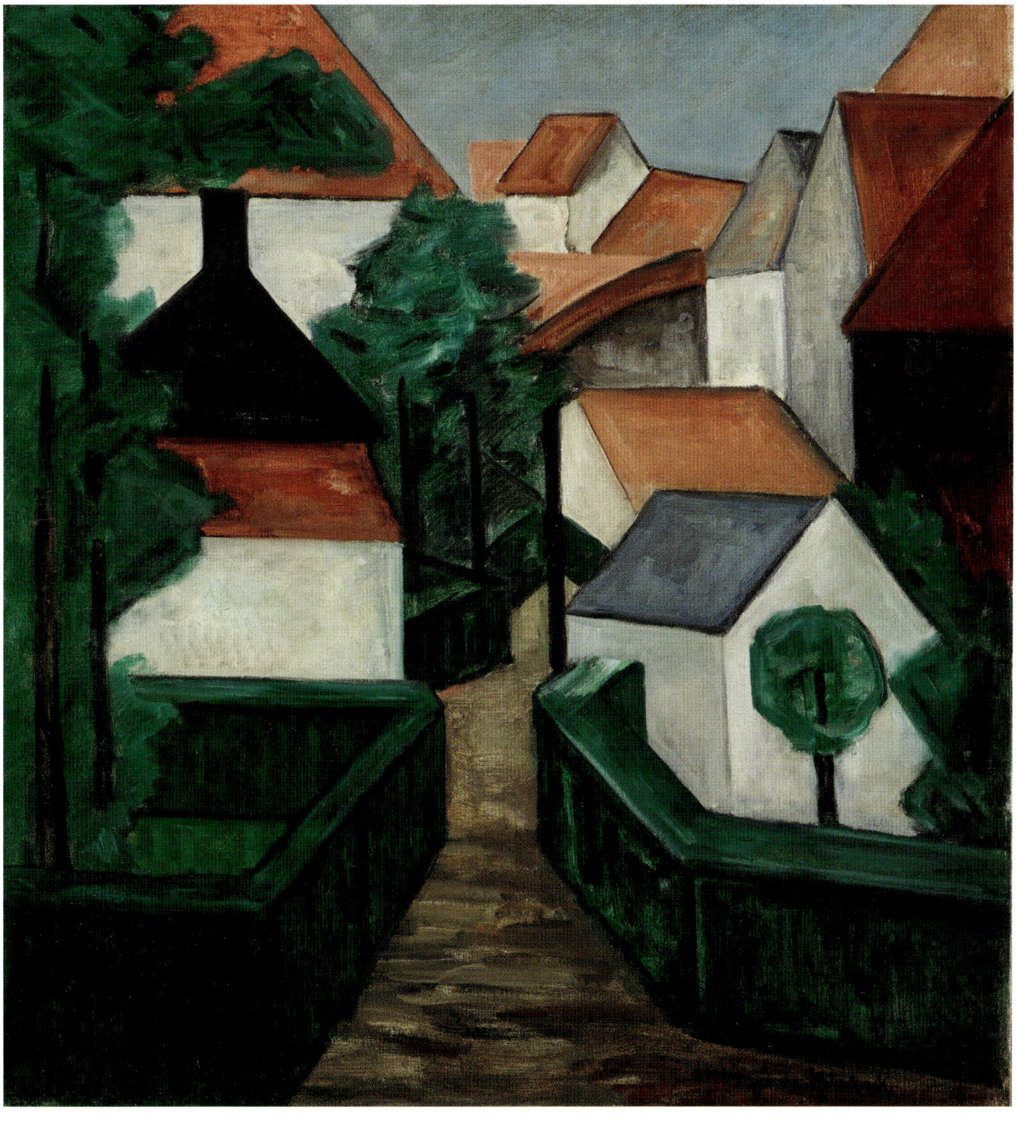

Compositie (Stilleven) |
Composition (Still life) 1914
Woodcut on Japanese paper
19,9 × 28,2 cm (sheet)

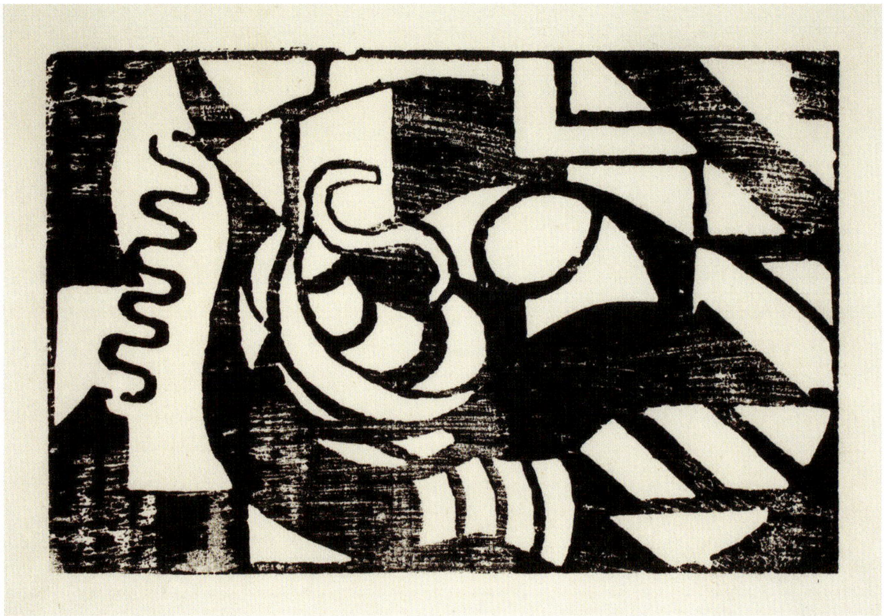

Bild no. 8 (Stilleven met kan) |
Image no. 8 (Still life with Jug) 1914
Oil on canvas
56,5 × 66,5 cm

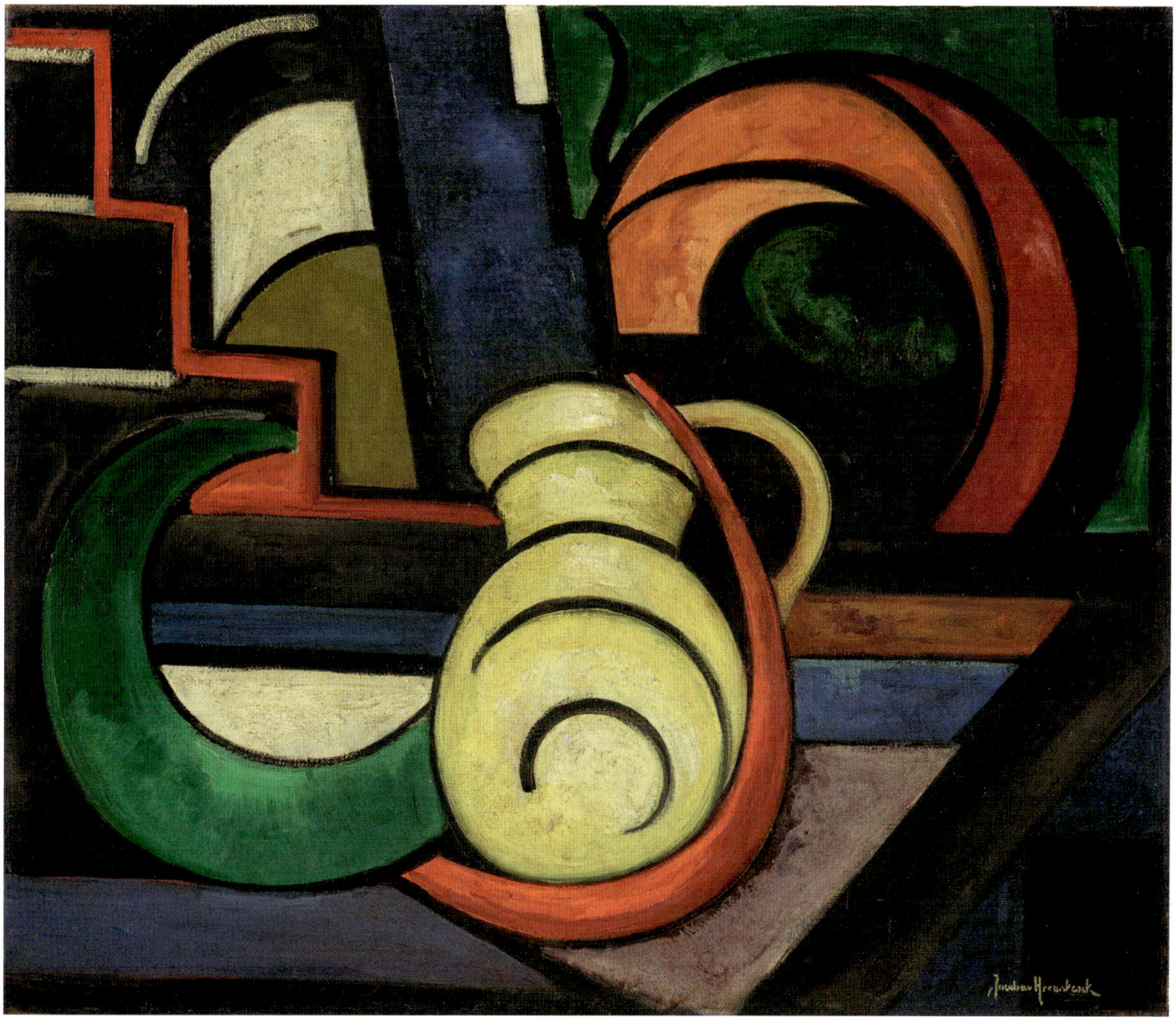

Bild no. 10 | **Image no. 10** 1914
Oil on canvas
56,1 × 48,3 cm

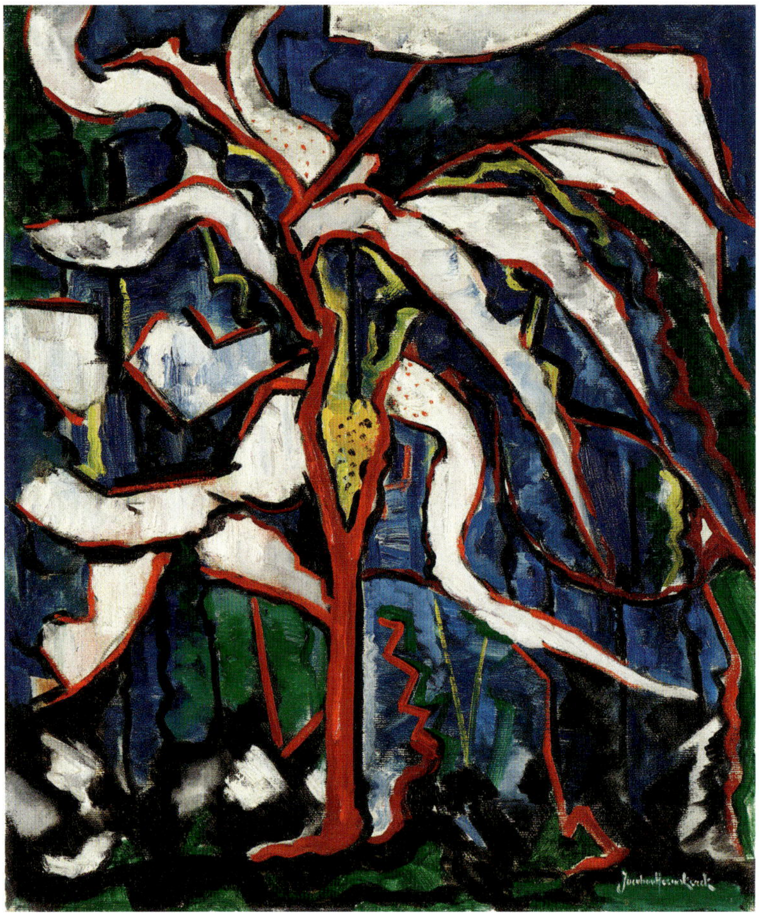

Compositie | **Composition** 1914
Oil on canvas
75 × 109 cm

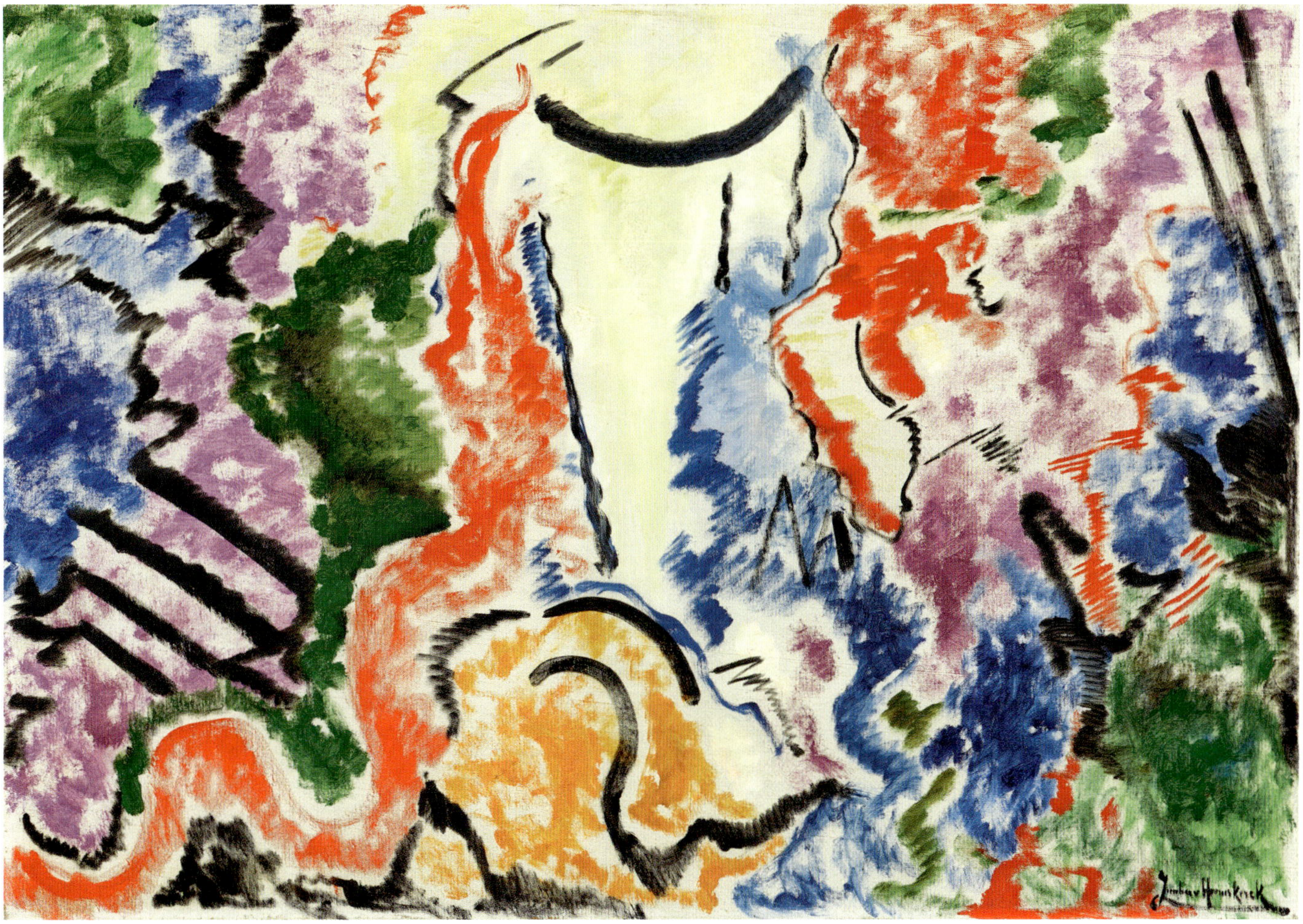

Compositie (Boom) |
Composition (Tree) 1915
Woodcut on Japanese paper
37,9 × 30,3 cm (sheet)

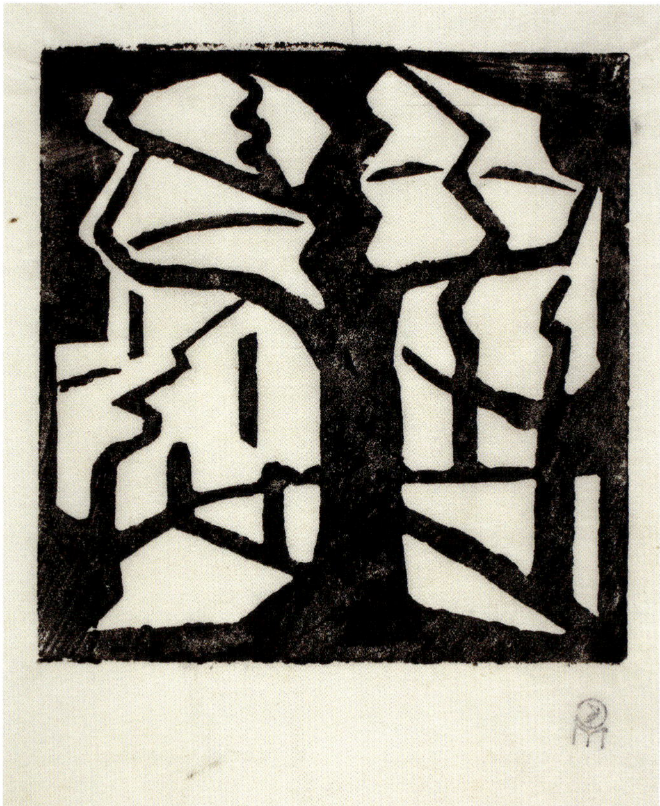

Bild no. 23 (Witte zeilschepen op een meer) |
Image no. 23 (White Sailing Ships on a Lake) 1915
Oil on canvas
111,1 × 130,9 cm

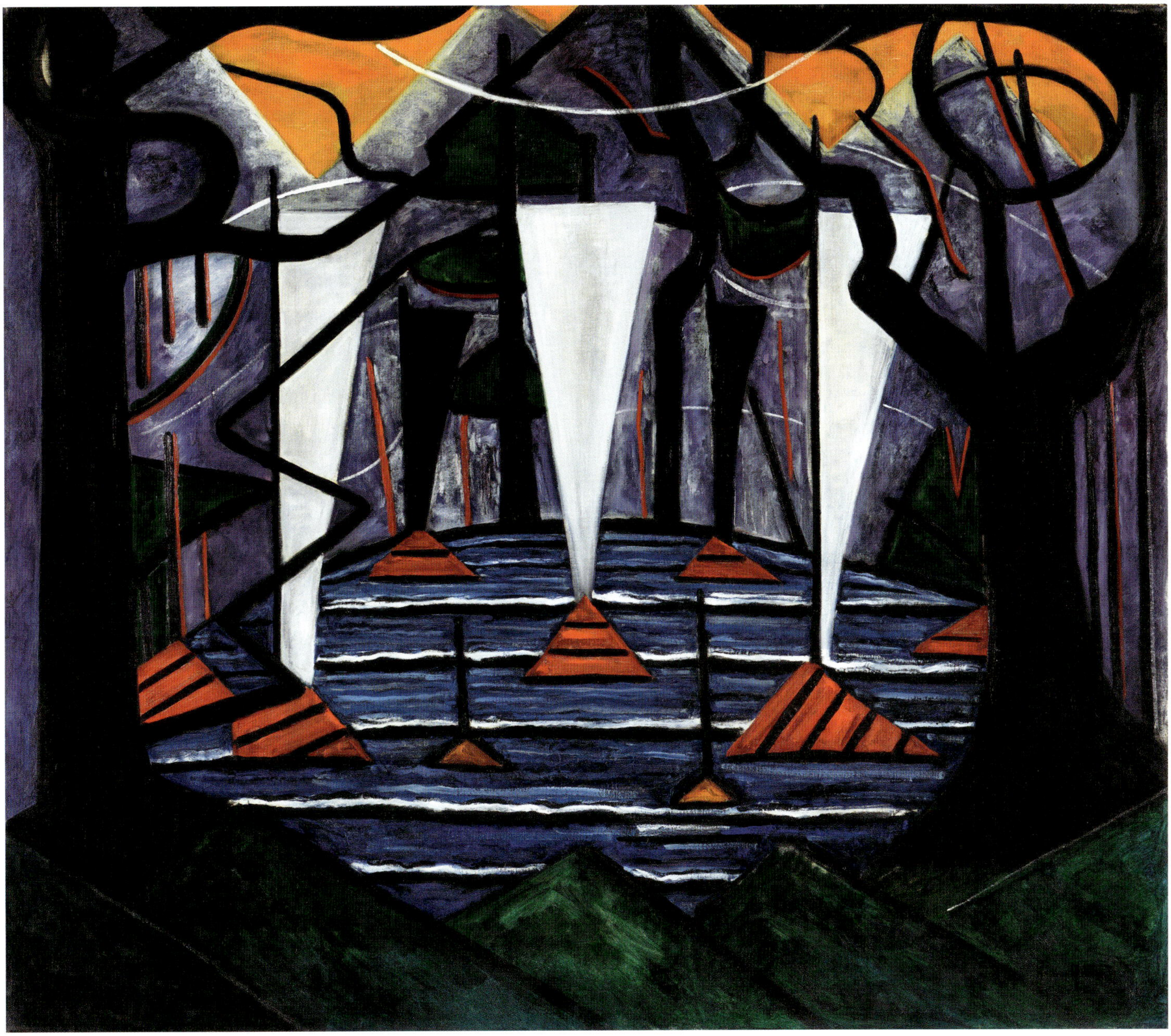

Compositie (Boten in haven) |
Composition (Boats in Harbour) 1916
Woodcut on paper
37,8 × 36,1 cm (sheet)

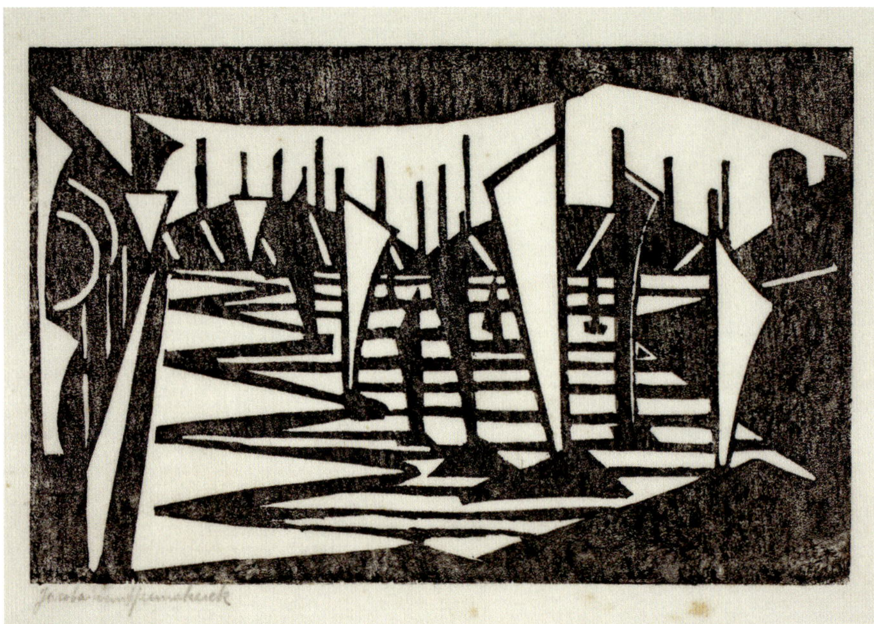

Bild no. 18 | **Image no. 18** 1915
Oil on canvas
87 × 77,5 cm

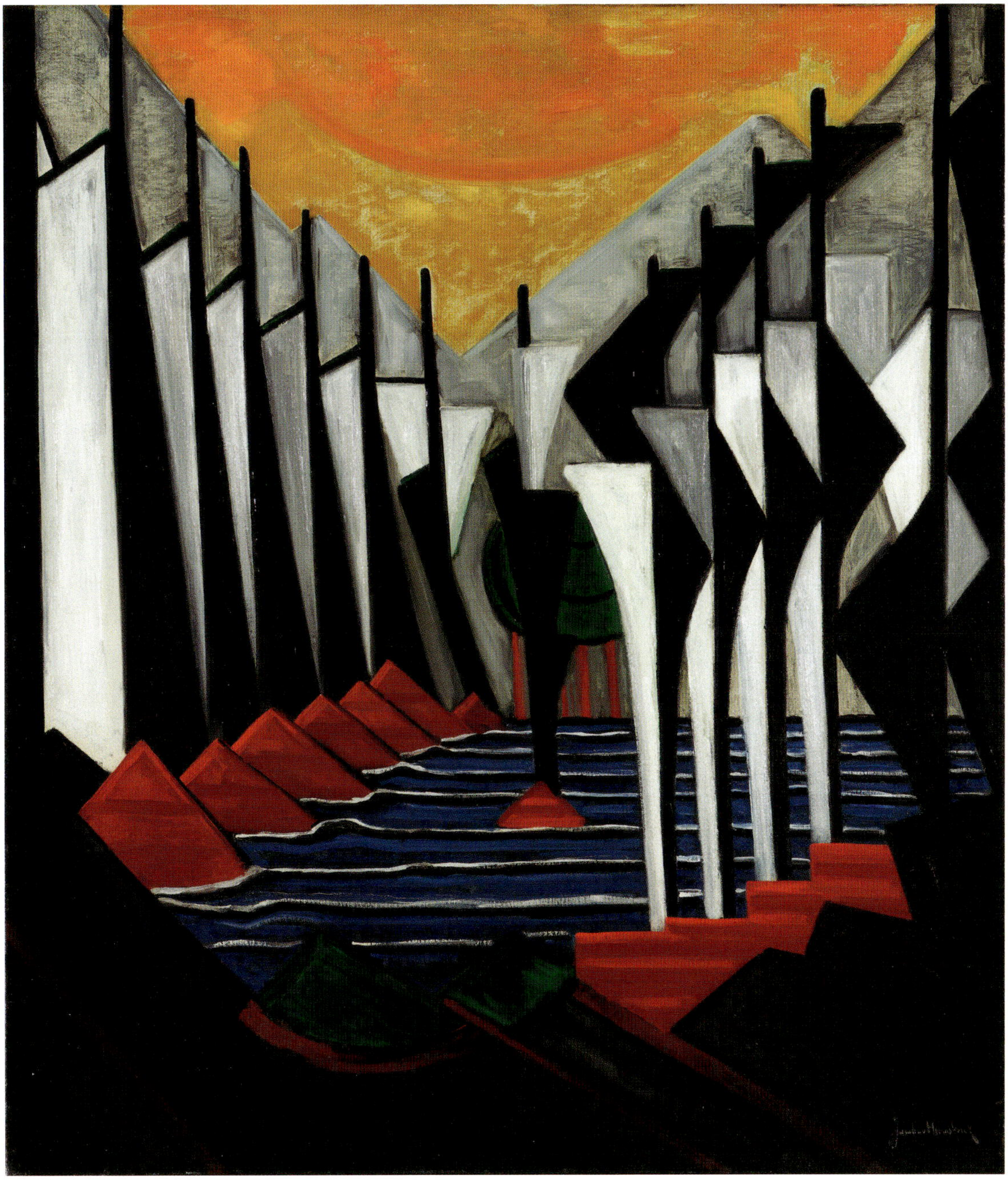

Compositie 9 no. 18 (Boten) |
Composition 9 no. 18 (Boats) 1915
Woodcut on paper
35,2 × 47,8 cm (sheet)

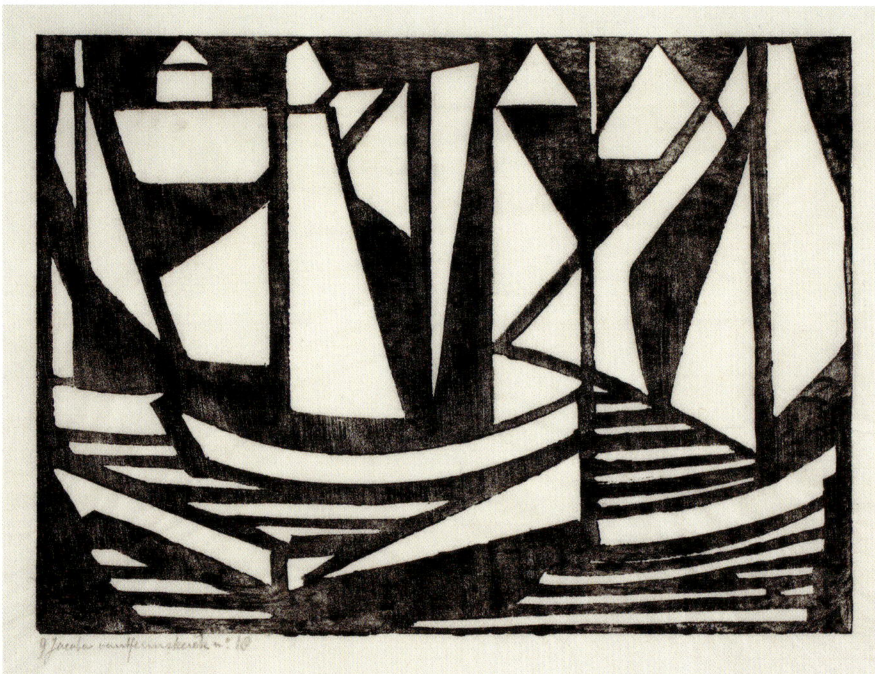

Bild no. 36 | **Image no. 36** 1915
Oil on canvas
57,3 × 44,2 cm

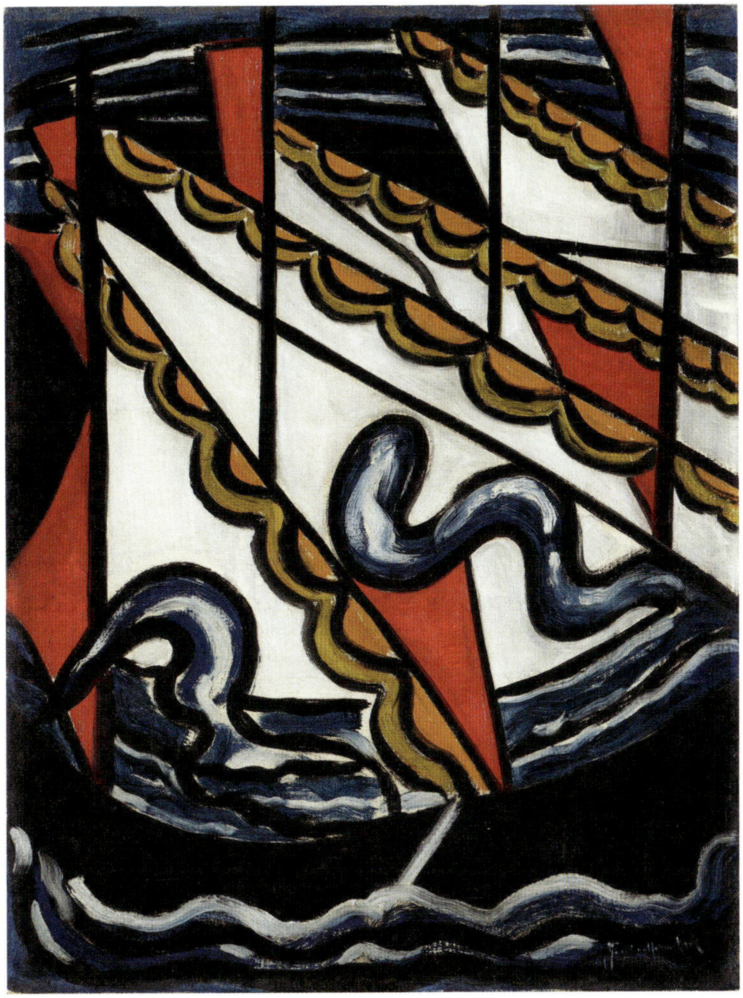

Bild no. 25 | **Image no. 25** 1915
Oil on canvas
112,6 × 193 cm

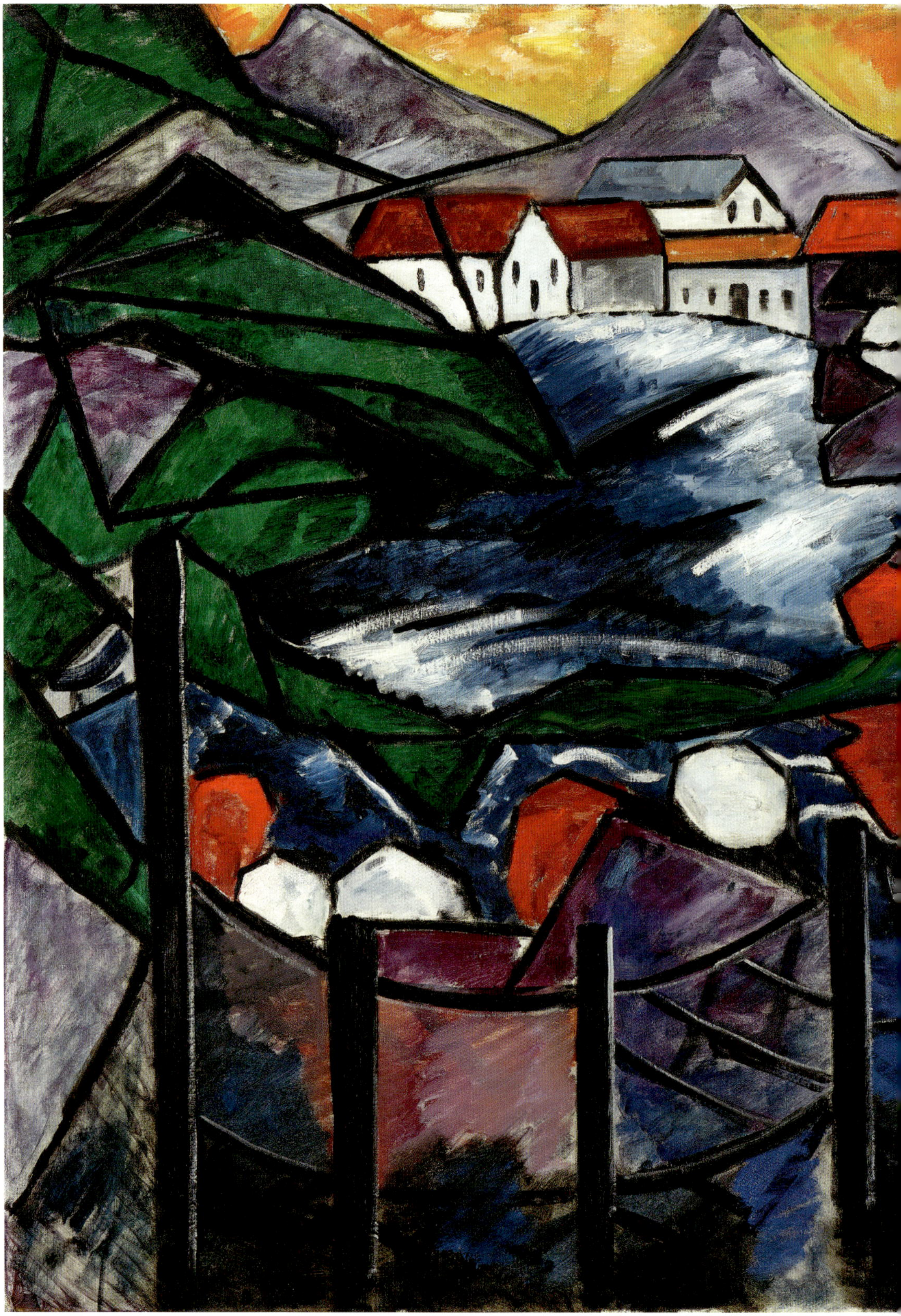

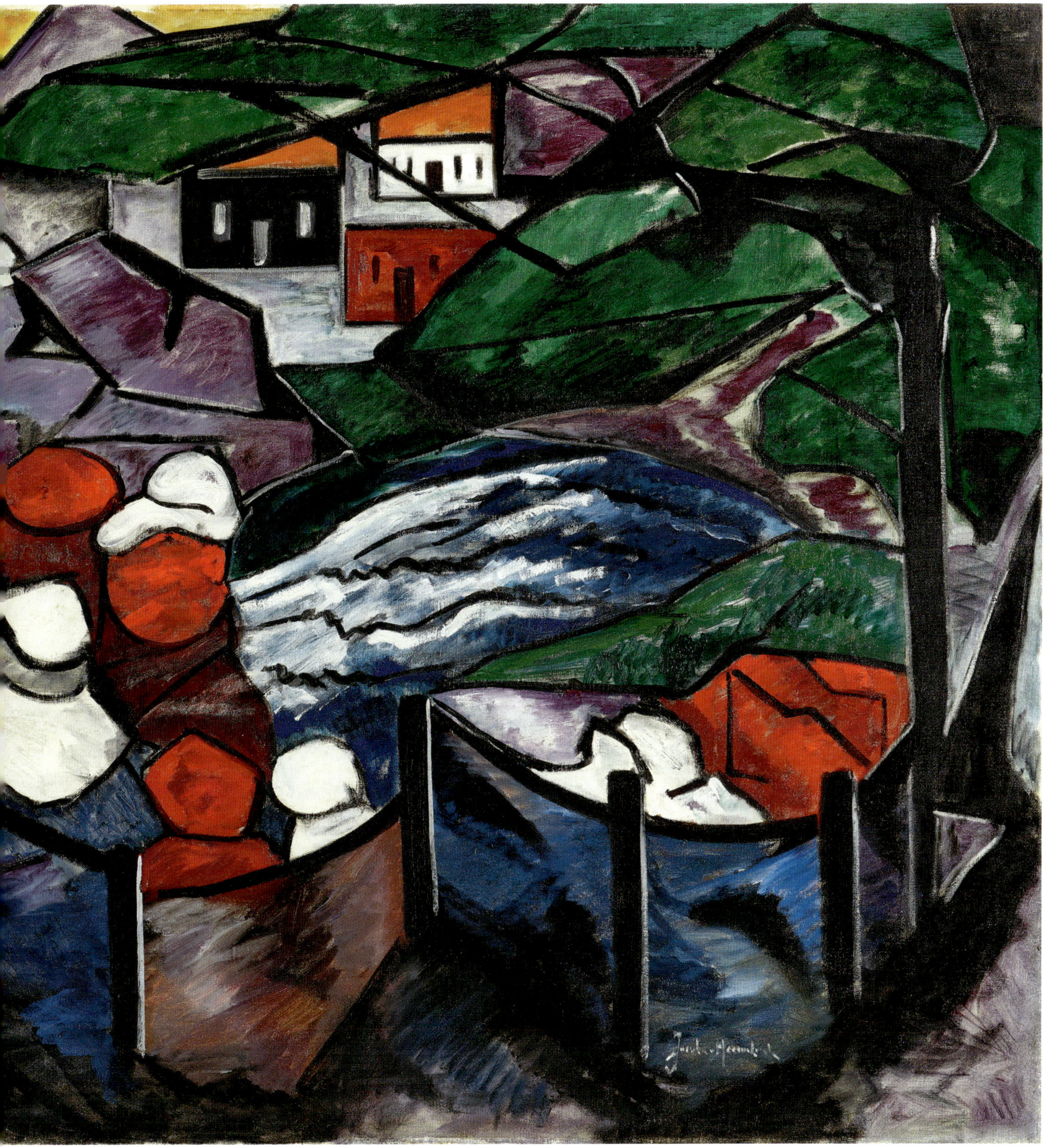

Compositie XVII no. 16 (Dorp aan de rivier) |
Composition XVII no. 16 (Village on the River) 1918
Woodcut and watercolour on paper
17,1 × 19,9 cm (sheet)

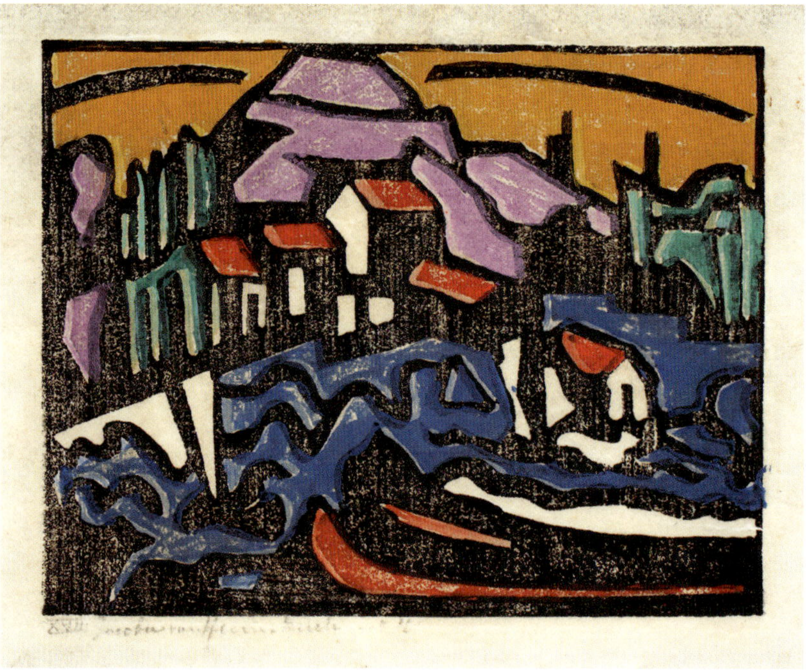

Bild no. 33 (Zee met schepen) |
Image no. 33 (Ships at Sea) 1915
Oil on canvas
80,5 × 100,5 cm

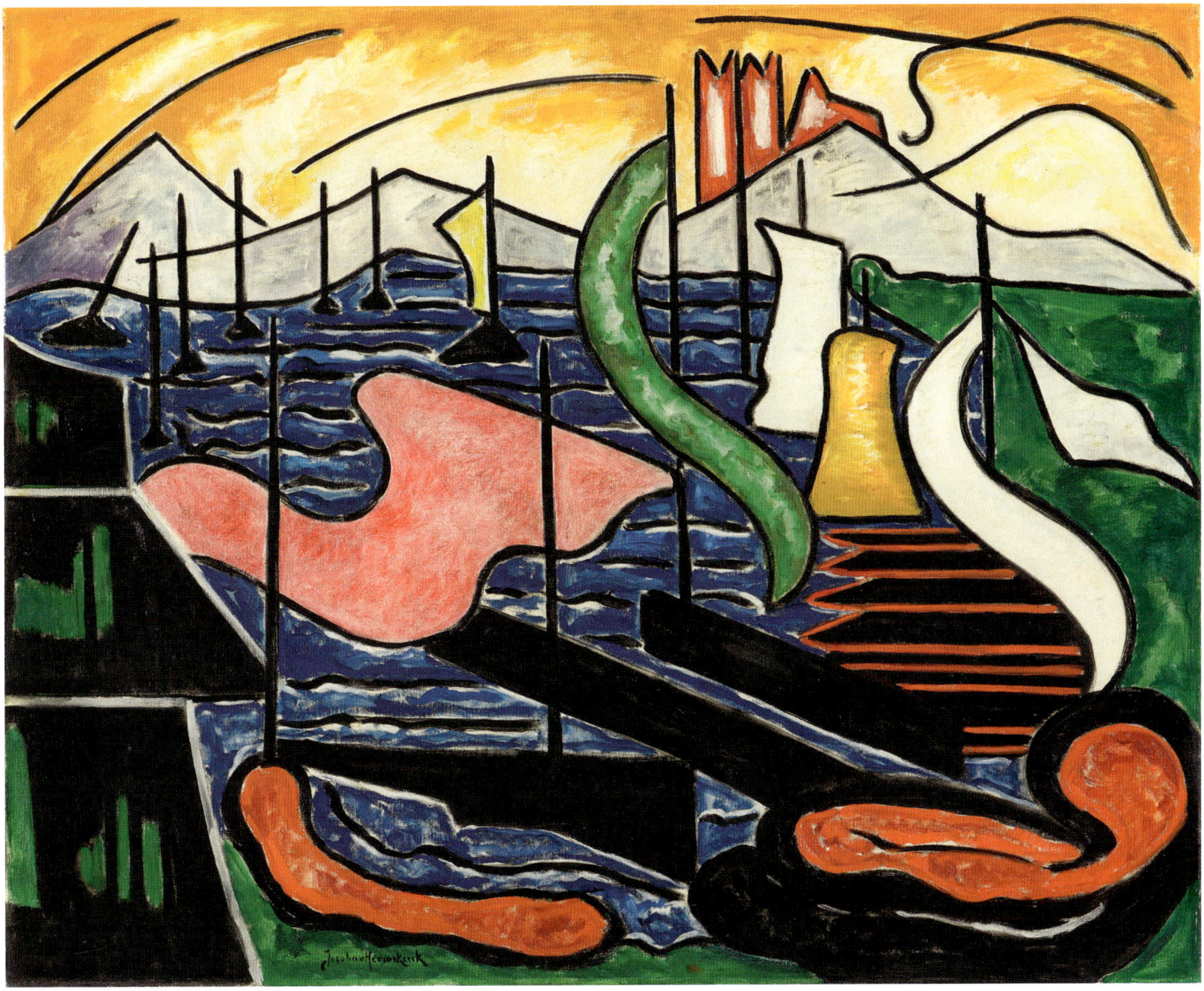

Bild (Landschap met bomen en bergen) |
Image (Landscape with Trees and Mountains) 1915
Oil on canvas
46,3 × 56,4 cm

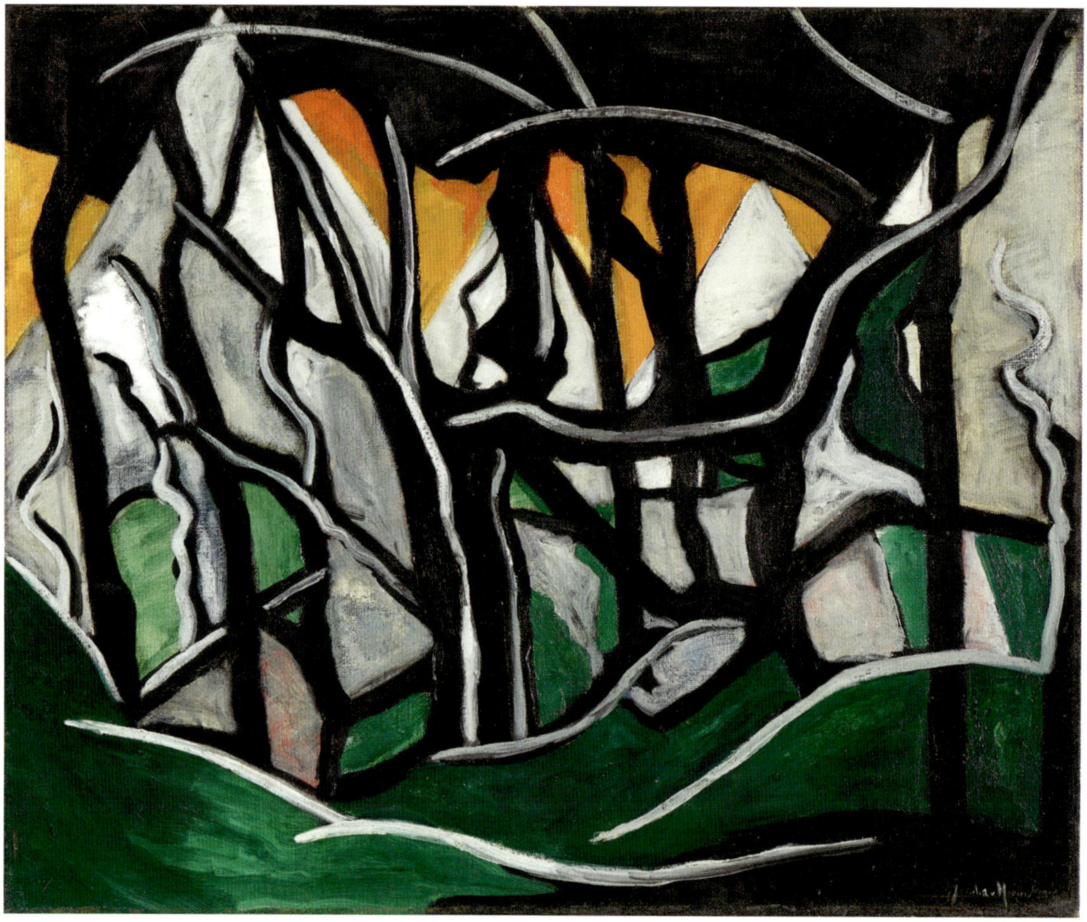

Compositie (Bosweg) |
Composition (Forest Road) 1918
Woodcut on Japanese paper
31,3 × 45,7 cm (sheet)

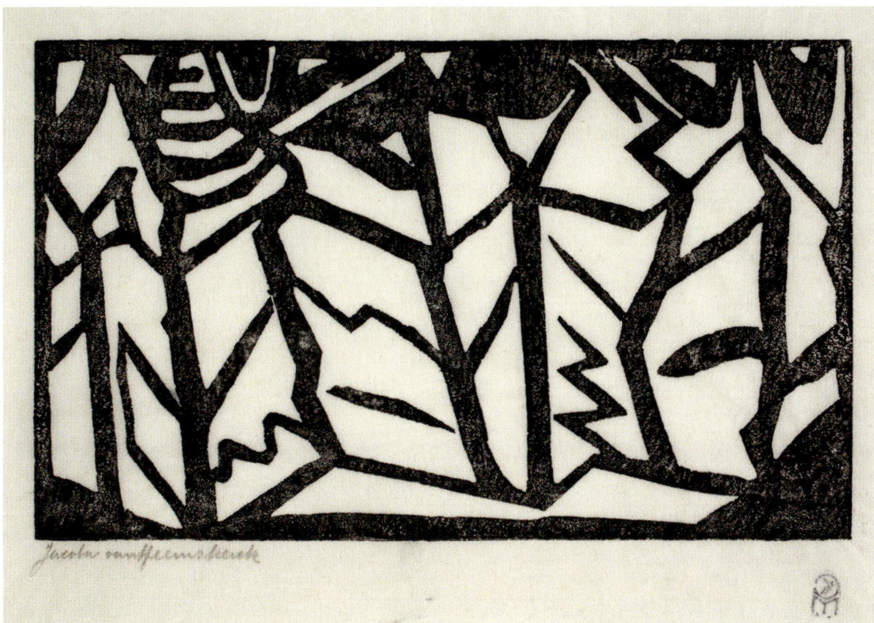

Compositie 6 no. 14 |
Composition 6 no. 14 1915
Woodcut on paper
32,3 × 50,6 cm (sheet)

Compositie no. 15 |
Composition no. 15 1915
Woodcut on Japanese paper
31,6 × 45,2 cm (sheet)

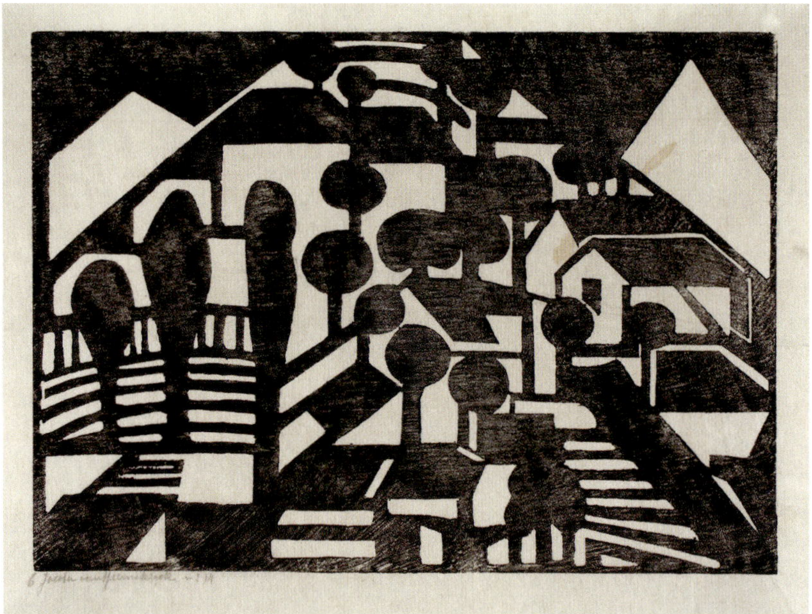

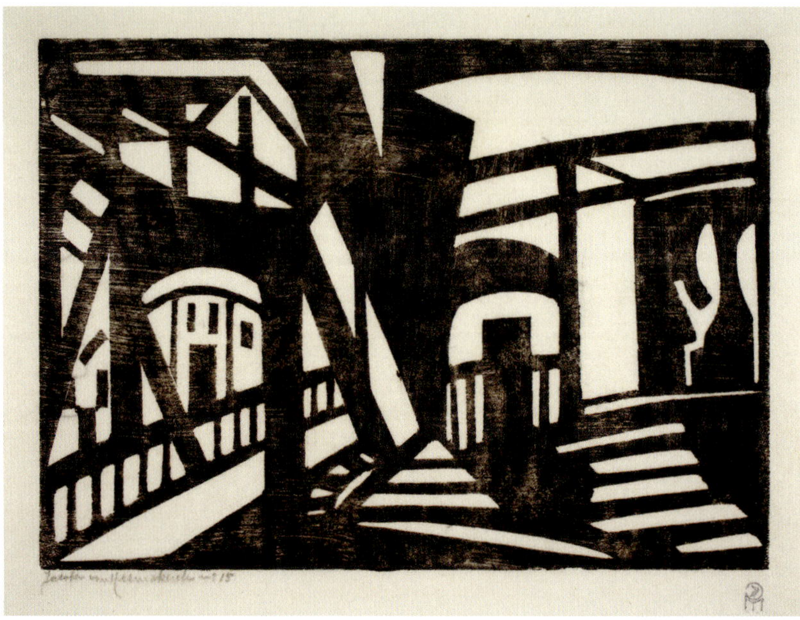

Bild no. 41 | **Image no. 41** 1916
Oil on canvas
105 × 78 cm

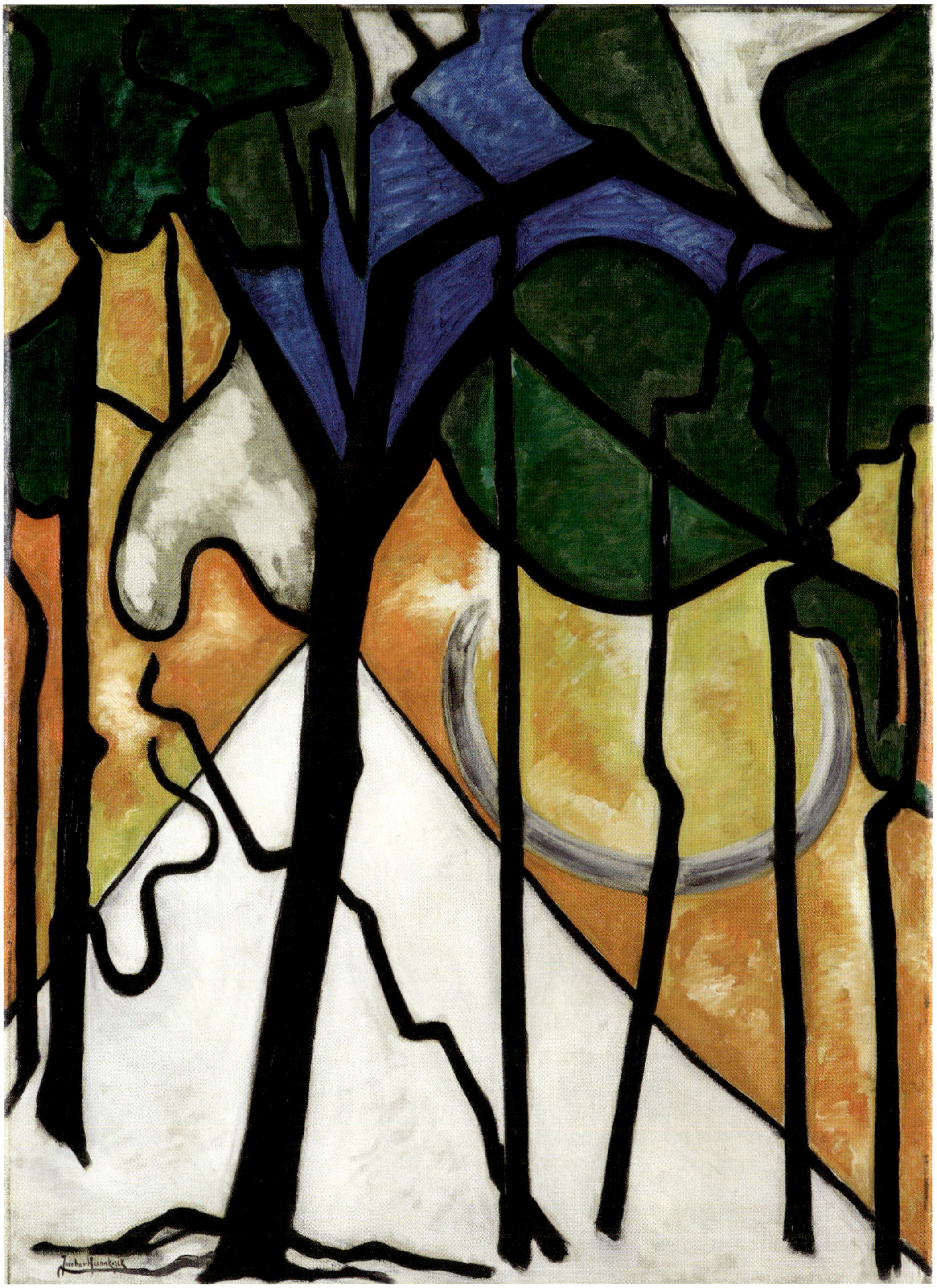

Compositie (Fjord) |
Composition (Fjord) 1916
Woodcut on Japanese paper
31,5 × 46 cm (sheet)

Compositie |
Composition 1916
Woodcut on Japanese paper
31 × 44,1 cm (sheet)

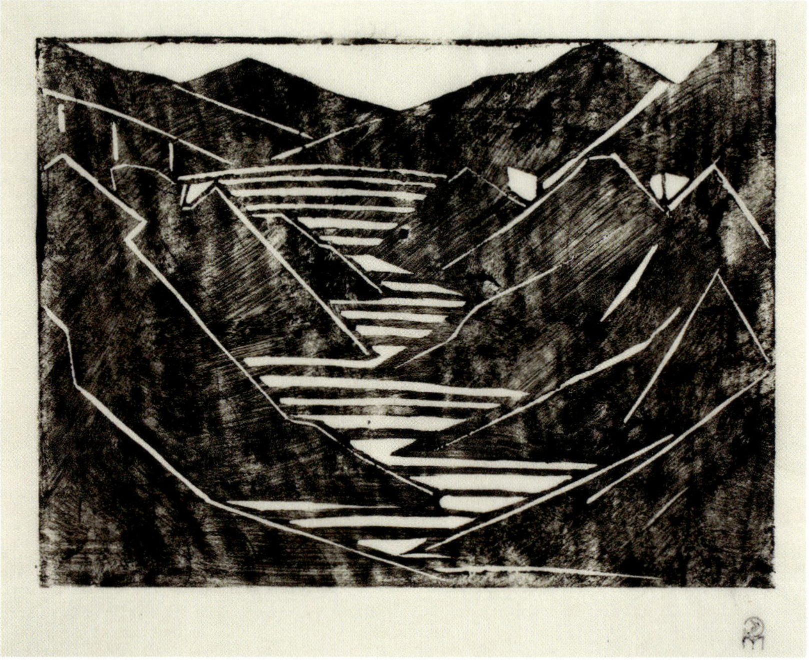

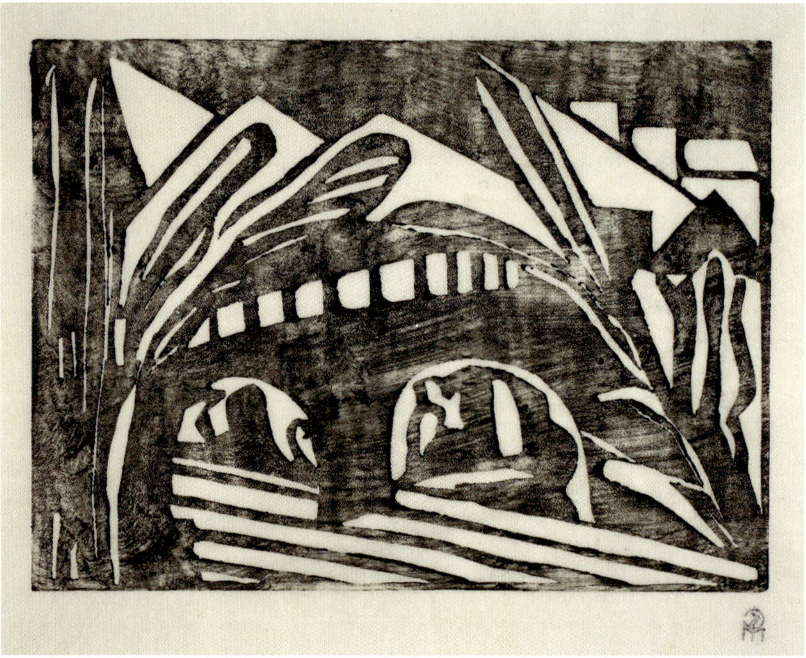

Bild no. 77 | **Image no. 77** 1917
Oil on canvas
75,7 × 75,7 cm

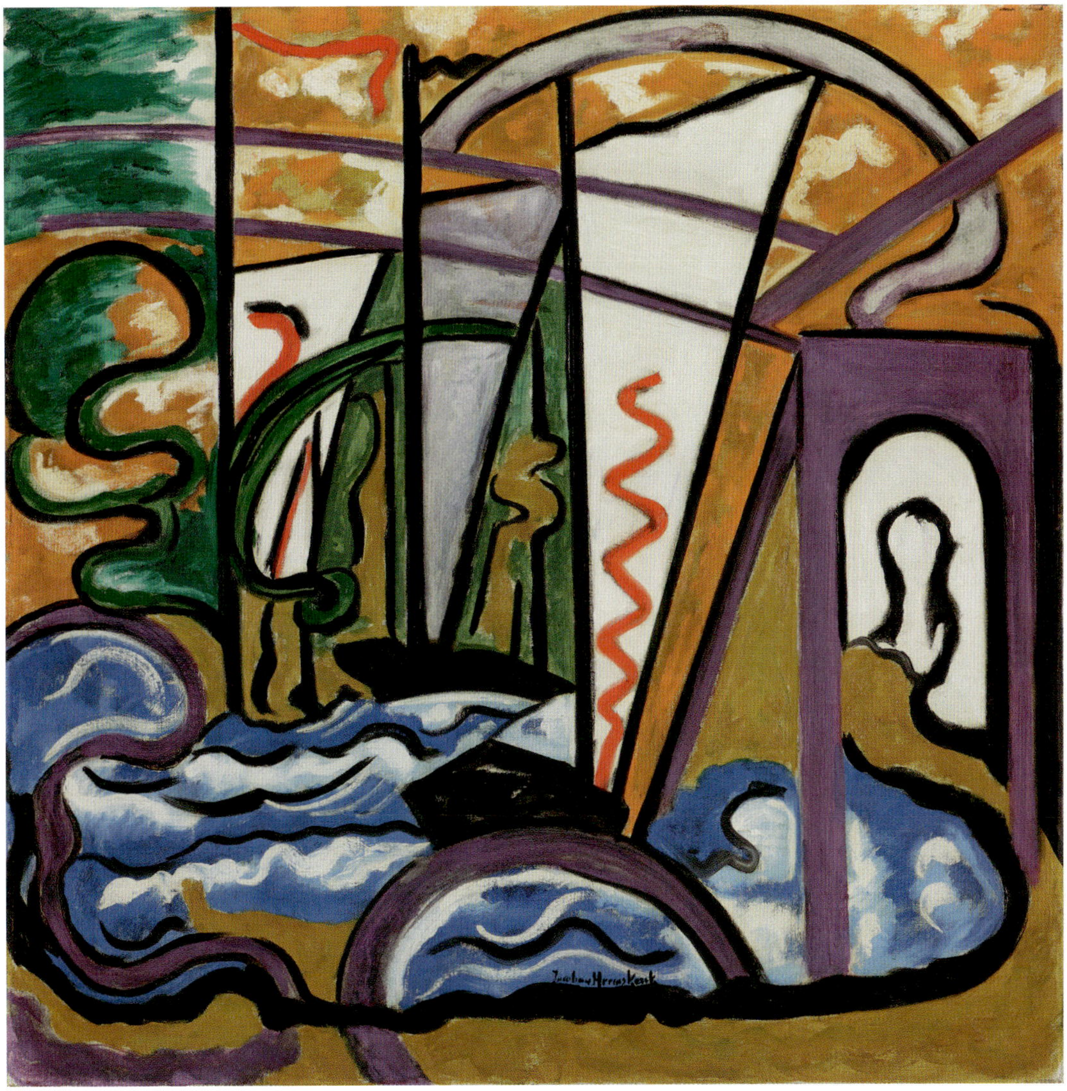

Bild no. 45 (Vissen) |
Image no. 45 (Fish) 1916
Oil on canvas
68 × 109 cm

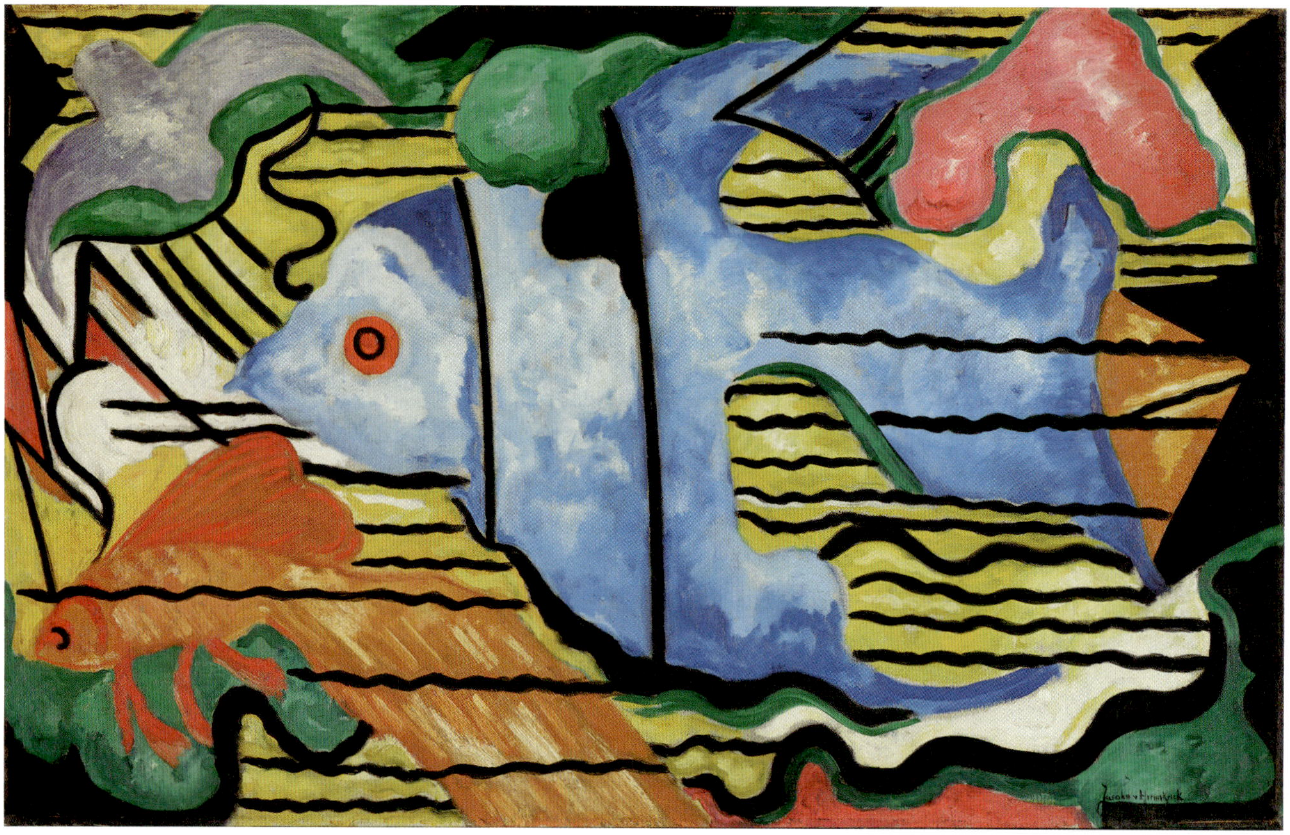

Bild no. 46 (Rog) |
Image no. 46 (Ray) 1916
Oil on canvas
95,5 × 72,5 cm

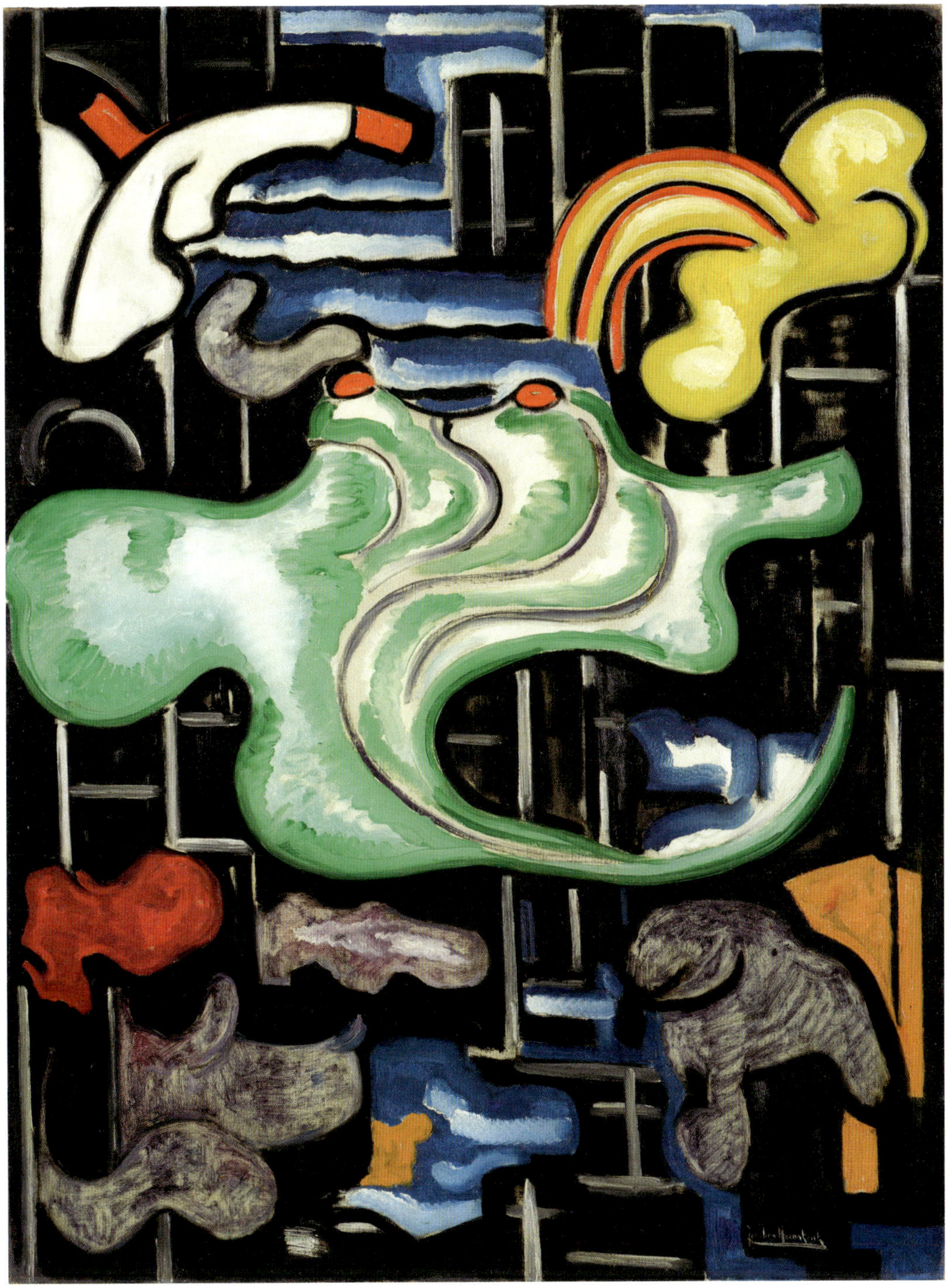

Bild no. 78 | **Image no. 78** 1917
Oil on canvas
77,5 × 135 cm

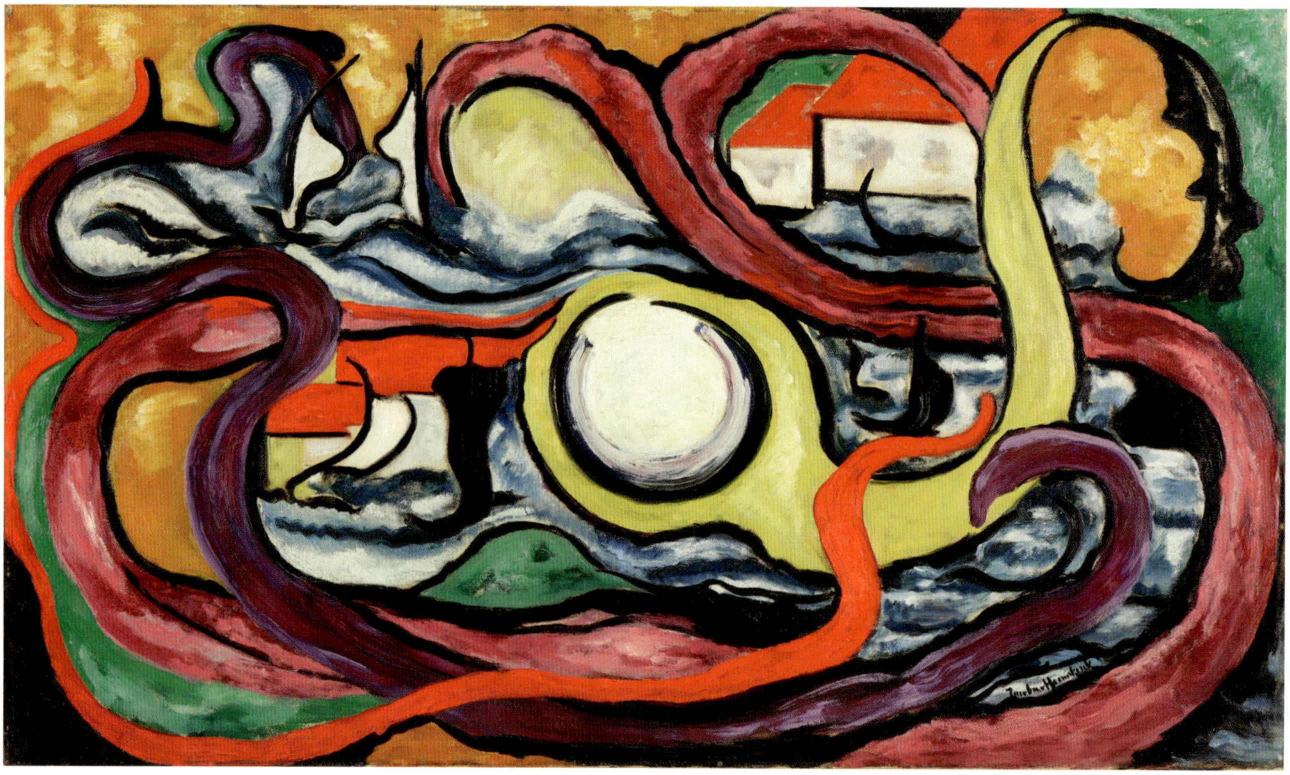

Bild no. 87 | **Image no. 87** 1918
Oil on canvas
81 × 100,2 cm

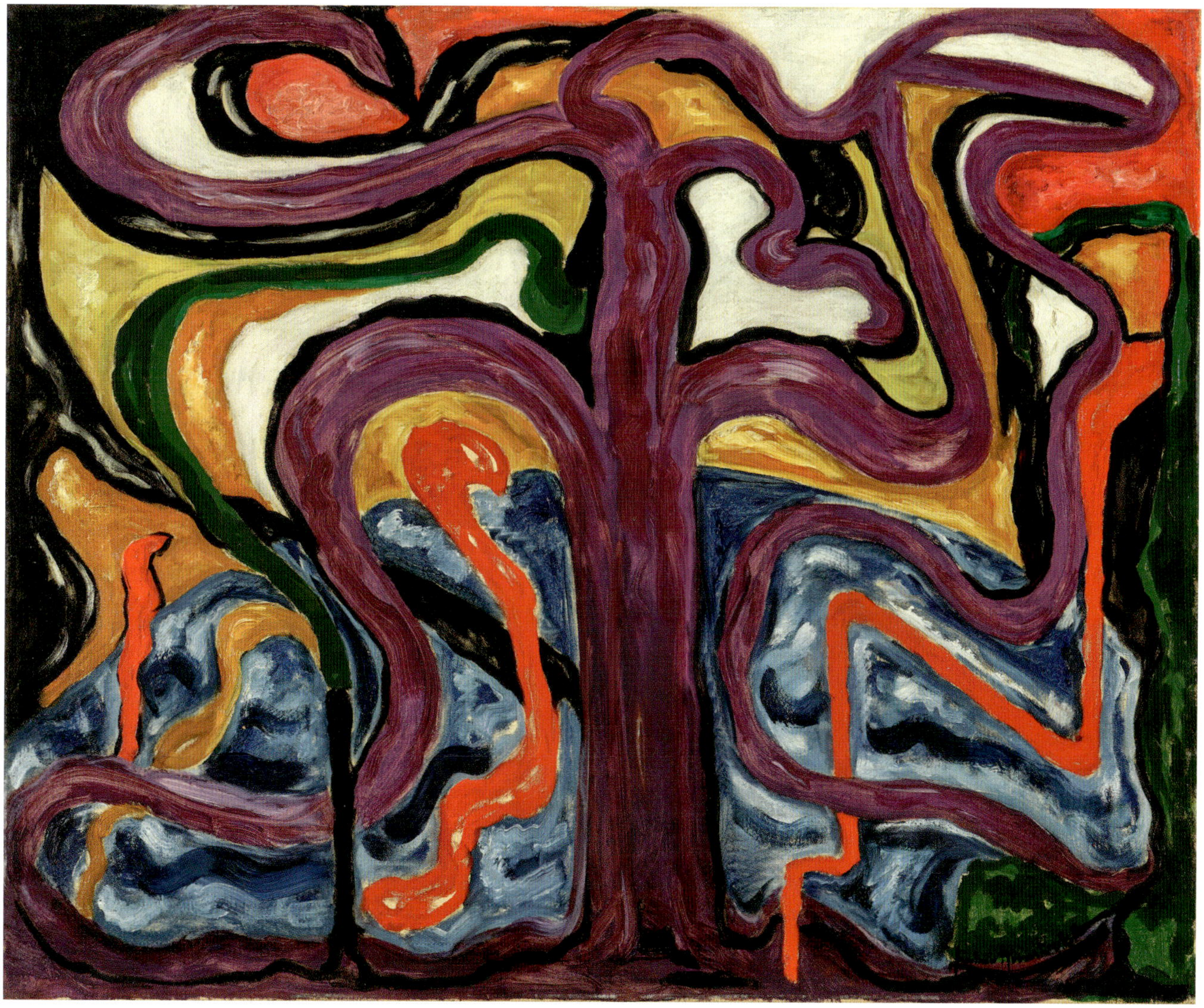

Compositie XVII no. 3 |
Composition XVII no. 3 1918
Woodcut on Japanese paper
41,3 × 55,2 cm (sheet)

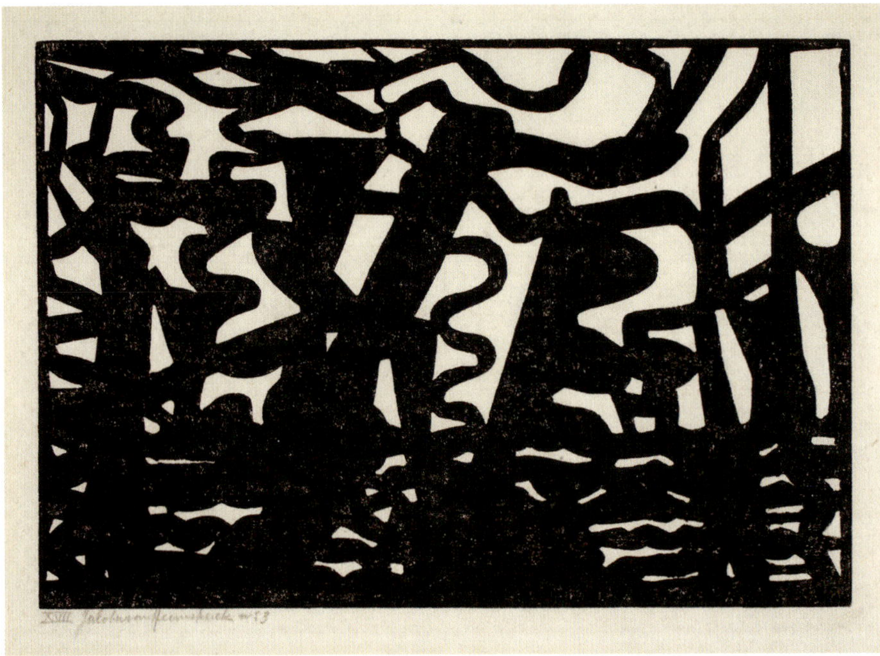

Bild no. 105 | **Image no. 105** 1920
Oil on canvas
100 × 80 cm

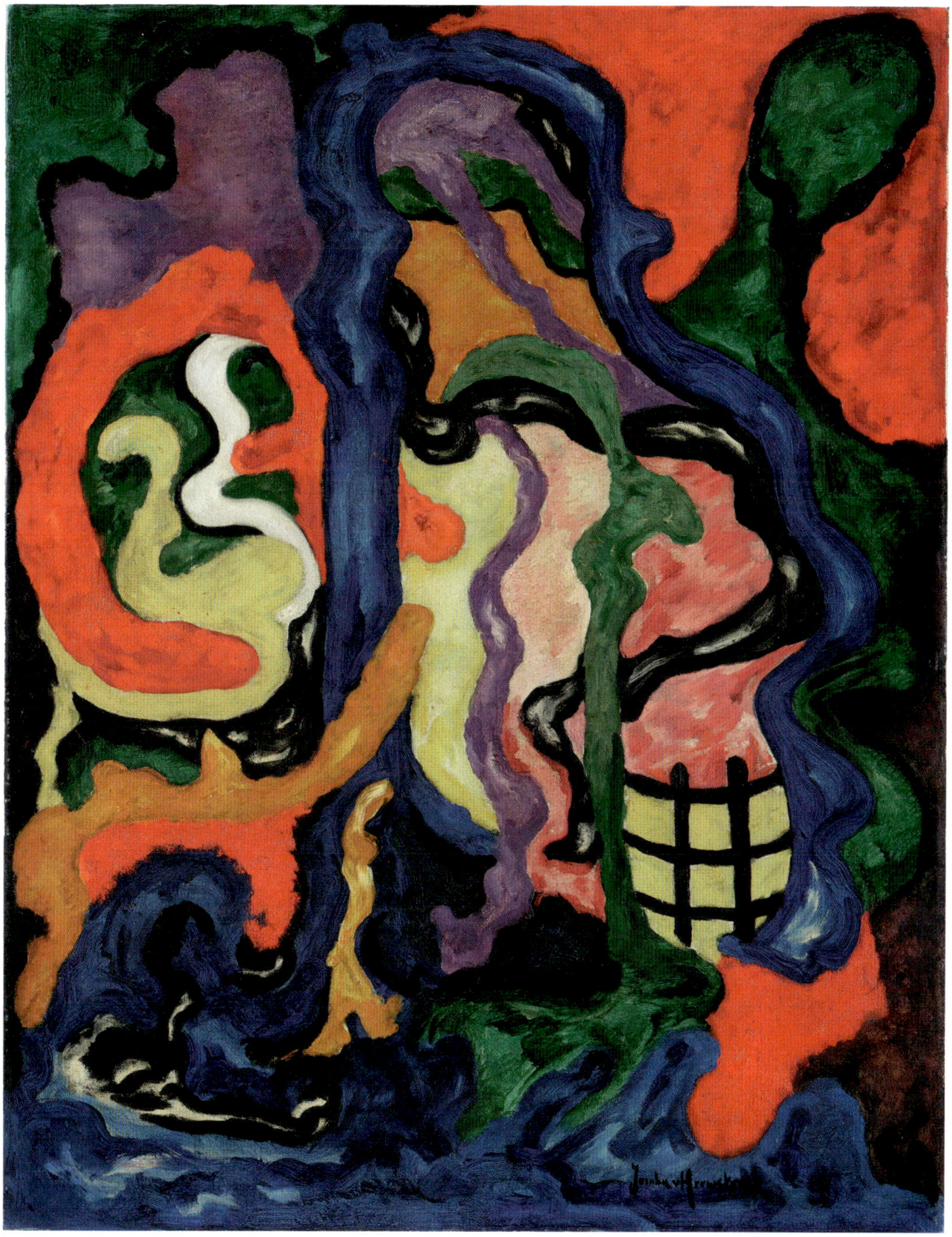

Bild no. 90 | **Image no. 90** 1918
Oil on canvas
60 × 76 cm

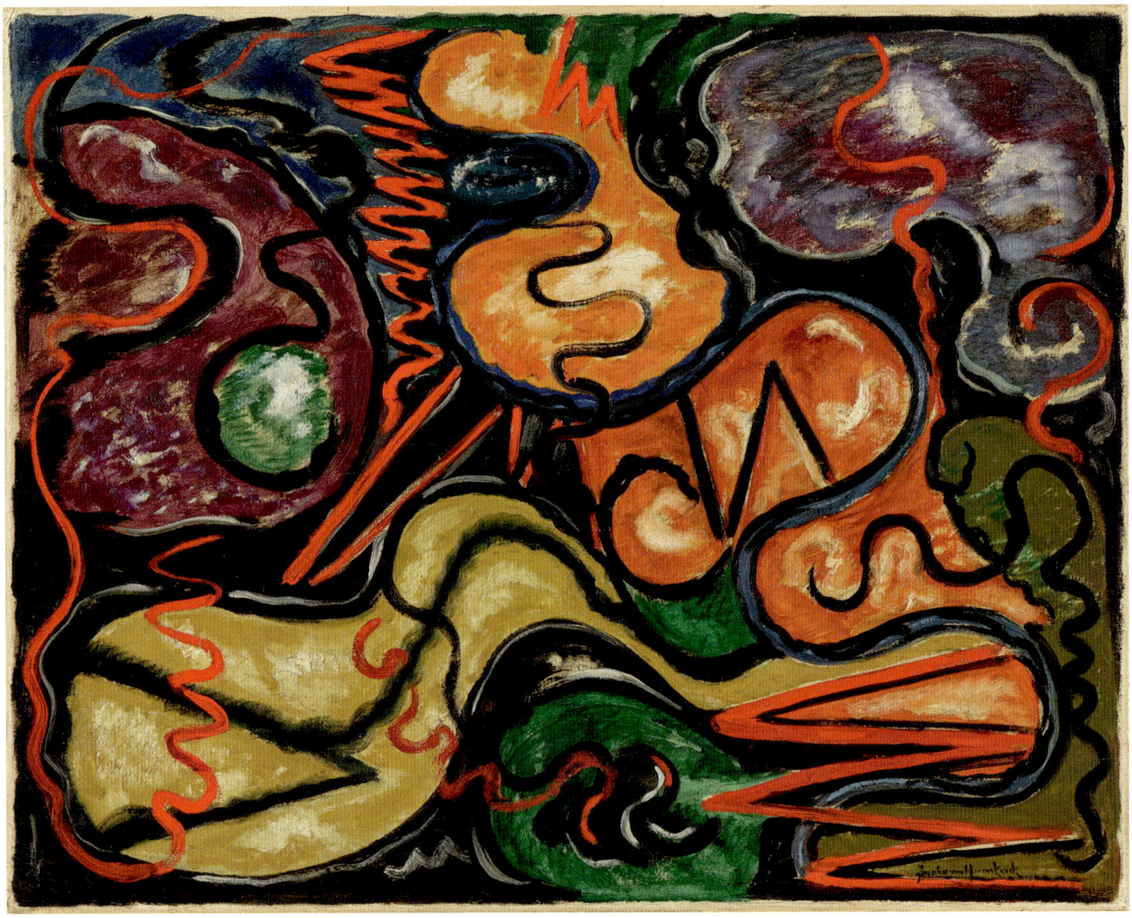

Bild no. 98 (Synthetisch portret) |
Image no. 98 (Synthetic Portrait) 1918
Oil on canvas
79,9 × 63 cm

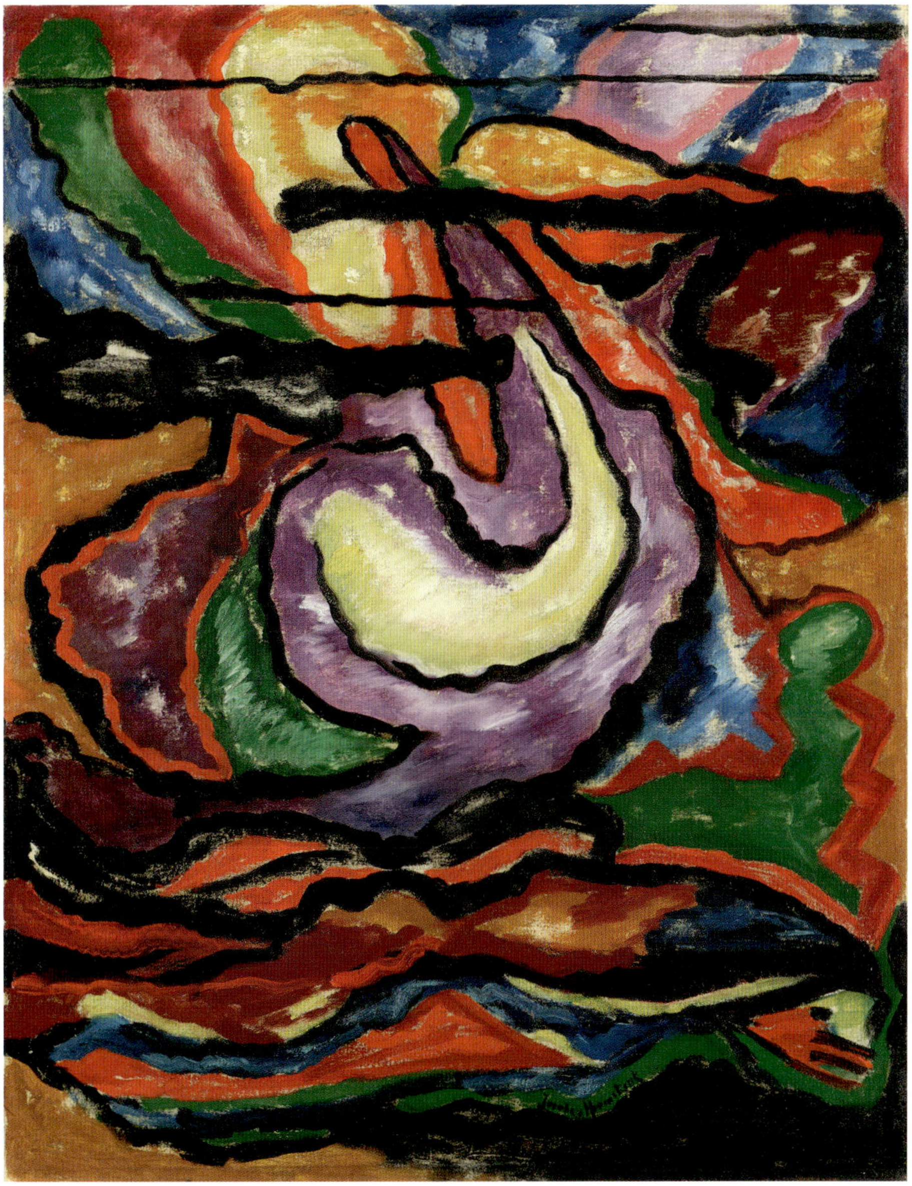

Bild no. 84 (Portret van een kind) |
Image no. 84 (Portrait of a Child) 1918
Oil on canvas
46,5 × 38,5 cm

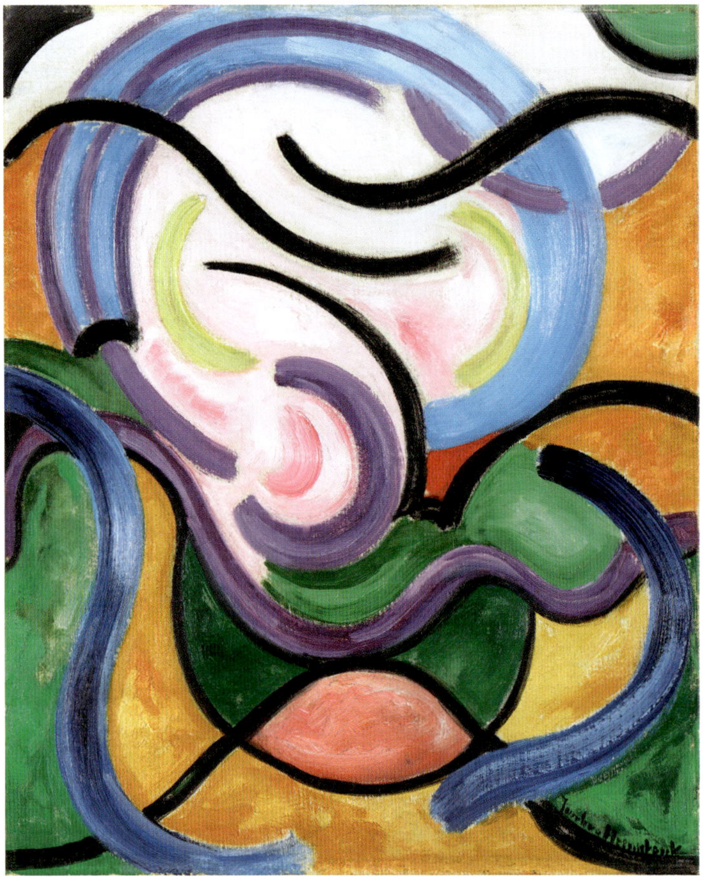

Bild no. 93 (Inktvissen) |
Image no. 93 (Cuttlefish) 1918
Oil on canvas
100 × 121,8 cm

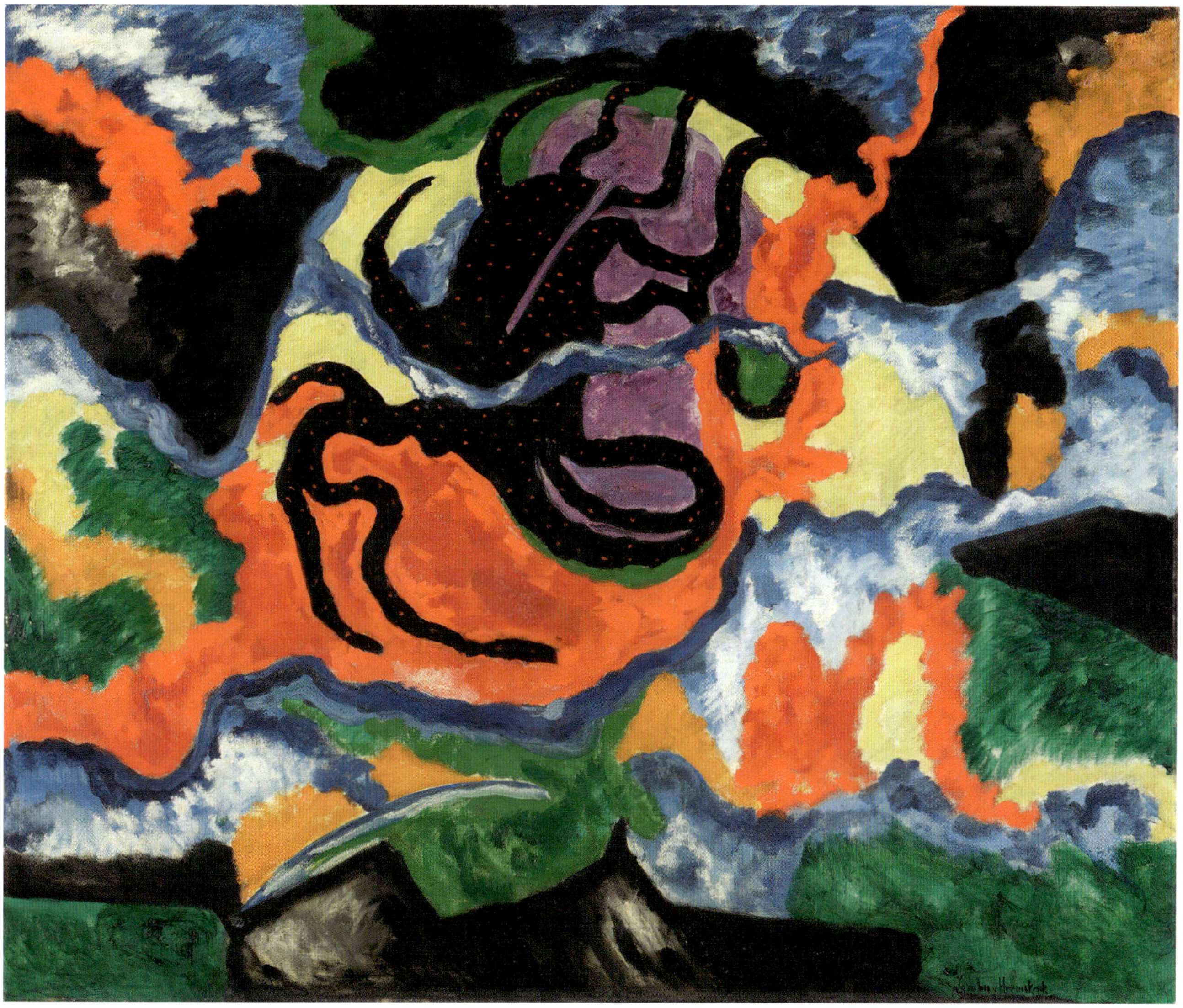

Bild | Image 1920
Oil on canvas
70,2 × 123,4 cm

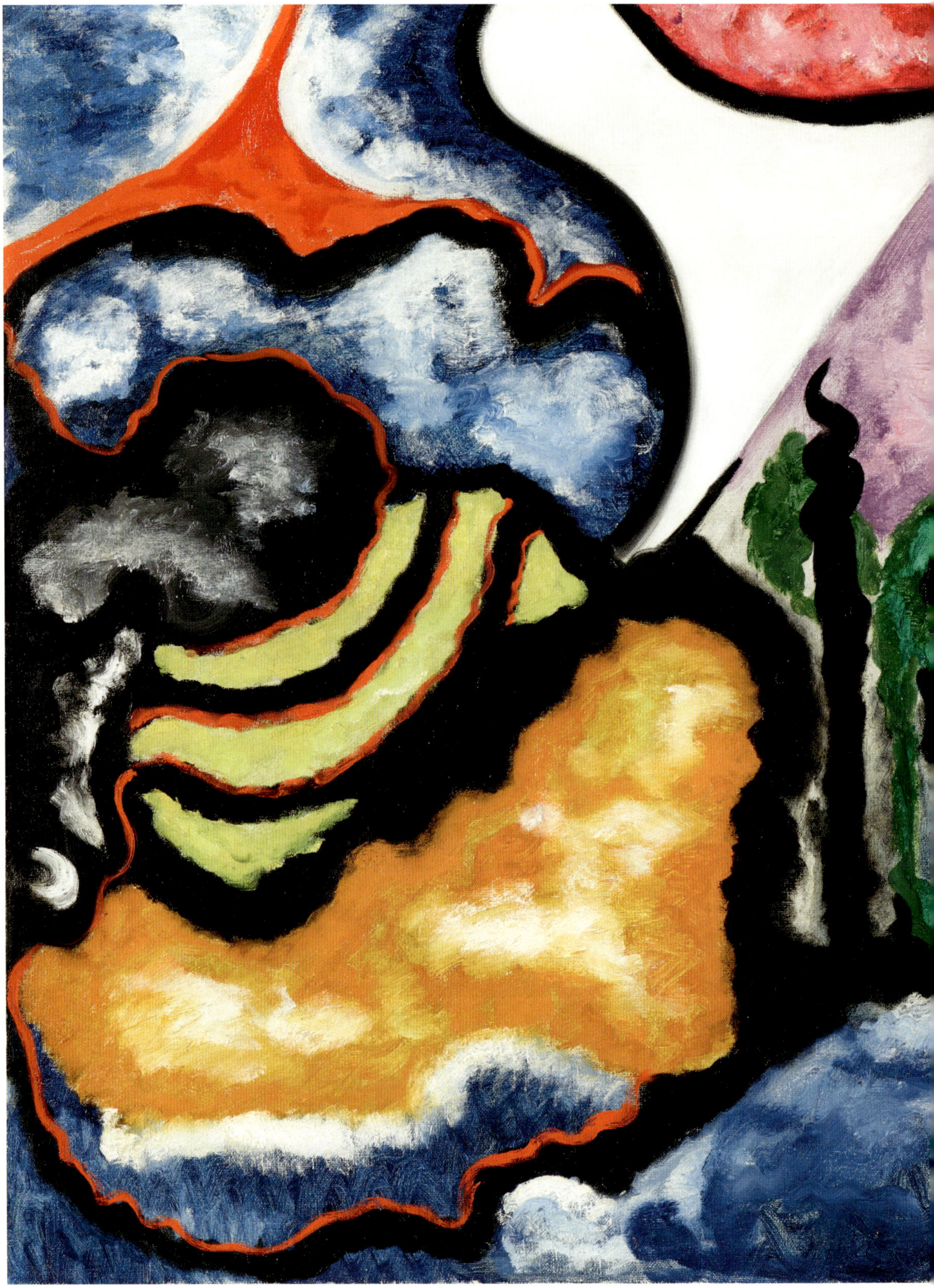

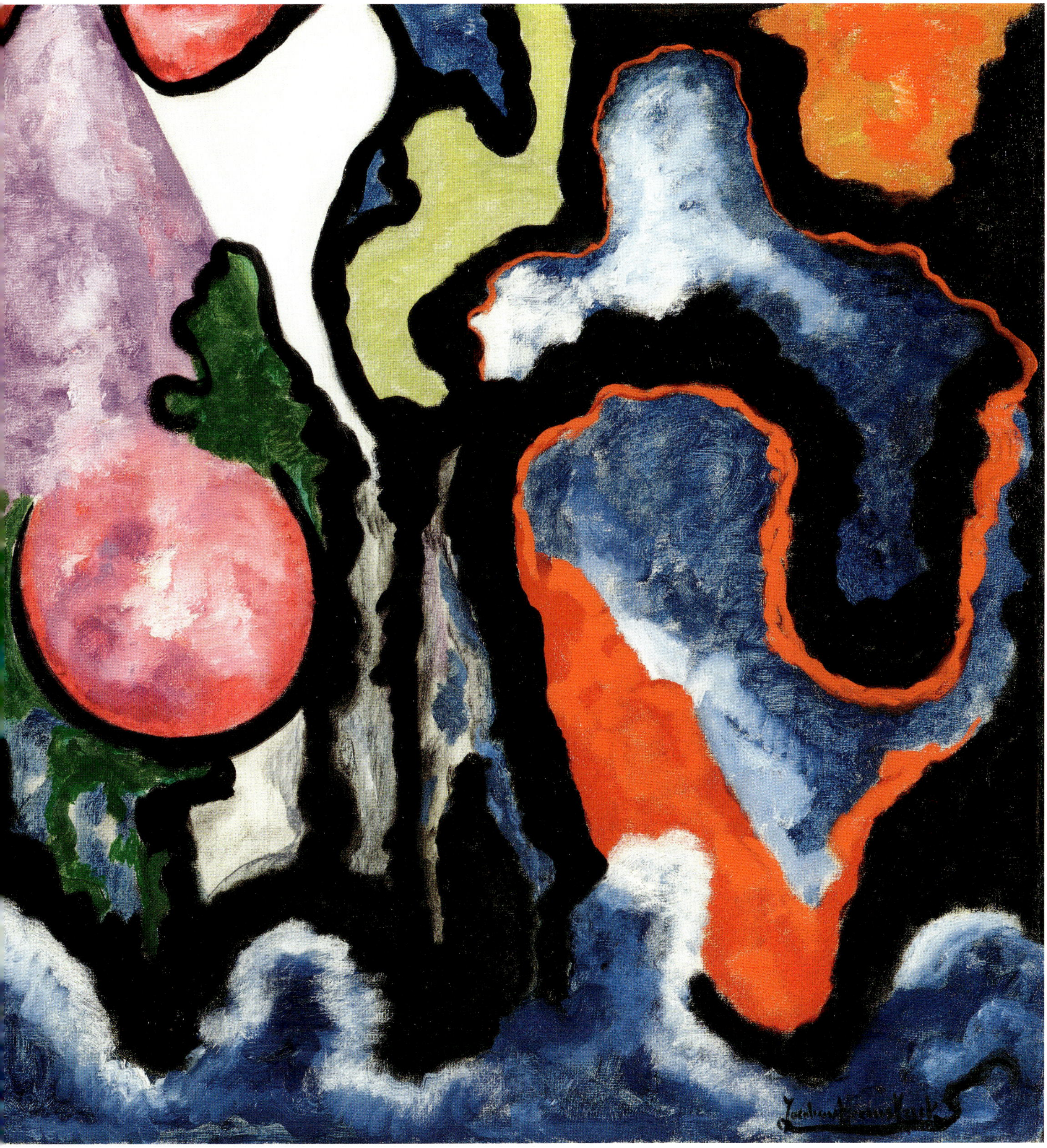

Compositie | **Composition** 1920
Stained glass
60 × 47,5 cm
Executed by Studio J. W. Gips, The Hague

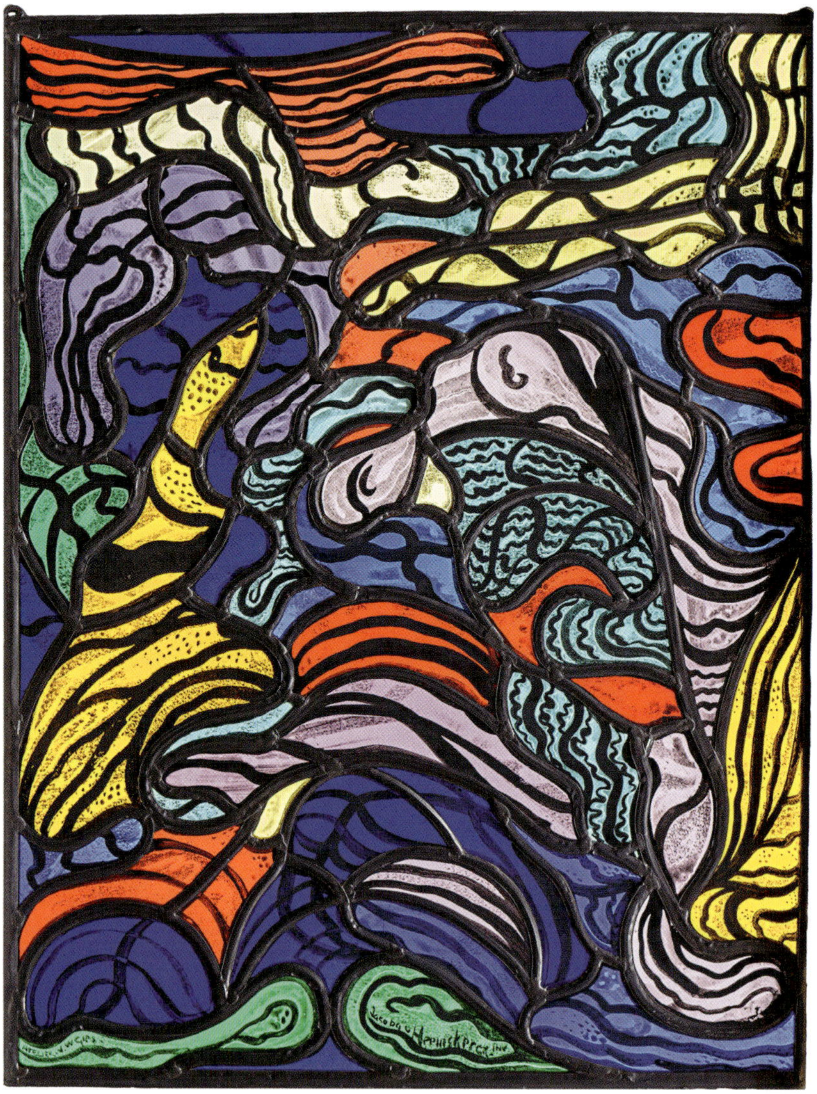

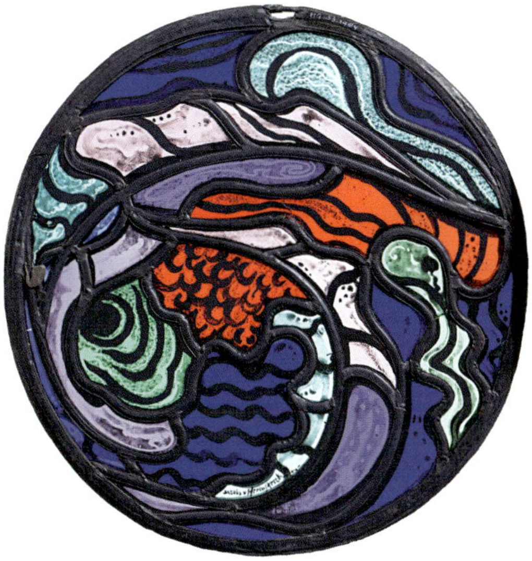

Compositie |
Composition *c.*1920
Stained glass
Diameter 27,5 cm
Executed by Studio J. W. Gips, The Hague

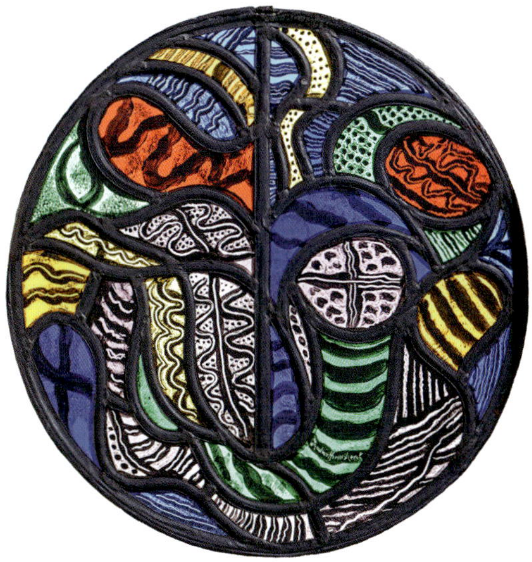

Compositie (Natuurmotief) |
Composition (Natural Motif) *c.*1920
Stained glass
Diameter 27 cm
Executed by Studio J. W. Gips, The Hague

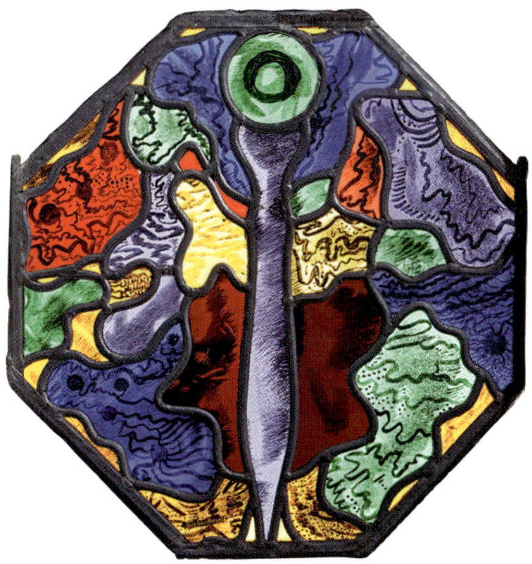

Compositie (Vlinder) |
Composition (Butterfly) *c.*1920
Stained glass
Diameter 29,2 cm

Compositie XXII no. 6 |
Composition XXII no. 6 1920
Woodcut on paper
39,6 × 26,6 cm (sheet)

Compositie XXIII no. 7 |
Composition XXIII no. 7 1920
Woodcut on paper
21,9 × 15,9 cm (sheet)

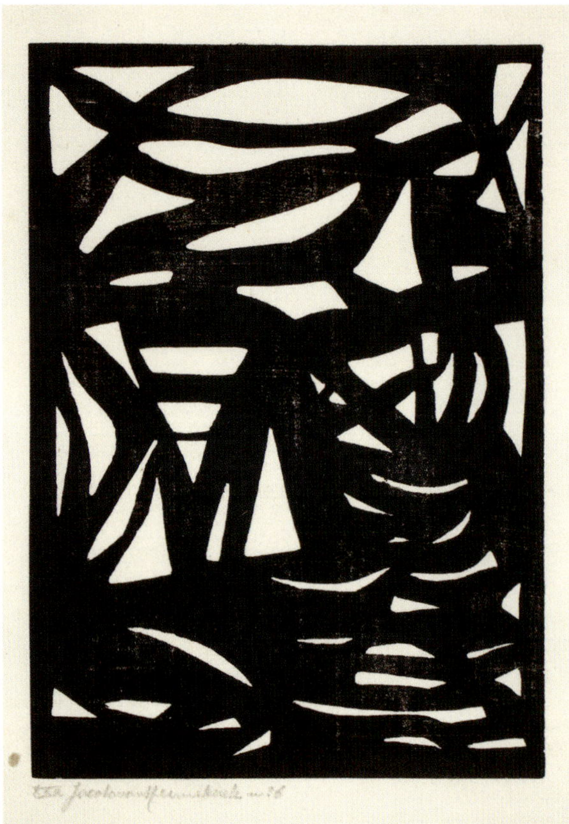

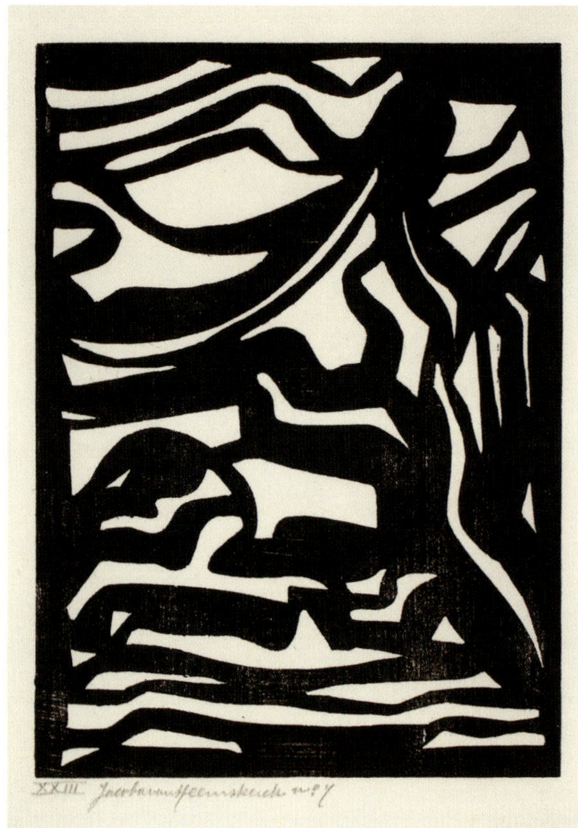

Compositie no. 2 (Boom) |
Composition no. 2 (Tree) 1920
Coloured woodcut on handmade paper
34,1 × 26,8 cm (sheet)

Compositie no. 15 |
Composition no. 15 1921
Woodcut and watercolour on paper
41,7 × 29 cm (sheet)

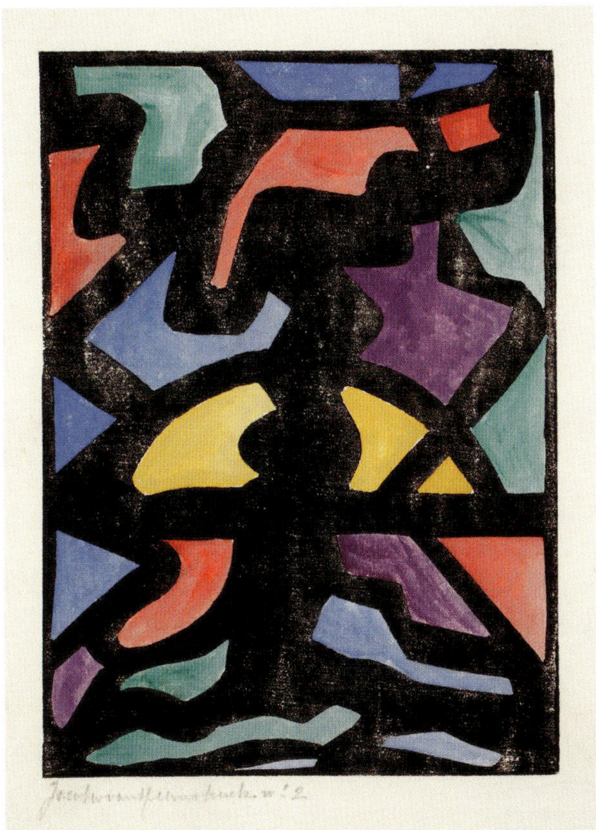

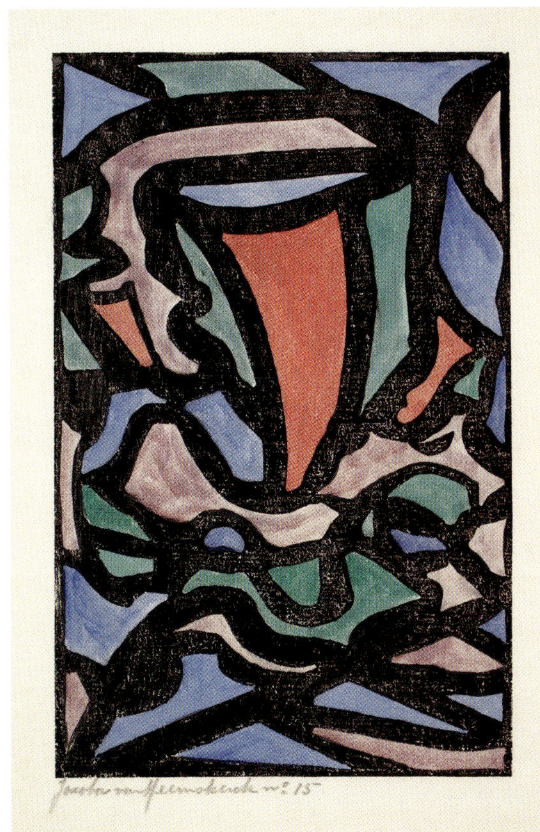

Glasfensterentwurf no. 25 |
Design for a Glass Window no. 25 1919
Indian ink and watercolour on paper
125 × 82 cm

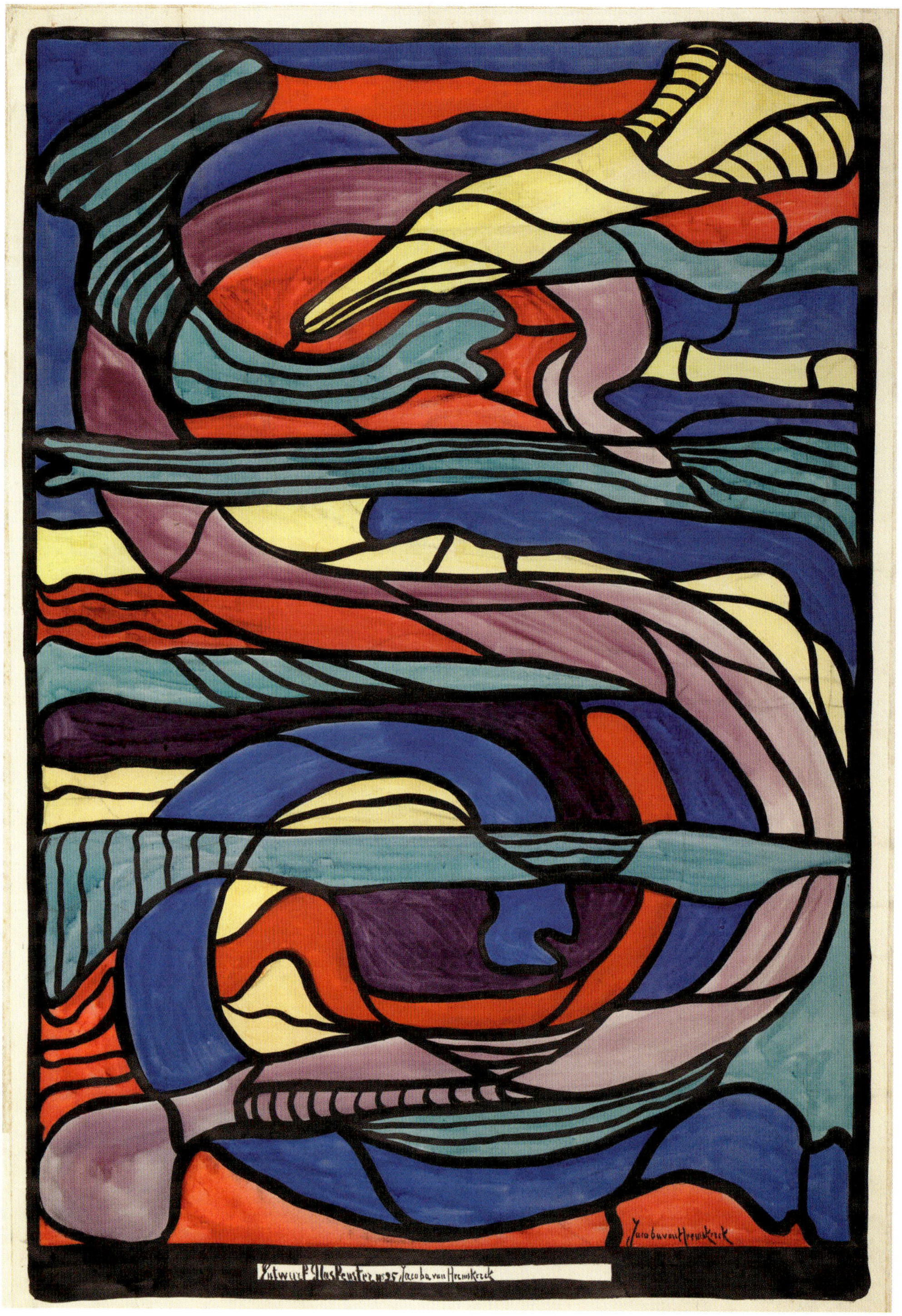

Glasfensterentwurf no. 24 |
Design for a Glass Window no. 24 1919
Indian ink and watercolour on paper
83,3 × 115 cm

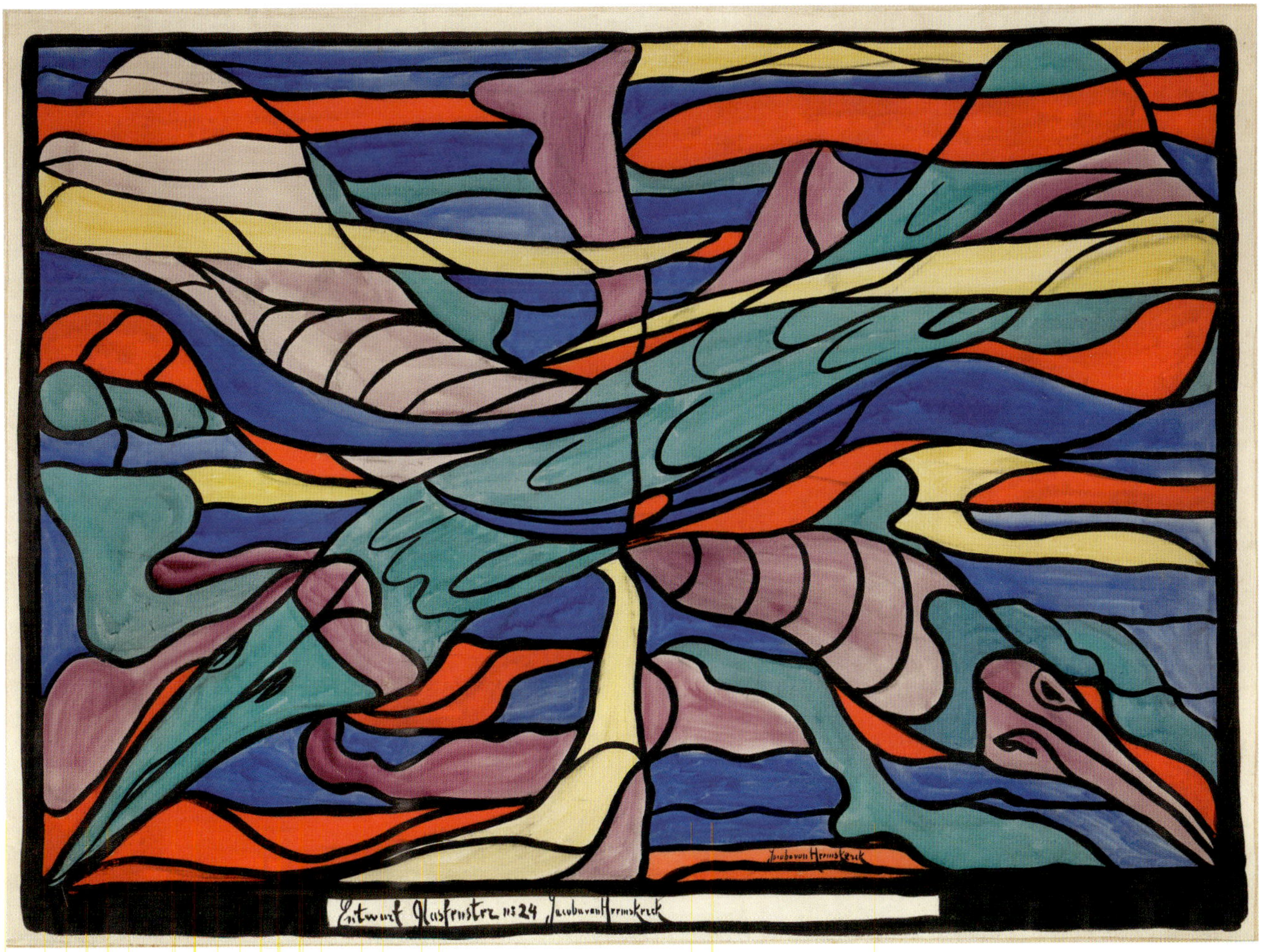

Compositie XIV no. 6 |
Composition XIV no. 6 1916
Woodcut on Japanese paper
31,6 × 45,2 cm (sheet)

Compositie XIII no. 16 |
Composition XIII no. 16 1916
Woodcut on Japanese paper
30,7 × 45,7 cm (sheet)

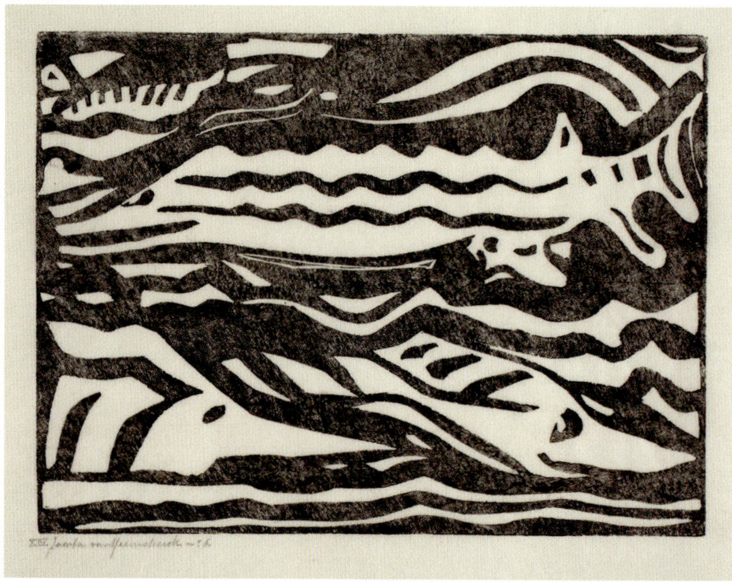

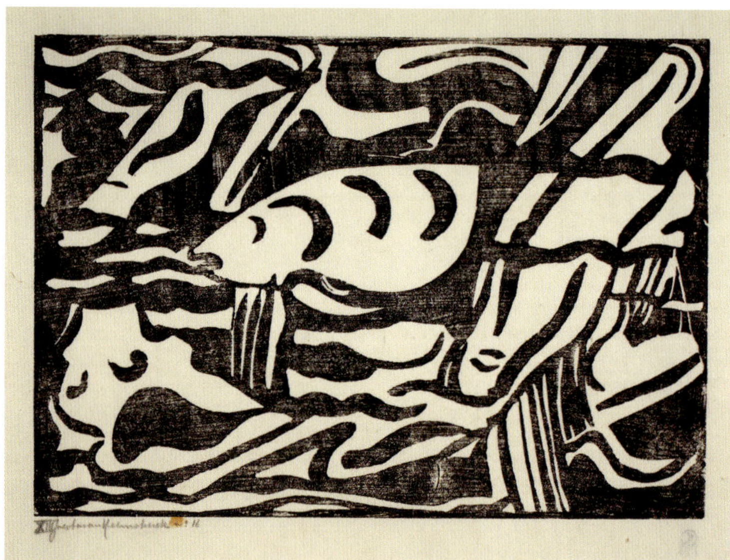

Compositie XI (Vissen) |
Composition XI (Fishes) 1916
Woodcut, watercolour on paper
39,5 × 51,6 cm (sheet)

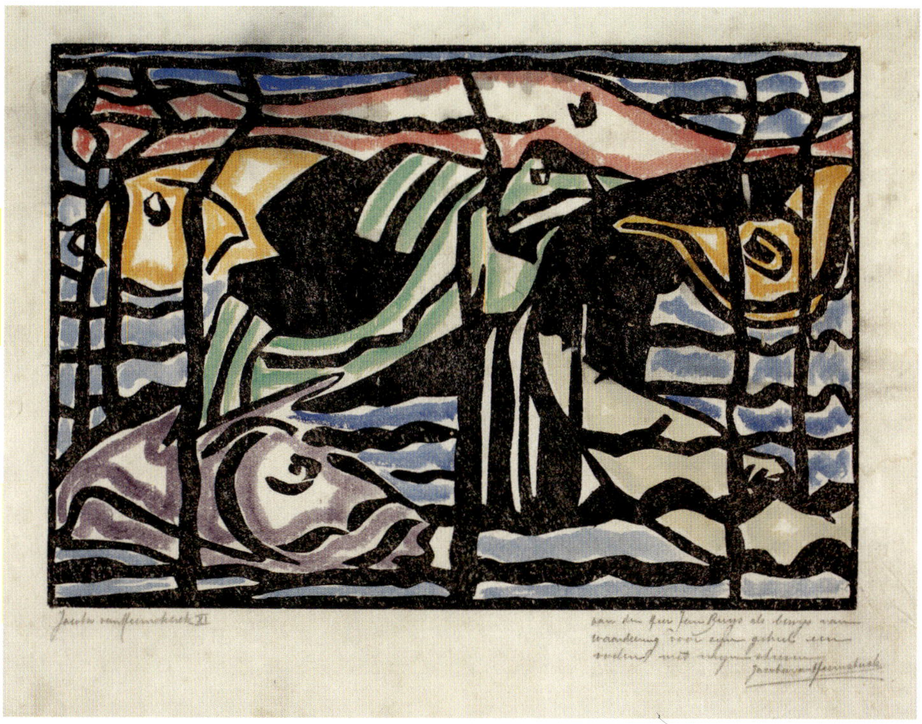

Glasfensterentwurf no. 21 |
Design for a Glass Window no. 21 1919
Indian ink and watercolour on paper
107 × 77 cm

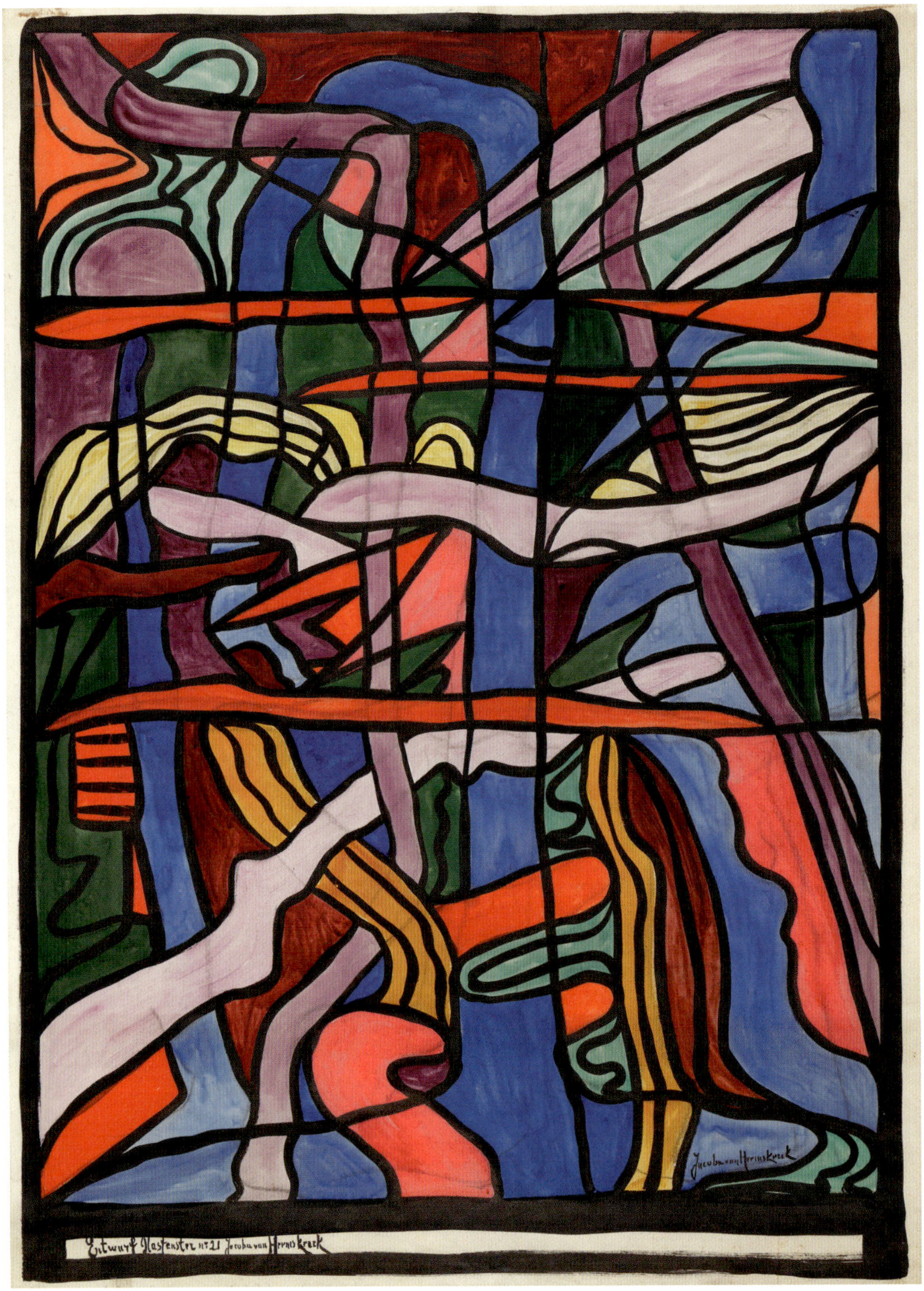

Compositie | **Composition** 1920
Mosaic of coloured glass
81,5 × 123,5 cm

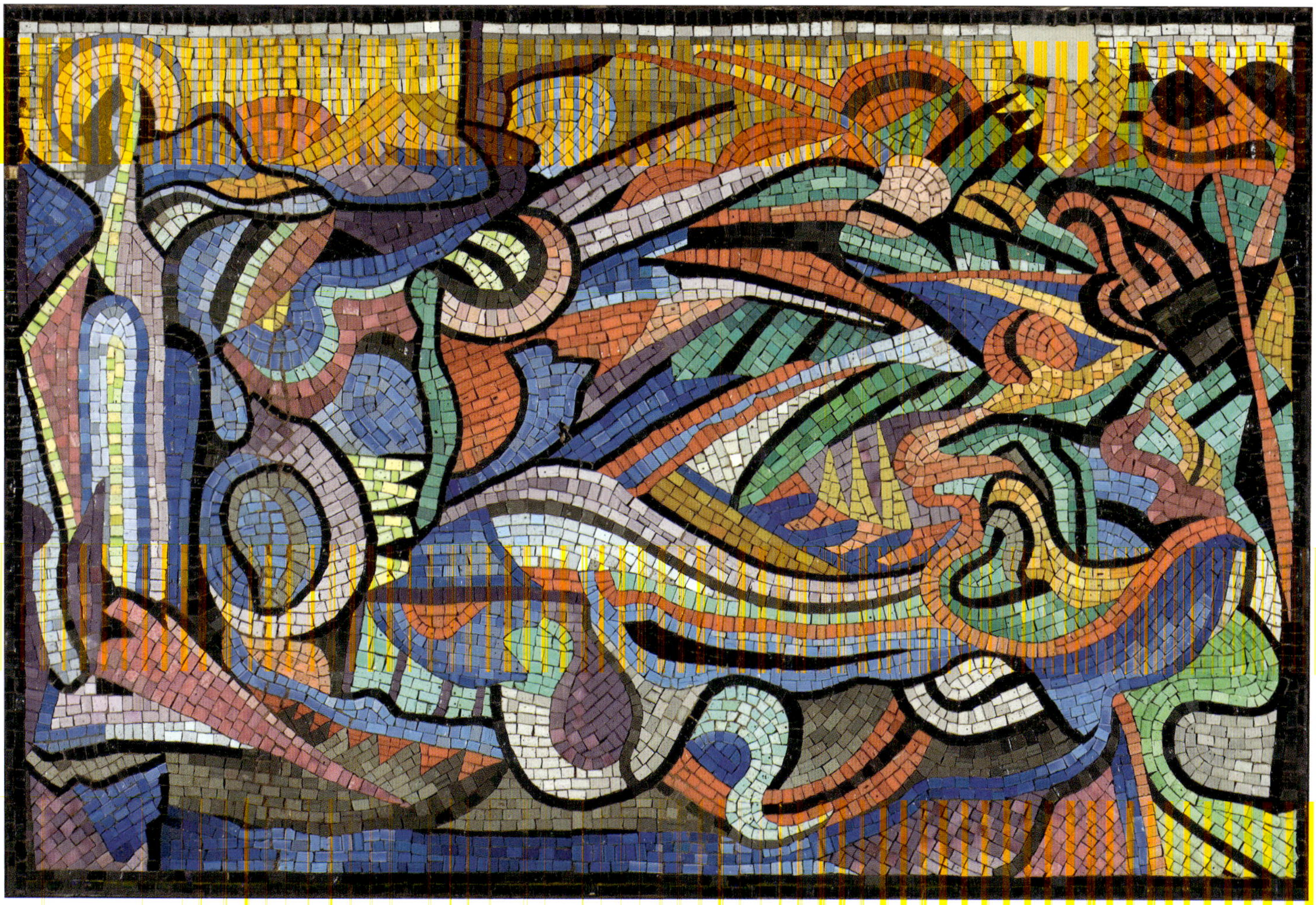

Bild no. 65 | **Image no. 65** 1917
Oil on canvas
111 × 130,5 cm

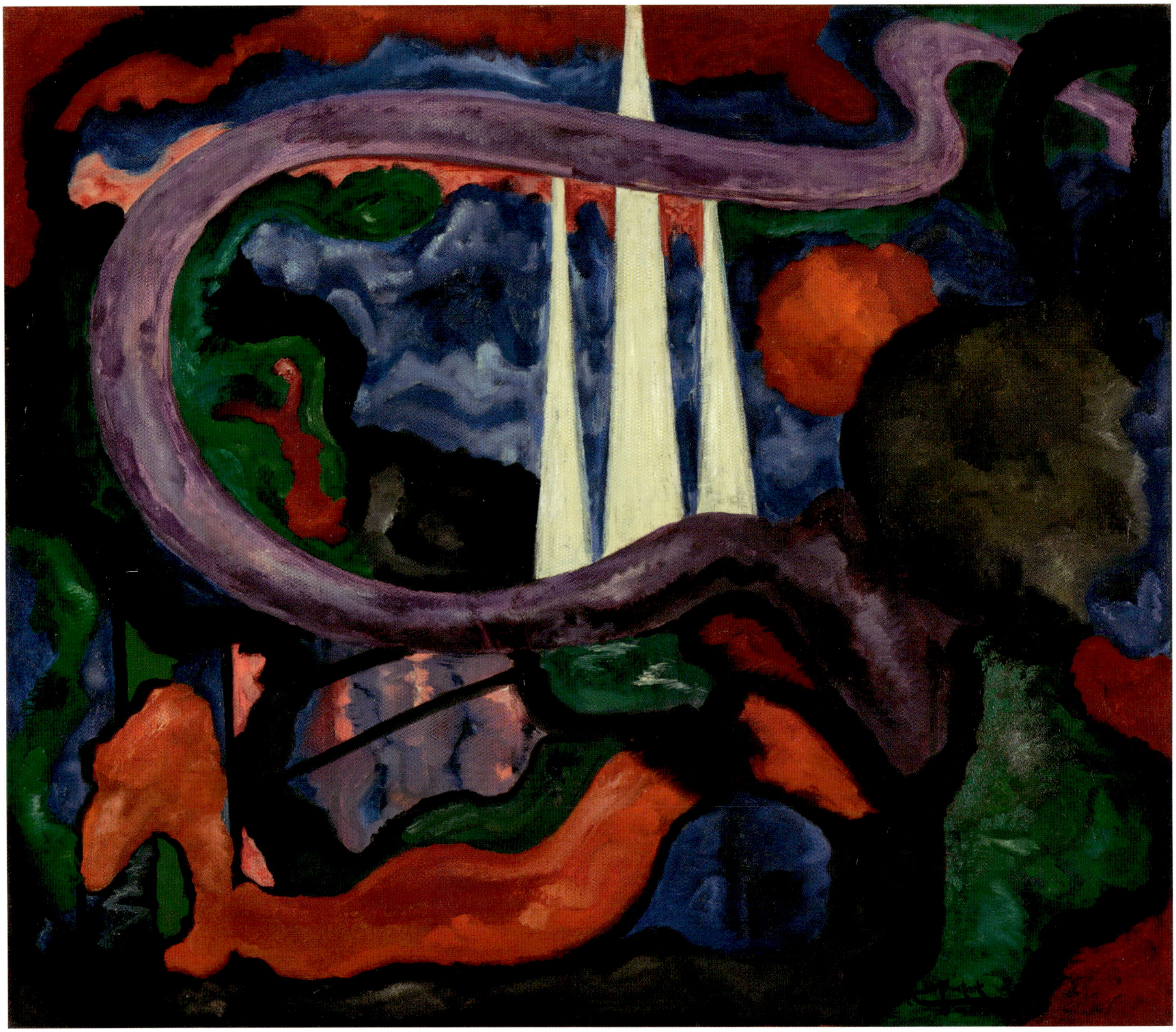

Bild no. 107 | **Image no. 107** 1920
Oil on canvas
95 × 75,5 cm

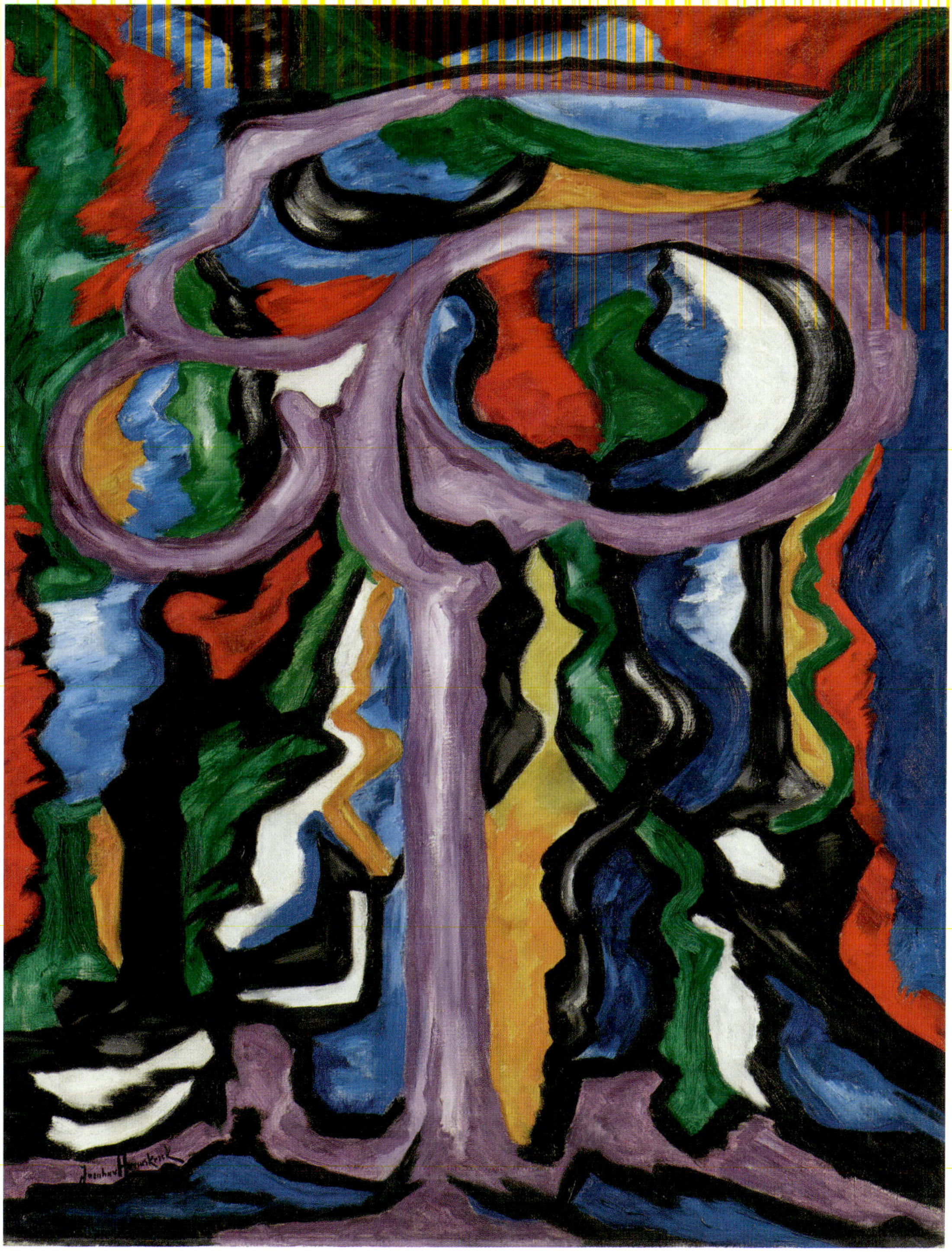

Compositie naar ontwerp no. 19 (Boom) |
Composition after Design no. 19 (Tree) 1920
Stained glass
107,5 × 80,5 cm
Executed by Puhl & Wagner – Gottfried Heinersdorff, Berlin

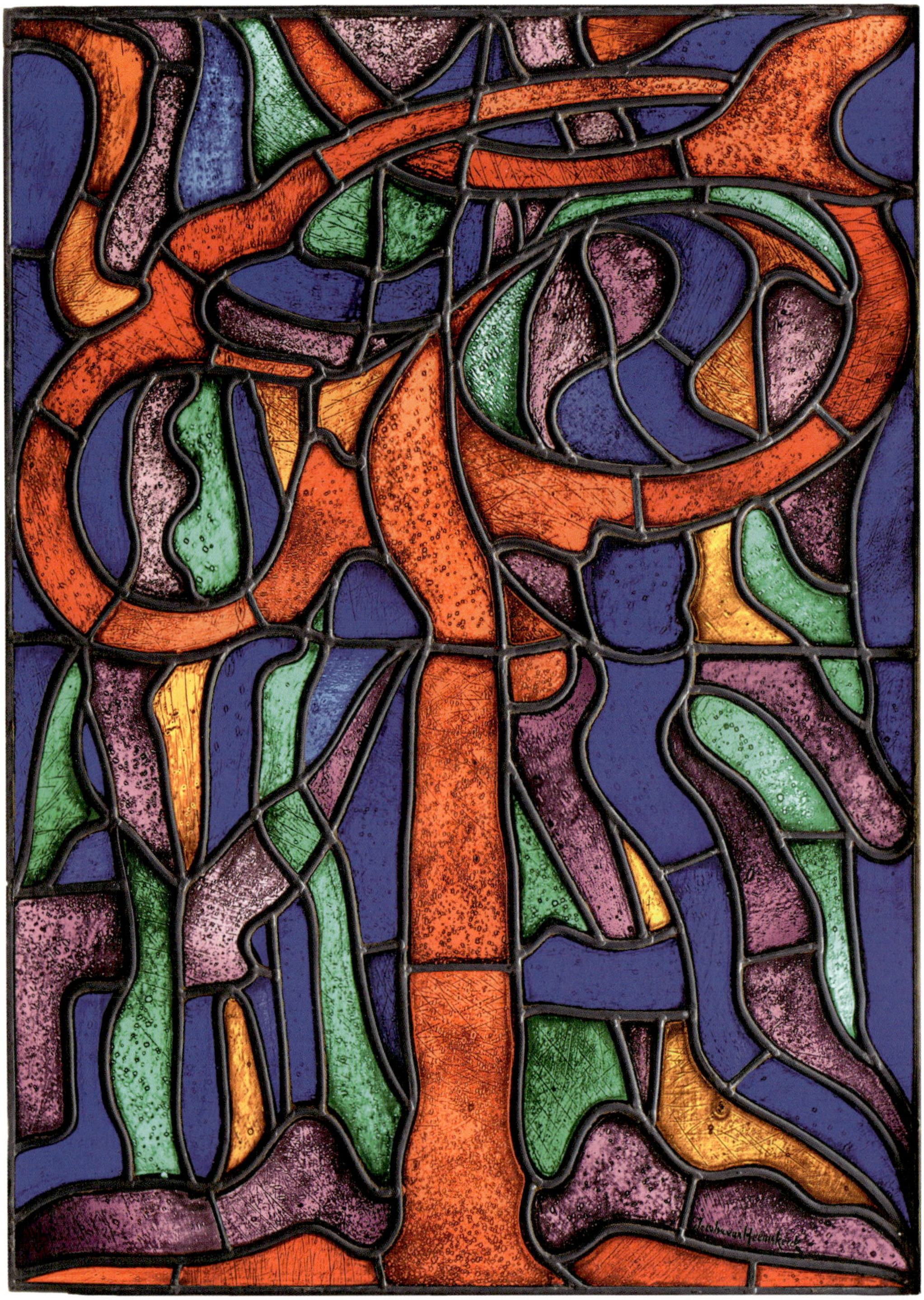

Compositie (Boom) |
Composition (Tree) 1920
Mosaic of coloured glass
107,5 × 93,5 cm
Executed by Puhl & Wagner – Gottfried Heinersdorff, Berlin

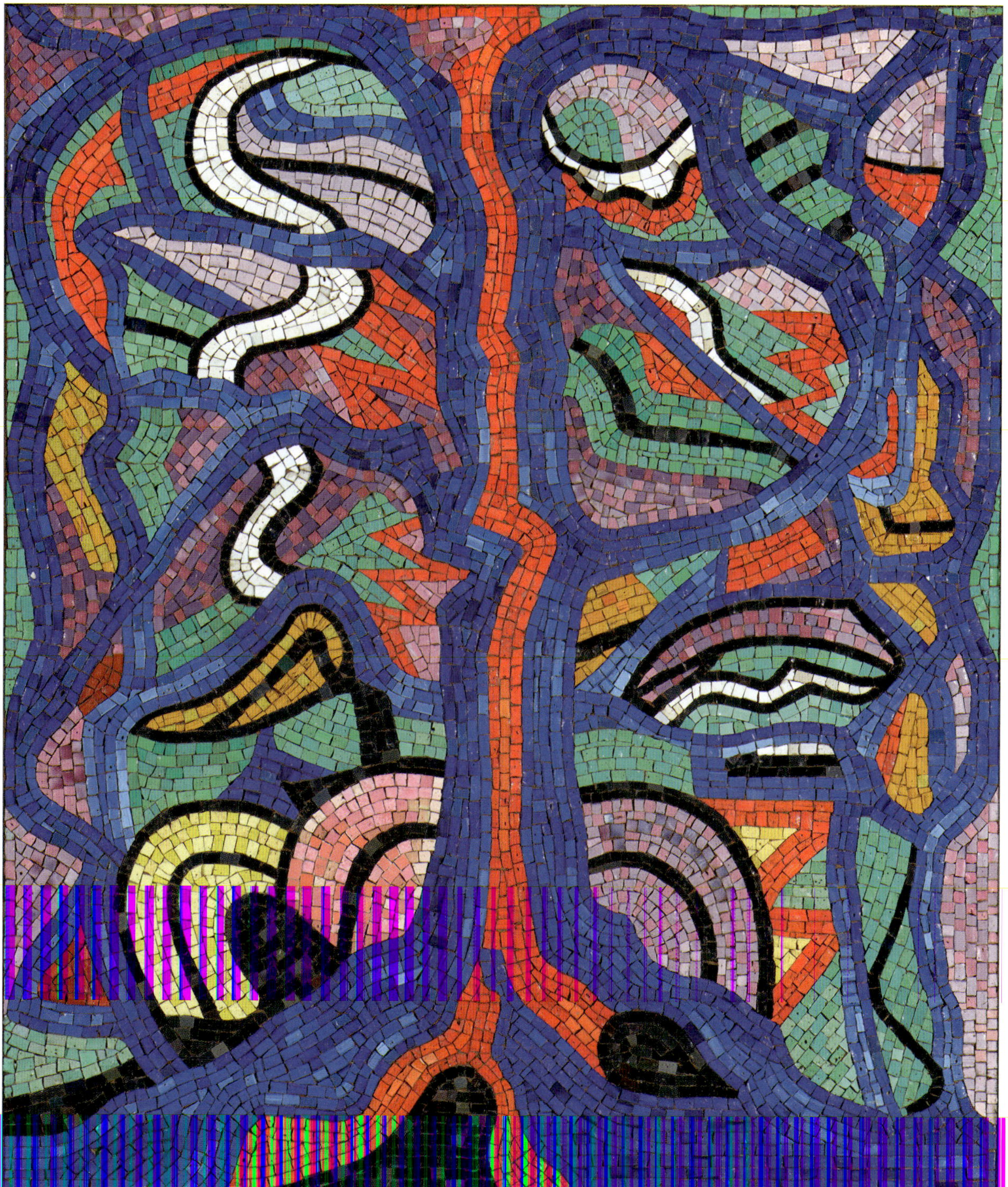

Compositie naar Glasfensterwentwurf no. 17 |
Composition after Design for a Glass Window no. 17 *c.*1920
Stained-glass window
106 × 76,5 cm
Executed by Puhl & Wagner – Gottfried Heinersdorff, Berlin

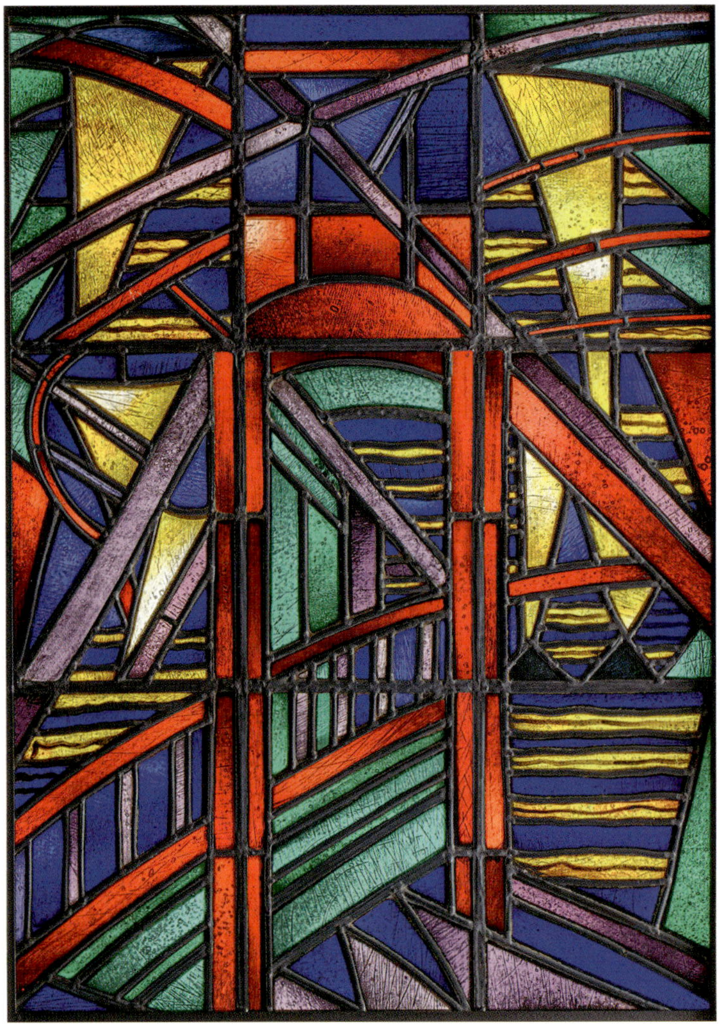

Vestibuleraam Villa Wulffraat |
Vestibule window Villa Wulffraat 1920
Stained-glass window
136 × 71,5 cm
Executed by Atelier J. W. Gips, The Hague

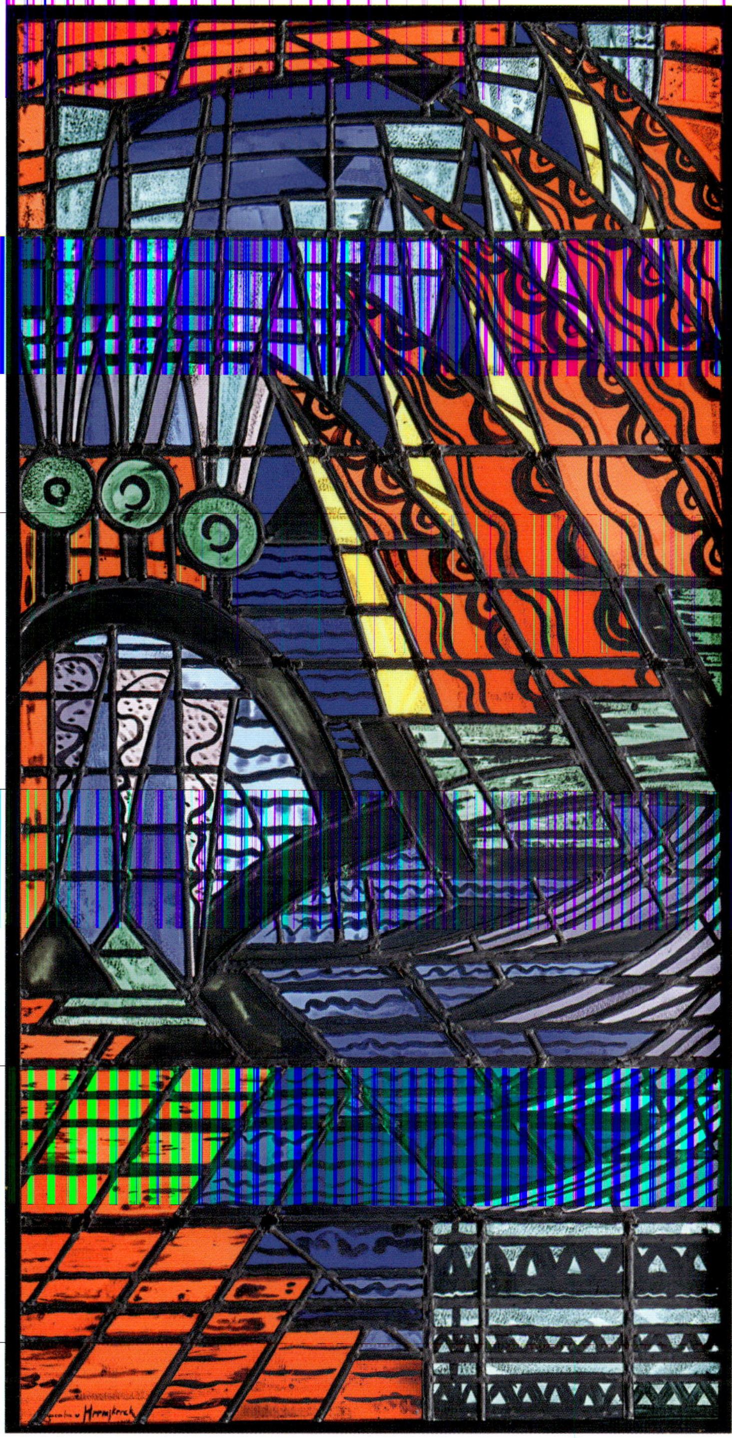

Jacoba van Heemskerck

Willem Zeylmans van Emmichoven

The Spiritual Direction in New Painting

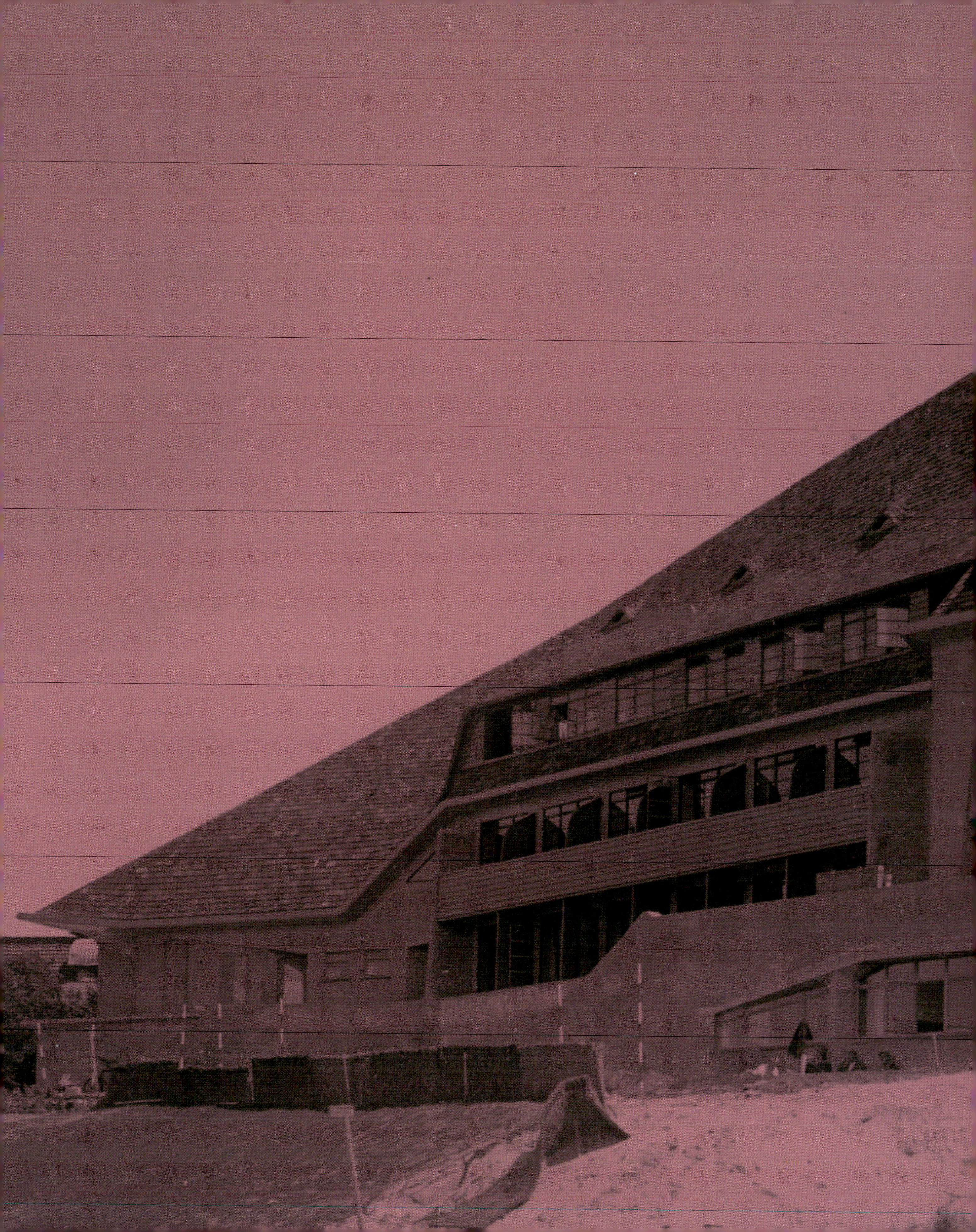

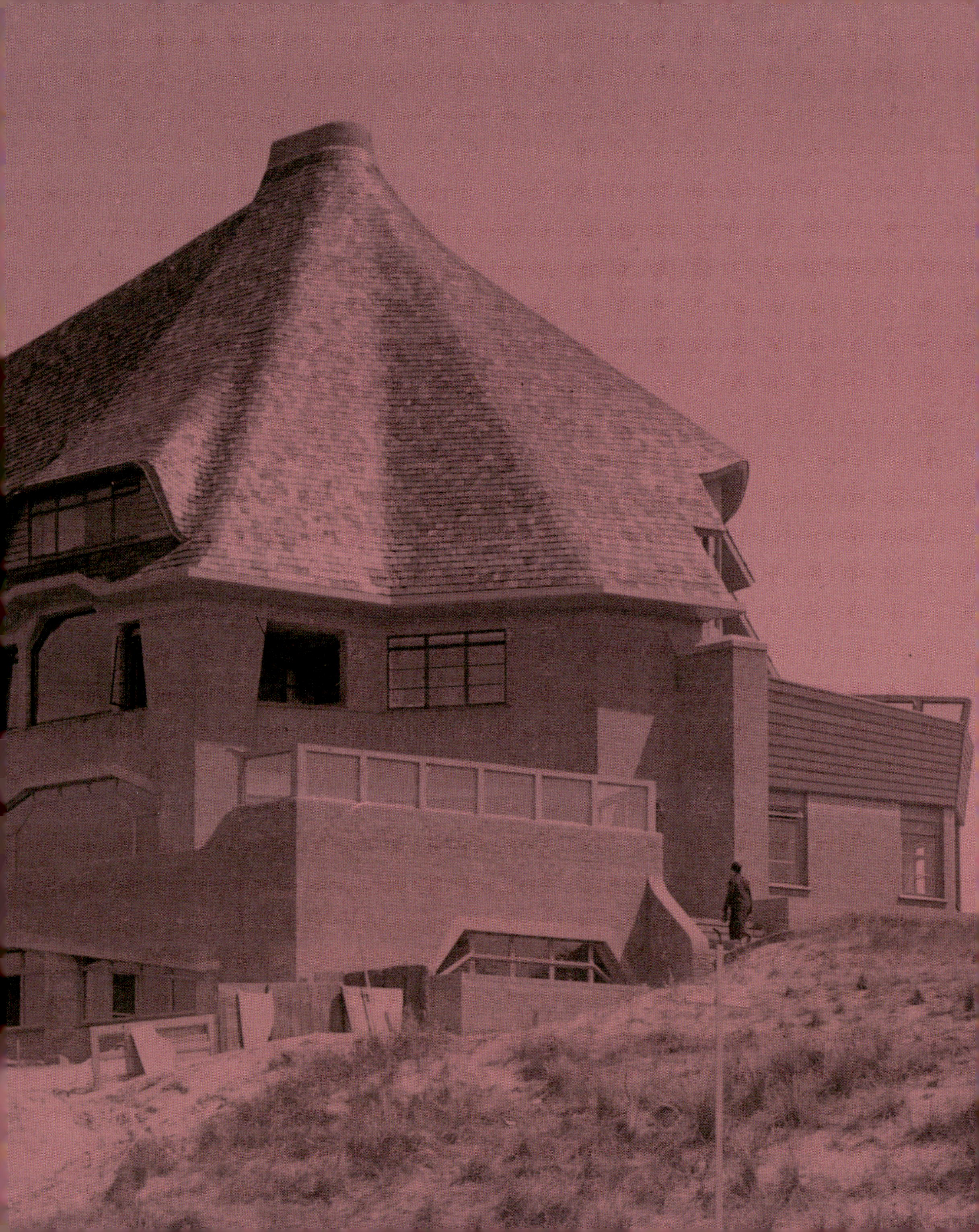

66 Rudolf Steiner-Klinik, The Hague (Architects J. W. E. Buijs and J. B. Lürsen), c.1928

Man's relationship with nature is defined by the continuous struggle for supremacy of the desire to become one with nature and the simultaneous and contradictory urge to liberate oneself from it. In the midst of these tendencies, both of which originate in nature itself, mankind seeks a way.

The desire to become one with nature is entirely spiritual. It comes from the longing of a single life to merge with all life, the longing to return to the peace, to the balance, that is the origin of everything. In that peace, matter is restricted entirely by the all-powerful spirit, for whom that balance is the only true life. The material resists this restriction, which appears to seek its destruction. That is why in all matter there is an urge to resist nature, an urge towards the unnatural.

Life is thus a battle against the unnatural, which draws its strength from an illusory satisfaction that lies in the growth and comfort of the material. Everything that lives seeks to free the essence from the illusion, the unity of nature from the multiplicity of unnatural desires. Life is therefore about imparting unity, which is peace, to the turmoil that life itself causes due to the presence of its constantly conflicting elements: matter and spirit. This unity is the style of life. *Art is a unified reflection of life.* Not of life as most of us know it, as a combination of small, everyday sensations, or of life as it is crassly symbolised in all that is shocking and sensational around us. No, art endeavours to depict life in its entirety: great and all-encompassing. First and foremost, therefore, the battle against the unnatural. A battle that is vital if we are to fathom completely the unity of life. And those who believe—and there are many of them—that it is possible to represent nature without this will never proceed beyond an endless repetition of their own delusion, their own smallness. To express visually is to restore to life.

The artist is a thinking, struggling intermediary between nature and artwork, whose creation evokes a revival of life. *An artwork is the representation of what the artist's spirit has found in the spirit of nature. The highest states of both thus meet in a work of art. Art therefore captures the highest spiritual values achieved by mankind.*

Clinging to the idea that art seeks to represent life, it would be logical to deem anything that does not, or does so only partially, not to be art. This is not customary. The stylish representations of life processes that are only part of life are also regarded as art, and so one begins with the lowest form of spiritual activity, with sensation.

Most people are still at the stage of development where they know only sensation. A sensation is an experience that the spirit perceives via the senses, accepts and undergoes without alteration or appraisal. An event is observed through the senses and the sole consequence is a surrender to the feeling evoked, whose intensity depends on the nature of the observer. Those who manage to represent these sensations in a unified way are the only artists fully comprehensible to this group of people, for they never present anything that they cannot feel with their entire being. Any other art presented to them they experience only in part, the sensation, which is present to some extent or other in every artwork. To them, this is the only thing that is visible, and they are deluded into believing that they perceive the artwork in its entirety.

The portion of humanity that has reached the next stage of development knows both

The text written in January 1917 by Willem Zeylmans van Emmichoven is the first comprehensive analysis of the art of Jacoba van Heemskerck during her lifetime. Moreover, it is a document of some of the perceptions of the zeitgeist and also provides insight into the ideas of Van Heemskerck herself, since it was written during a period of intense exchange between author and artist. The Ita Wegman Institut in Arlesheim, Switzerland, which houses the estate of Zeylmans van Emmichoven, allowed us access to the original manuscript. The resulting first-time translation is made available for research.

sensation and emotion. Simple observation is not enough for them. They deconstruct the feelings they experience. They participate in a spiritual event through their senses and their intellect. Observation and deconstruction of a feeling can produce emotion, if the depth and scale of the feeling lend themselves to it. Emotion is therefore a much higher form of participation in life. A much purer form, furthermore, for while sensation is nothing more than uncritical submission, the intellectual deconstruction inherent in emotion resembles other spiritual values.

Sensation can never, therefore, be of great importance for life because it is exclusively personal and, moreover, lacks any intellectual component. Sensation lacks reason. Spiritual value begins with emotion. The deconstruction of feeling immediately raises the question of why, and therefore leads to the acknowledgement, where appropriate, of the extent to which it lacks purpose.

However important the universality of emotion, mediated through the intellect, it still undeniably contains an element of the deeply personal. It is perhaps unnecessary to point out that this group of people have their art products which lie entirely within their spiritual reach, while all merely sensational art cannot satisfy them.

The third and final way of experiencing or creating an artwork is that which leads to rapture. Rapture is spiritually mediated construction following deconstruction. And it is this process of construction that is of true and immediate value to life. Passivity, which is sensation in its entirety, and emotion in part, has now made way for a fully activated spirit. *And thus begins true life, stretched to its limit, when the spirit actually comes into action.* When it no longer allows itself to be distorted and misshapen, but defines its own form, as a conscious part of the spiritual harmony of nature.

Rapture is the highest form of engagement with life. Alongside intellectual deconstruction, we have here full collaboration between feeling and intellect engaged in an act of construction that seeks to transcend the limitations of the individual; an act of construction in which the personality, having penetrated the deepest essence of nature, voluntarily reveals its intrinsic self. Those who know rapture are small in number, and the artists among them are but few. But this is the only state of mind which can bring forth art that can serve as a guide to mankind. The only art, ultimately, that shows man not his own smallness, nor the limitations of his soul, but elevates him to a life above himself and his battle against the unnatural. A life in which he is at one with nature.

In our time, there is a growing recognition that painting has been through a long period that has known little rapture, or at least only by way of great exception. We must in fact go back to the Primitives* to find the highest point reached by art, from where it proceeded in a series of directions that took it to astonishing technical heights, while its intrinsic value gradually diminished.

For the Primitives the ideal was to express in art the highest that life gave them, to capture the result of years of religious contemplation. To them, the ultimate goal in life was to feel as one with the deity, as they imagined it. Mary, the birth of Jesus, his crucifixion and descent from the cross —these were the ideas they believed connected them with their god. In their thoughts and feelings, it was Jesus and the salvation he brought mankind that captivated their spirit and continually prompted them to seek, to delve further into the mysteries of life. Many schools of art have followed the Primitives, but in none of them did that high-minded and serious attitude to life, that deep and sacred longing to know mankind and his place in life exist in any great measure.

From that point on, painting began to concern itself with things that lay immediately to hand. The outward appearance of nature, the landscape or a sensational, sometimes emotional event, replaced the spiritual quest of the Primitives. The inward aspect of life was supplanted by the outward. This was in very large part due to scientific and technological progress, which had outstripped the human mind. With pride, man declared he had freed himself from nature's forces. Man began to feel human *in opposition to* nature, which he now set about subjugating, in order to exploit it for his own benefit.

The self-conceit of mankind grew to such proportions that man could not see that all those forces are used by nature itself in the service of its great, unfathomable purpose and that the use of those same forces taught him nothing about that purpose. The only progress, if it may be referred to as such, lay in the fact that material prosperity could be acquired faster and with less effort.

Spiritually, however, mankind remained as poor as ever, his own conceit keeping him further removed than ever from the inner essence of nature. This was accompanied by the loss of the element required for a full appreciation of art: intuition. Intuition is unconscious construction in a spiritual process. It is an unreasoned conjecture, residing in the spirit, concerning that which is valuable to the development of that process. It is that which precedes and initiates any conscious synthesis. Understandably, the entire materialistic world resisted with all its might this spiritual element that frequently judged with such painful sincerity. Even science, however valuable the service rendered to it by intuition, found it safer largely to deny its existence, and otherwise to subjugate it to reason. This was the death of intuition. As the justification for its existence was called into question, one could not expect its development to be valued in the slightest. And it certainly gives no pleasure to discover how a vital element of life is found in our time almost exclusively in artists and children, who are generally unaware of it.

For a moment, impressionism offered the promise of liberation from this age of general decline and spiritual impotence. It succeeded to a certain extent. The Impressionists' quest to represent an event not by means of reality, but according to an impression, the inward experience of the event, did indeed deepen art, albeit only in the manner of representation. One might say that Impressionism pointed out to the new art that absolute freedom of representation is just as necessary for the completeness of the painting as for the spiritual growth of the artist. What Impressionism was not able to give art was great ideas, life symbols. The Primitives depicted their greatest passion. In their lives they felt incomplete unless they were in the closest possible contact with God. The Impressionists never reached those heights. They remained strangers to rapture.

Today's humanity is gradually becoming aware that its spirit is not faring well. However persistently the so-called blessings of materialism have spread, it has not managed to suffocate all higher human consciousness. And once the word 'intellectual' has come to sound as exaggerated as 'sentimental' has for some time, then there is a much greater possibility that the human spirit will develop harmoniously.

All things considered, these are not new ideals. They are ideals from the past, long known to the Primitives, and, before them, to the Ancients, re-emerging now in a form more suited to our time. Ideals which, it is now acknowledged in painting, are still worth striving for. It is precisely this acknowledgement that is so important. The fault lay not with the lack of ideals suited to our time, but with mankind today, grown accustomed to focusing his attention on the apparent development and happiness surrounding him.

The desire to become one with nature, the origin and continuous source of all life, is the same at its core as the more simply symbolised longing of the Primitives to devote their lives and their art to the service of God. In both there lies a need to bring mankind in his quest into harmony with life, from which he stands apart, yet also within. Both are expressions of the highest and purest desires that mankind can cherish. *The only ones, moreover, which can ever elevate mankind to the ideal of leading a conscious, natural life.* The revival of awareness of this truth has been a great driving force in painting, which has brought about a mighty reversal.

It took a long time before the chaos of newly emerging movements could be fully comprehended. But now that a large proportion of them, including the most bizarre, have died an early death, and many others, even newer, though they have not brought anything new, merely languish, it has become considerably easier to chart a way through the apparent confusion.

And it seems clear now that the 'Sturm' movement that has grown in Germany encompasses the most important and valuable elements for the more recent art. It cannot readily be referred to as a 'style', as it concerns a collection of artists who, although driven by the same impulse, all differ in their views and procedures. Der Sturm is a combination of entirely heterogeneous personalities, brought together by the largely negative realisation that the quest and the work of painters today left them dissatisfied. This lack of precisely defined principles gives the movement great alertness. It protects the artists from imitation and thus from the death of their original spirit. It prevents the self-satisfaction of apparent security. It gives them all complete freedom and, furthermore, constant stimulation as they observe other innovations.

Although not constrained by fixed theories, a series of guiding notions can nevertheless be discerned, which define the character of the whole. First and foremost is the acknowledgement of the impotence of current artistic expression which has become mired in lacklustre realism as a result of the loss of higher spiritual ideals. To bring about a change in this was the great driving force that brought the Sturm movement into existence. Damning criticism, merciless ridicule, combined with the creation of generally startling, sometimes exaggerated, but always truthfully expressed artworks —it was this with which they confronted their astonished audience. And of course, to most, the sarcasm and the exaggeration were the main thing—the only thing, even—that distinguished these new artists from what had gone before. But for those who looked further, it was the basic ideas—new light, new force, new movement in all areas of art—that were paramount.

Is this not the fate of all movements that attempt to find their way in a world of outdated ideas and lives reduced to drudgery? The general public see only the eager faces of these warriors, hear their perplexed and plentiful cries. They see only the outward appearance, the temporary… and they condemn it. Beneath this, however, burns the flame of inner conviction, the light of reform, seen by only a few. The Sturm movement quickly became famous in Germany. In other countries, and certainly in Holland, its name continued to be associated with excess, with senselessness. This is not the place to explore why this is so. A certain rigidity, a lack of interest in spiritual processes, coupled with an undeniable mistrust of anything new, are undoubtedly at play.

One of the most important features of the movement is its universality. Der Sturm is involved in every field of art. Painting and literature are the foremost, but theatre, recitation and music have also been drawn into the focus of the new light. This universality is a defining feature. It was rightly appreciated how deadly monotony and narrow-mindedness must be for an artist. How a creator of new, unique life needs nothing more than to be among the great contentious issues that surround him. It is no secret that both painters and musicians are regarded as foolish. This defines today's art just as much as art defines the artist. Art is engaged in as a profession. A profession in which one can acquire a certain skill through training, for which of course a certain talent, taste, understanding of style etc. is vital, though these factors are in fact only secondary. Versatility, universality, knowledge of real life—these are the things that the more recent artists regard as vital to every true artist. The artist as the creator of new life! Can a creator be monotonous, narrow-minded?

Der Sturm showed itself to be versatile, revealed the fruits of its versatility to the entire world. Exhibitions took place in Germany, Austria, in the neutral countries. Exhibitions that attempted to present a full impression of what this diverse group of painters produced, as well as individual exhibitions of the work of some of the greatest. The literary products appeared in the movement's journal and in a large number of books and pamphlets on art, criticism, architecture etc. Plays, poetry and songs also appeared in print. Small evening gatherings were arranged at which the artists were able to present their own and other new work. Reform of the theatre and musical drama, of architecture and interior design was contemplated. There was no area that the Sturm movement did not illuminate with its bright light, attempting to bring clarity to the many dark, shadowy corners and denying neither criticism nor synthetic labour.

It is gratifying to see that the most progressive in every country are now beginning to show an interest. It is also proof that not everyone admits defeat in the face of the great difficulties associated with the correct assessment of contemporary painting. The modern and hypermodern movements are still great in number, albeit reduced, and to distinguish good from bad, honest from dishonest intentions, occasions entirely unexpected and peculiar difficulties.

The unreality of the images renders the verification of the abilities of the artist, so long practised with such ease, impossible. One cannot therefore investigate these moderns too meticulously, cannot appraise them too closely. In almost all cases we find we are dealing with art that conveys mood purely, to some extent or other, art that rarely proceeds beyond sensation, and never beyond emotion. Art, therefore, of the lowest rank, that uses a so-called modern technique only to mislead the public and perhaps also the creator himself. To inform the public, moreover, endless series of highly abstract, apparently philosophical tracts are published, extolling the virtues of the recently invented style.

These artists prefer to depict mood. The defining characteristic of mood is submission. A submission that is entirely passive, that is completely devoid of resistance, of fight. A feeling aroused by sensation, whereby the spirit remains ineffectual. A dead, and thus meaningless age, for art. A mood can be of the greatest importance for the artist himself, but it is no less than arrogance to believe that depicting it might mean something to others.

The weakness and, in terms of criticism, inconstancy of this art, is defined by the word '*aanvoelen*' (sense), which emerged simultaneously, an entirely nondescript word open to any interpretation. It is used in an attempt to suggest that it is not possible to say how one experiences a work of art, that one simples 'senses' it. But if this truly is the only possible encounter with the work, it is proof that the sensation depicted is so vague and meaningless that it cannot withstand deconstruction and will therefore never evoke an emotion, let alone rapture. Precisely in view of this abundance of hollow, and moreover largely perverse, art, one cannot be too keenly aware of how to fathom the inner essence of every work of art. One must not fear harsh appraisal. The genuinely good can withstand anything, and there is nothing more prevalent in the world than the mediocre.

Among the more recent artists, **Jacoba van Heemskerck** is one of those whose art, by virtue of its great seriousness and sincerity alone, is worthy of the greatest interest. Her work revives the urge for all-encompassing nature. The urge to find what nature gives us, not as landscape, but as spiritual truth, in its lines and colours. Nature captured as it emerges in the artist's mind, as a symbol of the expression of life.

What she presents are her thoughts on being, prompted and influenced by the forms and colours around her. She depicts not what exists, what is real, *for every merely realistic depiction is lifeless in itself*. It is only when natural motifs in the broadest sense are re-created that they begin to have importance for art. To arrive at the point of re-creation, however, requires profound study. Not study in the academic sense, an exercise in naturalistic copying, which leads to a certain level of technical skill; no, a study of all that nature has to give in terms of inner richness, of what life has to offer in terms of spiritual events, and of the effect of both—nature and life—within and upon each other.

For everything that happens in life has no value by virtue of the mere event itself, only by virtue of the symbol behind it, which connects it to the grander scheme of life. Each event, each act, is a revelation about life. But it is a revelation whose meaning is not presented to anyone, so it must be understood through profound and extensive study. It is certainly worthwhile, in this context, to consider the different periods in Jacoba van Heemskerck's life and work.

Having completed thorough academic studies, she soon began to grow aware of the poverty of and the great restrictions imposed by the system of copying nature. And it certainly says much about the logical line that can be discerned throughout her development as an artist that she began as a strict Cubist. The work from that first period is typified by a constant search for a strict mathematical rhythm. Just as in our time everyone is in a certain sense a victim of a measure of scientific progress, so too is the artist, certainly at first, as he seeks the greatest simplicity. He will find it impossible to reconceive the rich basic forms of nature other than in the form of geometric planes and space. Inability to re-create them in the image of one's own spirit means the endless proliferation of forms are necessarily constructed with the help of scientific progress. An intellectual rather than a spiritual synthesis, therefore.

It is strange in this context to note the fact that artists generally tend to create a rhythmic whole using only horizontal and vertical lines. And so we see a complete deconstruction of random line movements into their most extreme components. At this point, the artist has come so far that he can impart harmony, not to the forms of nature itself, but to the product of its most radical deconstruction. A more elementary stage, therefore. It is no wonder that the colour in Jacoba van Heemskerck's work displayed few interesting properties at this stage. Mankind has more affinity with form, after all, than with colour. Firstly, because as well as being visible, forms can also be discerned by touch, but above all because mankind, living within certain dimensions himself, more directly relates to all forms, while colour is more abstract for him, and thus more difficult to fathom.

The colours that Jacoba van Heemskerck uses in these works are generally dull and misty. There is a certain note of hesitation, a reluctance to express as true colour, a largely dream-like state in which the fear of growing awareness is manifest. The majority are shades that comply with certain demands of balance, but do not presume to offer anything of value as colours in themselves. The greatest importance of these works derives, however, from the fact that they clearly indicate the main direction of the artist's quest. Firstly, in the simplicity and austerity of the forms, and in the colour which, though hesitant, has already been liberated from the academic palette, but above all in the ever-present balance that predominates in all of Jacoba van Heemskerck's work.

The first requirement of any completed spiritual process is that it should bring peace, that its result stands firm, like nature itself, solid and in balance, in the great sum of turmoil and conflict. For an artist to understand this is of inestimable value. Balance, both in the movement of the lines and in the value of the colours, is the foundation of a work of art.

In the subsequent period of Jacoba van Heemskerck's development we begin to discern a great change. A change partly in the rhythm, but above all in the colour. Strong, personal colour begins to dominate, in place of the muted, hesitant shades of the previous period. A certain measure of constraint is still discernible, a restriction of the form-freedom, but this gives way to a greater, deeper wealth of line movement. The entire composition of the painting is then subordinated to the symbol, albeit to some extent subconsciously. Not the symbol in the narrow sense, whose articulation has given its name to an entire school, but the symbol that is nourished by the development of the human spirit, which has learnt to see it, how it figures in life, as a symbol among symbols, all subordinated to the great, unknown purpose of nature.

In this period Jacoba van Heemskerck's colours, too, assume a symbolic power, and it is this in particular that lends her palette its personal quality. *Every colour has a spiritual value*. It is largely the same for every observer, although there remains some individual effect. A certain kind of deep, dark purple will not make one person lighthearted and glad in contrast to almost all others, just as a scintillating red will not cause misery except in certain highly specific circumstances. Smaller nuances can however prompt very important differences in the individual.

Combining different colours can make these influences less personal. *While one colour has a spiritual value, several colours together prompt a spiritual process, whether it be conflict or harmony. The study and resolution of these processes has become one of the foremost objectives of the truly new art.*

If we now consider which colours and colour relationships dominate in Jacoba van Heemskerck's work in this period, we find that the drab, faded shades have disappeared, and made way for predominantly strong, warm colours whose personal and animated quality distinguishes them from those of the solar spectrum. There is red, the colour of strong passions, the colour of burning desire, almost fatal in its intensity. In contrast to that there is green, the colour of silence, of harmony in nature, the balanced foundation of all life, of all struggle. These two colours are the elements that can convey the clash of primal forces in life, the smouldering, sensual desires and the quiet, calming power of nature. They reflect this struggle in the work of Jacoba van Heemskerck, too, where they generally symbolise the earth, in all its turmoil and turbulence.

Then there is keenly radiant yellow, harsh and intense, the symbol of the constant urge to move forward, further and further, to find all the unexplained mysteries of life. The colour of reason, of cold but restless searching. In this sense yellow is like the human spirit which, in its ignorance, ceaselessly strives to relate correctly to life through deeper knowledge. Alongside this we have blue, cool, cautious blue, which has no passion and no conflict. The colour of self-reflection, of quiet contemplation. Dark purple, and beside it flaming, all-consuming orange, reflect the conflict of the greatest stirring of the soul, the clash between the surging power which erupts in bold sparks, ready to do battle with anything that stands in its way, and against that deep purple: the gloom, the sorrow, the endless melancholy. Thus mankind longs to experience, to enjoy, every unparalleled delight the earth has to offer. But in response there is the melancholy at the dissatisfaction every new gratification leaves behind, each time more intense.
But apart from this deep purple, there is also violet, lighter and more rarefied which, with its pale glow, symbolises the firm, serious will, and appears among other colours with an elevated spiritual quality which, though less warm and forceful, transcends them like the wide beam of a serene light.

Finally, at the extremes, black, absolute colourlessness, and white, the highest and purest radiance, the sum of all colours. While black represents nothing, the start of all things, white is the possible end state, the absolute peace which, devoid of passion in itself, contains all passion, all the colours of life. These are the two extremes of being. The Primitives would symbolise them simply as God and earth, as heaven and hell, grace and sin.

Jacoba van Heemskerck gives us in her work all these colours, in their endless variations and nuances, in their continuous clashing and harmonies, resolving them into one grand balance, a complete vision of life.

Like colour, form also has value as a means of expressing thoughts, particularly the curvature of line, the movement of lines. In a painting, lines have two functions. Firstly they provide rhythm, dividing the image into balanced sections. The line is an aid that defines the boundaries of the colours, thus giving the plane its form value. This function of the line has long been known.

In the more recent art another, highly valuable, property of the line comes into play. While colours symbolise the different spiritual states, the lines, in their own expression, denote movement within or between those states. They thus indicate the passing, or the divergence, the exaltation or the decline, that the entire image is intended to express. And in those curvatures of the line lie endless possibilities to represent the smallest nuances of spiritual experience. Seen thus, the unfolding of all processes lies in the movement of the lines. They indicate the path travelled by the artist's thoughts and feelings, while the colours symbolise what those thoughts and feelings were. One might simply say that the colours and their position indicate 'what' has been achieved, and the lines 'how'. These two things are necessary in a work of art, and one is entirely worthless without the other.

So it is that in every painting the effect of the movement and countermovement of the lines is of the greatest importance for the balance of the work. Particularly the countermovement, for while everything conceivable inevitably has its opposite, and the ideal of peace is not to eliminate it completely, but to achieve harmony in precisely those contrasting factors, so in a painting movement in the lines, against the prevailing direction, is indispensable for true peace in the composition.

The majority of Jacoba van Heemskerck's work in this second period displays that peace, that harmonious unity, whereby though the rhythm is still more or less strictly intellectual, it remains logical and always balanced. From this point the value of the colours does not undergo further change, at least not in terms of the main relationships. Even in her latest work, it remains a clash of primal forces, a struggle between flaming passion and quiet contemplation, between profound, quiet sorrow and burning spiritual power. But above all the eternal struggle in which the all-suffusing white light of spiritual harmony attempts to overcome the endless night of human tragedy.

While, in the colours, these remain the dominant symbols, in the forms and lines a further progression can be seen, as they work themselves free of the bondage in which they were held. Jacoba van Heemskerck has grasped and deconstructed all the forms that fascinated her in the great game of nature. She has studied the motif of boats on the water. The longing in the sails reaching up towards heaven, the calm they represent when, white and gleaming, they stand motionless against the distant sky. And the endless firmament, as it arcs over the world, taut and all-sheltering. She saw how the heavy dark trees lift up their arms beseechingly, and how the long, capricious branches twist downwards, exhausted.

In her search for the soul of things, she considered all the strangeness and mystery that nature has to offer: the slender bodies of fish darting through the trembling water, the monstrous and grotesque movements of sea creatures, terrifying and ridiculous at the same time. She brought the vibrant turbulence of the water dwellers into harmony with the element that surrounds them. And then the colours and strange rows of eclectic floral figures, and the wondrous embroidery with which nature adorns the wings of butterflies. She sought through all of nature, the forests and water, the high, bustling cities and the quiet villages, knowing that every form and every colour carries in it a truth about life, because they are revelations that have grown in nature, there for anyone who seeks earnestly and with all his soul to find.

For every revelation that is important to life must reside in nature itself, in its greatest purity. Jacoba van Heemskerck made many such finds, though not all are of equal value. For humanity, the scale and greatness of the values found is of paramount importance, but in our age the very fact that the new art devotes itself to life in this way will be of greater import.

Jacoba van Heemskerck does not name her paintings. They are merely numbered, to distinguish them one from another, in the order of their creation. This is a phenomenon common in the more recent art that deserves a moment of our attention

A word generally has two meanings—its actual meaning, and a symbolic meaning. A word can thus readily be used in daily life and in literature, for example, by way of a symbol. The rest of the sentence will indicate which meaning is intended. A title of one word or a short phrase beneath a symbolic painting would be of no harm to the viewer with immediate understanding, as he would promptly incorporate it into the meaning of the painting. But just as it would not harm him, nor would it help him to any great extent. And such a title can set a viewer without immediate understanding on the wrong path, as he will not know how to interpret it. Which meaning he chose would depend entirely on his nature. To prevent this from happening would require a full description of the artist's intention. An attempt to approximate the image in literary form, therefore. But this would require the artist to be in possession of such descriptive talent, and this is not generally the case.

The only remaining path would therefore be for a writer to attempt to characterise the paintings, which he understood entirely, as briefly and accurately as possible, in a language more comprehensible to the majority of people, giving the impression that he sought to interpret the painting. But this too would occasion many problems, of course, so that for the time being the omission of any title is the purest way, albeit for many the most difficult. For the lack of any designation will be a great obstacle against those for whom the more recent art is still inaccessible growing closer to it.

The custom of including in every painting a representation that, outwardly at least, conforms to daily life, a custom that has existed for centuries, has made countless numbers of people almost entirely unreceptive to non-realistic colour and line symbols. The question of whether omitting any representation of reality introduces greater purity to painting has been discussed by numerous proponents of the more recent art, and many have found this to be the case. Their arguments are that painting should adhere entirely to the elements at its disposal, colour and line, which are always sufficient to express what the artist wishes. This is certainly the case, but it would be incorrect to see in this a reason for anything that still seeks to reflect the realistic image as such, or freely altered, to be deemed impure painting. Just as realism in literature does not render it impure art. For the purity of art depends not on employing the smallest possible number of means, but solely on the way in which they are used, and to what end. The difference between abstract and realist art is that the former uses more direct psychological expression, while the latter expresses itself by means of images and comparisons, and thus indirectly. This does not however detract from the purity of painting.

In the art of Jacoba van Heemskerck the abstract symbol dominates, yet there is always a reference to a real event, albeit incorporated entirely into the idea being expressed. And that is precisely one of her greatest gifts, that she depicts reality in such a way that, first and foremost, we encounter the harmony, the spiritual balance of the whole, while for the understanding viewer there is not the least inducement to delve further into that reality. A closer inspection of some of the works reproduced here will make this still more clear.

Image no. 23 (fig. 67). This cannot be characterised any more simply than as eternal truth revealed to humanity. At the centre the motif of a ship gliding through the water, with a brilliant white sail, like a saint opening both arms to heaven to receive the wisdom of the divine. Beside this, and following the first, two others, also with spotless white sails, though their inner aspect is not fully developed. And so they proceed, silent and sure, over the rippling surface of the water, towards suffering humanity. For in the background are the mighty purple mountains on which a bright orange glows. The deep melancholy, the sorrow of he who hoped to find, but found his powers wanting. Yet above this, alive and glimmering, the desire to persist, to continue seeking and struggling. Perfectly symbolising mankind, restlessly torturing himself in his powerful urge to know everything that eternity conceals from him.

In the foreground, on either side, two powerful, heavy black tree figures, the branches twisted and reaching for each other, forming the gateway of misery and suffering through which must pass anyone who wishes to give to mankind something that might help him. Beneath that, depicted in hefty angular blocks, is the earth from which the trees grow, the earth and its fertility. Here, Jacoba van Heemskerck has resolved this main idea with the balancing auxiliary figures into pure colour harmony.

Image no. 56 (fig. 68). Ideas about labour, the restlessness of the spirit. The main motif is a windmill of simple and

67 Jacoba van Heemskerck
Bild no. 23 (Witte zeilschepen op een meer) | Image no. 23 (White Sailing Ships on a Lake) 1915
Oil on canvas, 111,1 × 130,9 cm
Kunstmuseum Den Haag

68 Jacoba van Heemskerck
Bild no. 56 (Hollandse molen) | Image no. 56 (Dutch Windmill) 1916
Oil on canvas, 56 × 60 cm
Nationalgalerie, Staatliche Museen zu Berlin

69 Jacoba van Heemskerck
Bild no. 60 | Image no. 60 1916
Oil on canvas
(whereabouts unknown)

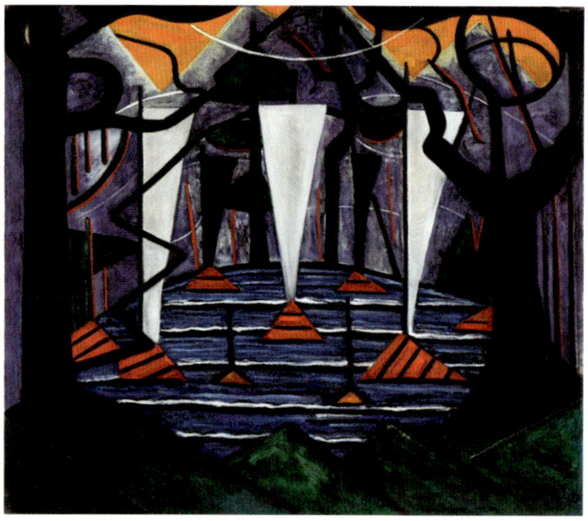

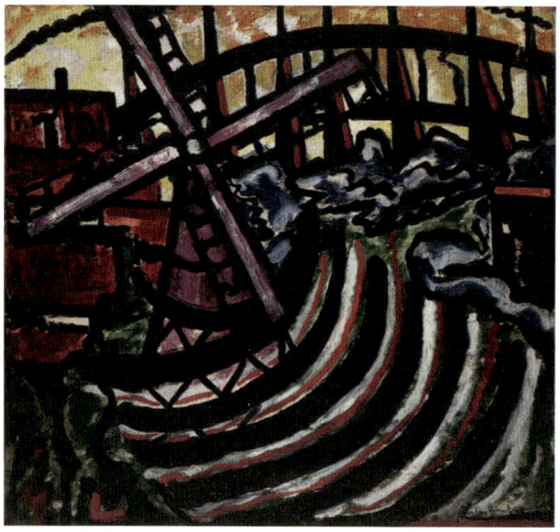

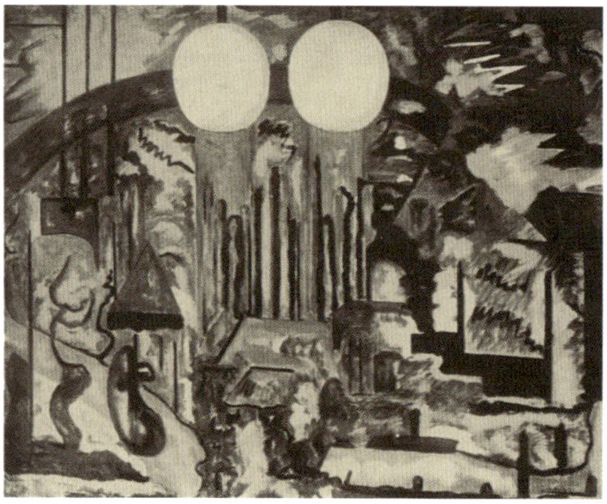

robust construction. The sails appear to be still, but beneath are mighty arches, black and orange which, repeated, and varying in appearance, prompt thoughts of tireless toil, the constant turning of the sails. Around this, in red and green, the play of human emotion and of passion in the midst of life as it moves inexorably forward. Among all this, the windmill rises up, pale violet, symbolising the value of labour, the sacred and redeeming task of mankind. In the background looms the black arch of a bridge under which slim, dark spires rise, representing the elevating power of restless labour and the joy and peace that comes when it is done.

Image no. 60. The turmoil, the commotion of urban life. At the bottom red and green clash once more, the life of labouring man, who believes he can find fulfilment only in the satisfaction of his passion for his work. A vibrantly coloured tangle of endless industry, of rugged, jolting power, of searching smokestacks and heavy, bleak blocks of houses. And through all this the surging orange flame. The desire for more than the constant turmoil of labour. In the midst of this rise slender, violet towers, tall and confident above the rattle and clash of the hubbub. The silent voice of eternity, speaking above the chasms of life, pointing to the radiant calm of spiritual harmony. On top of the pale violet towers, two blinding white balls of light. The light of truth. And over the entire city, in its vibrant turmoil, spans a heavy black arc, apparently attempting to encompass all of this enslaving life in its bleak power. But the radiant lights break through the dark arc, pointing the way to a higher and better life, to liberation.

These are some thoughts evoked by the aforementioned paintings. It is by no means the intention that these should be regarded as the only possible or correct interpretations. Anyone who understands the works will find other words that mean more to him, according to his nature or way of thinking. The intention is merely to apply the general observations made above to a number of examples. The desire is not to give a generally applicable explanation (this would after all be possible only for the most common symbols, used daily by all), merely to indicate a path one might take in approaching these works of art.

The value of the work of Jacoba van Heemskerck has thus been sufficiently illuminated. Firstly the purely pictorial value, as found in the strict balance and the deep colour and form resolution in almost every one of her paintings. But above all, the immense value to all of mankind of the revival of this art. *An art in which the most sacred quest is once more to trace the deepest origins of the spiritual revelations of life, to then construct them, re-create them, in a great living harmony. The harmony of the unified spirit.*

January 1917

(Translated from Dutch by Sue McDonnell)

* The word 'Primitives' refers here to artists of the fourteenth and fifteenth centuries, for example, 'Les Primitifs Français' (the French Primitives); they could be seen at the 1904 Paris exhibition *Exposition des Primitifs Français* au Palais du Louvre, which Jacoba van Heemskerck probably also attended. See A. H. Huussen Jr and J. F. A. van Paaschen-Louwerse, *Jacoba van Heemskerck van Beest 1876–1923: Schilderes uit roeping* (Zwolle, 2005), 16.

Biography

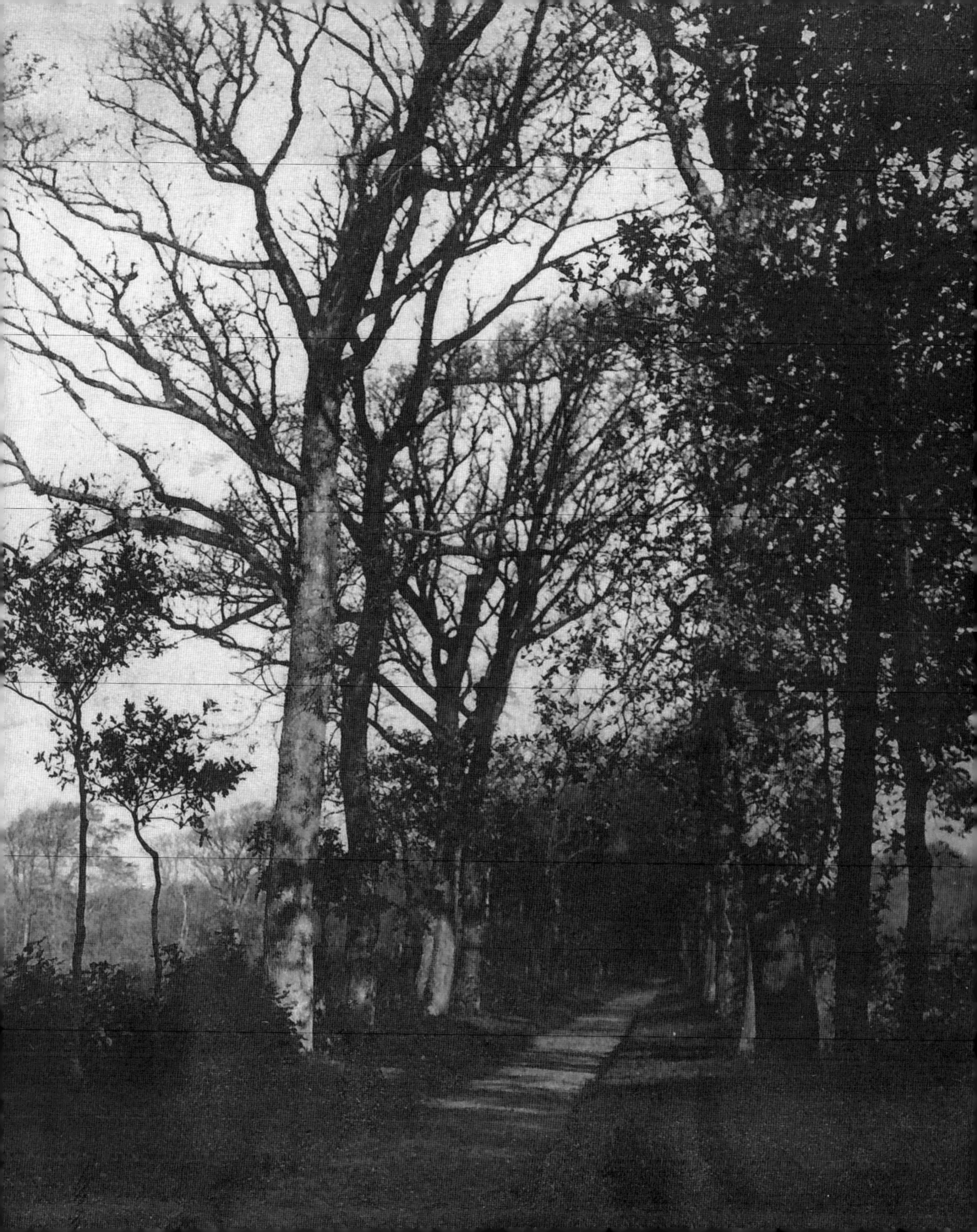

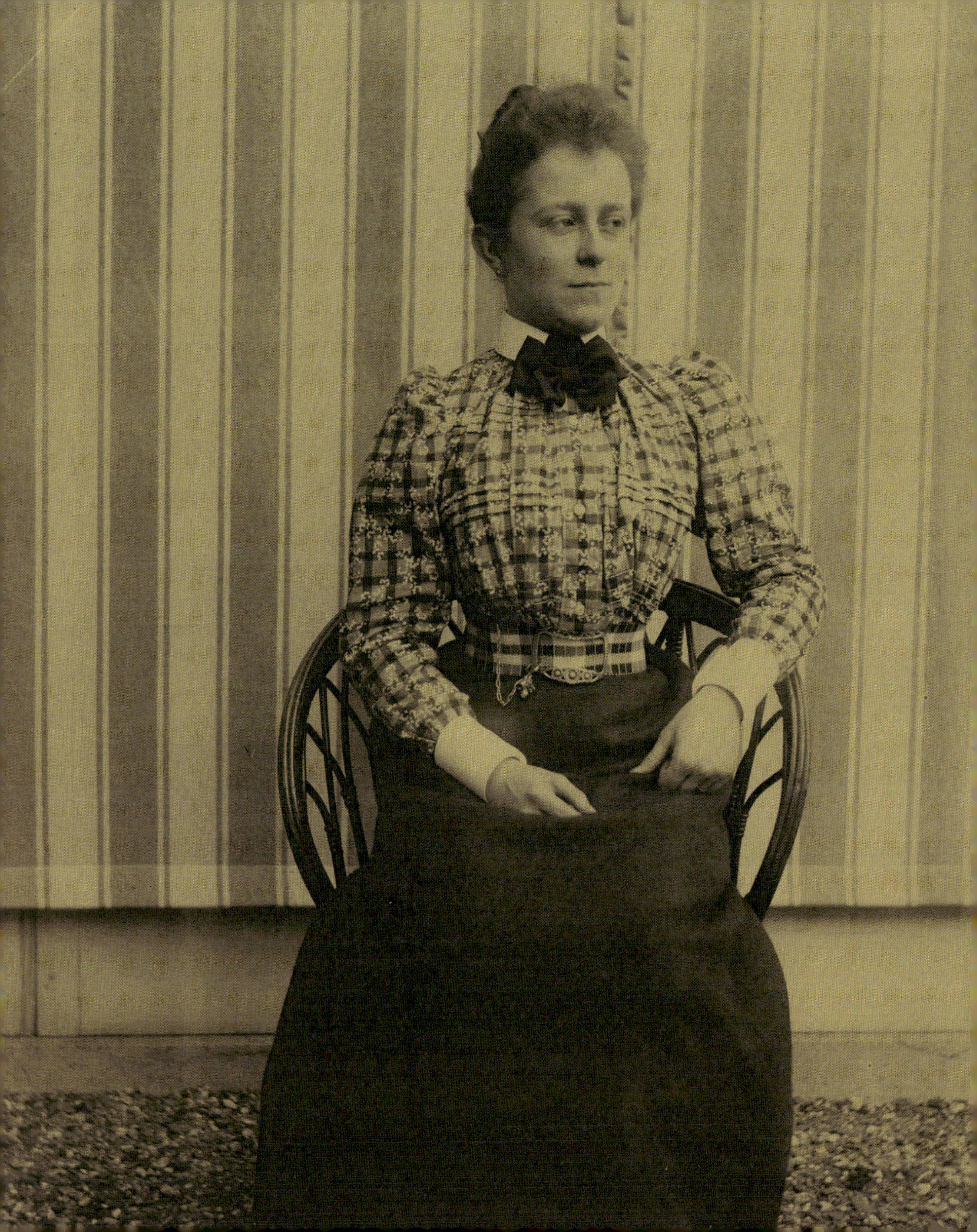

70 Lijdijkse weg, Oostkapelle (detail)

71 Jacoba van Heemskerck, 1917
Private collection

1876
Jacoba van Heemskerck is born in The Hague on 1 April, the youngest of six children. Her father, Jacob Eduard van Heemskerck, is a navy officer and a renowned painter of seascapes.

1897
She begins studying art at the Koninklijke Academie van Beeldende Kunsten in The Hague.

1901
After the death of her mother, Van Heemskerck and her sister move to Hilversum, near Utrecht. She becomes a student of Ferdinand Hart Nibbrig in the artists' village of Laren, taking lessons in printmaking and drawing. In the following years, she sojourns often in the art capital of Paris, attending classes at Eugène Carrière's studio.

1905
She moves to The Hague to be close to her friend Marie Tak van Poortvliet. From then on, she regularly participates in the St Lucas artists' association's exhibitions at the Stedelijk Museum in Amsterdam.

1906
Both women begin spending the summer months at the seaside in Domburg, where lively exchanges among young artists occur.

1910
Van Heemskerck joins the Theosophical Society.

1911
From this point on, she exhibits annually at the Moderne Kunstkring in Amsterdam, at the Domburg summer exhibition in Jan Toorop's pavilion, and at the Salon des Indépendants in Paris.

1913
She shows four paintings at Herwarth Walden's *Erster Deutscher Herbstsalon* in Berlin, one of the most important exhibitions of avant-garde art in the pre-war years. This marks the beginning of a friendship with Herwarth and Nell Walden, the founders of the Sturm movement, to which Van Heemskerck feels connected until the end.

1914
Van Heemskerck has her first exhibition for Der Sturm, and she begins making numerous woodcut designs for its magazine. She gives Herwarth Walden the exclusive right to exhibit and sell her art and begins numbering her work. She retreats from the Dutch art scene.

1915
Jacoba van Heemskerck and Marie Tak van Poortvliet become members of the Anthroposophical Society.

1916
Van Heemskerck meets the medical student Willem Zeylmans van Emmichoven, with whom she carries on intense discussions about Rudolf Steiner's anthroposophy; subsequently he authors a text about her work *The Spiritual Direction in New Painting: Jacoba van Heemskerck.*

1917
Van Heemskerck undertakes Sturm activities in her studio in The Hague. She gives lessons once a week, in the spirit of the Sturm art school. She also explores the theatre and a puppet show.

1918
Together with Zeylmans van Emmichoven she performs empirical experiments on the emotional impact of colours on viewers, and creates her first studies for works in glass, an idea that the artist had previously explored in 1914.

1920
Jacoba van Heemskerck produces large stained-glass works, including for the Villa Wulffraat in Wassenaar. Like many other artists, she gradually distances herself from Der Sturm. On her own she organises exhibitions in the Netherlands and elsewhere, and her stained-glass art meets with great accolades.

1921
The artist receives a large commission to design stained-glass windows for the Marinekazerne in Amsterdam. In this year and the following, Van Heemskerck plans exhibitions in the United States, as well as in Amsterdam, Brussels, and Paris.

1923
Van Heemskerck dies at the age of just forty-seven on August 3. Herwarth Walden organises a huge commemorative show in her honour. As a posthumous tribute, he also publishes the *Sturm-Bilderbuch VII* (1924).

Marie Tak van Poortvliet, who built an important collection of art that included works by Jacoba van Heemskerck, bequeathed part of it to the Kunstmuseum Den Haag, which owns the largest collection of her works today. Other works can be found at the Museum Boijmans Van Beuningen in Rotterdam, the Kunstmuseum Bern, the Berlinische Galerie, the Landskrona Museum near Malmö and at the Marie Tak van Poortvliet Museum in Domburg.

Der Sturm Magazine 1914–23

From above left to below right

1914 vol. 5, no. 9
Cover Jacoba van Heemskerck
1914 vol. 5, no. 15/16
Cover Heinrich Campendonk;
figs. Jacoba van Heemskerck;
texts Aage von Kohl, August Stramm
1915 vol. 5, no. 19/20
Cover Jacoba van Heemskerck

1915 vol. 5, no. 23/24
Cover/figs. Jacoba van Heemskerck;
texts August Stramm, Adolf Knoblauch,
Kurt Heynicke
1915 vol. 6, no. 9/10
Cover Aloys Wachlmeier; fig. Jacoba van Heemskerck; text Adolf Knoblauch
1915 vol. 6, no. 13/14
Cover Jacoba van Heemskerck

1914

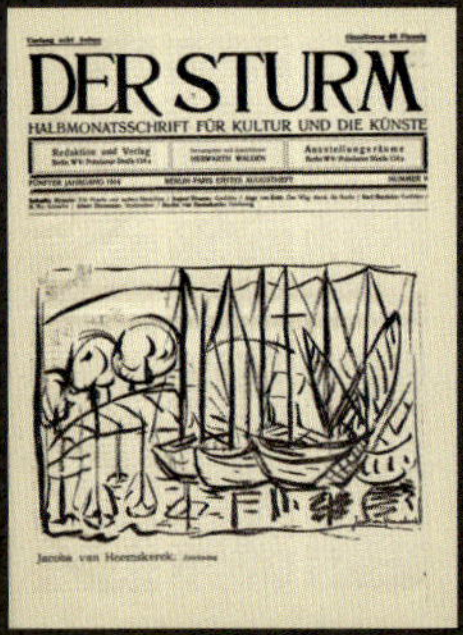

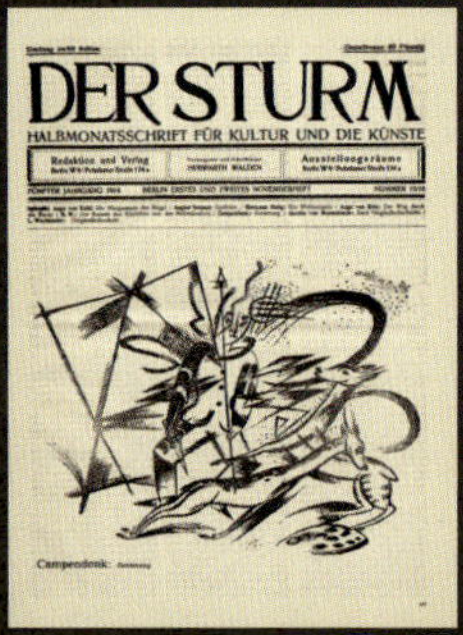

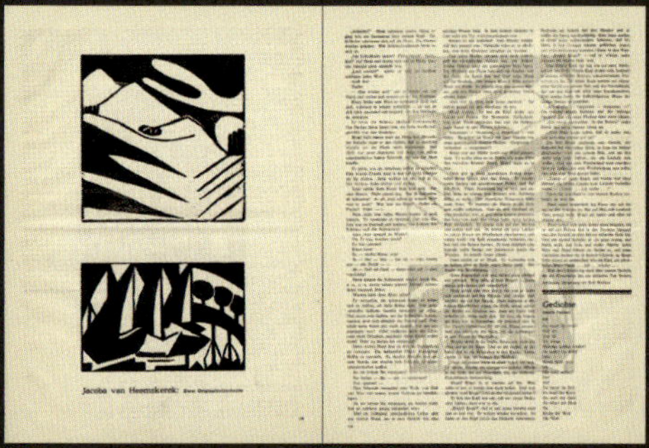

1915

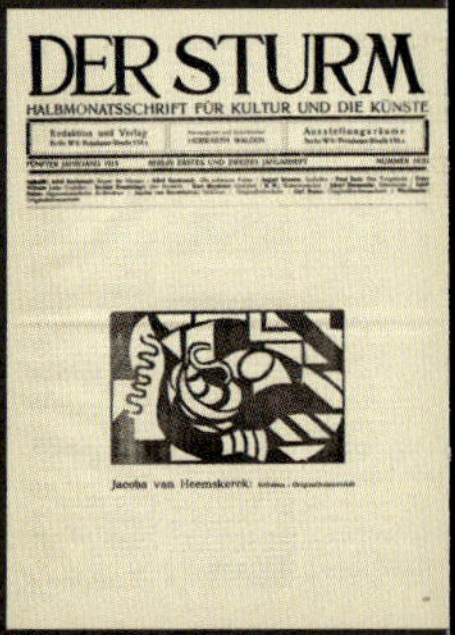

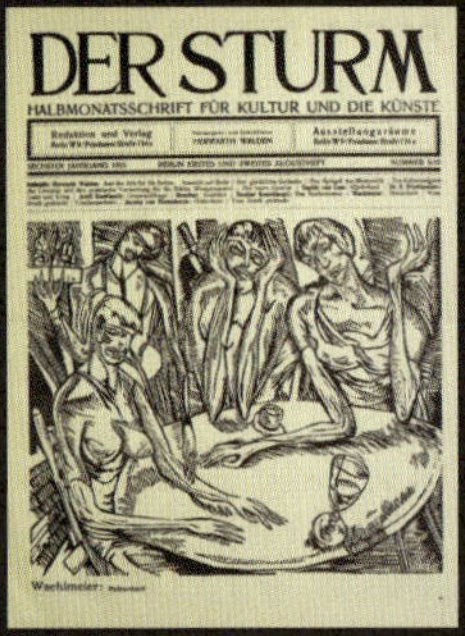

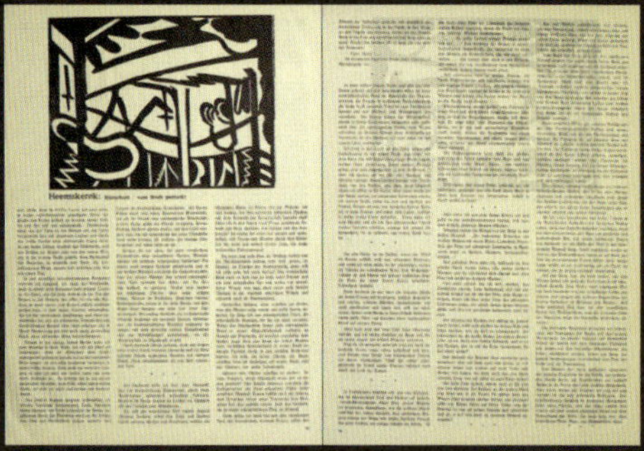

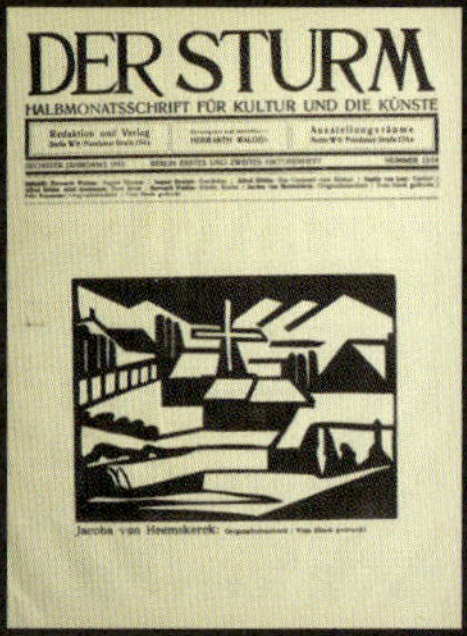

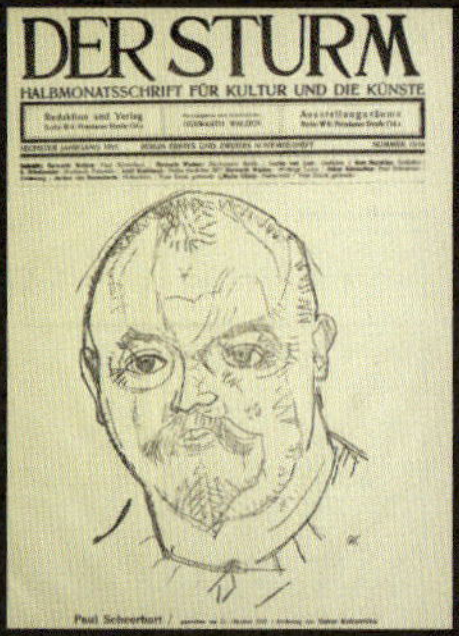

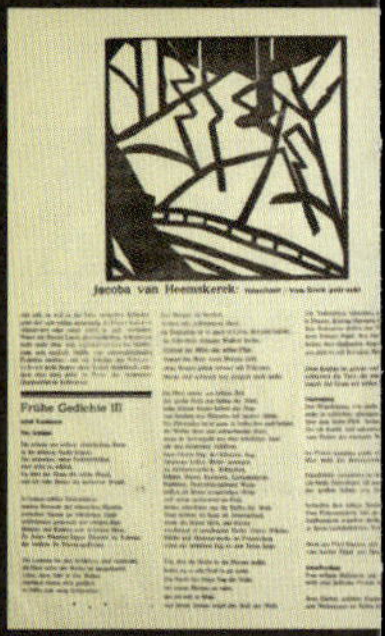

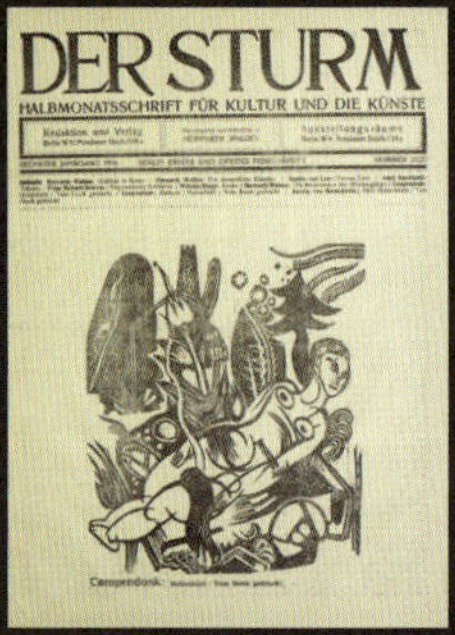

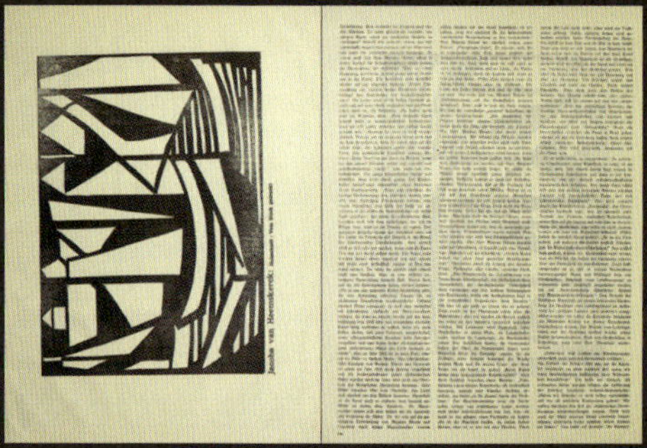

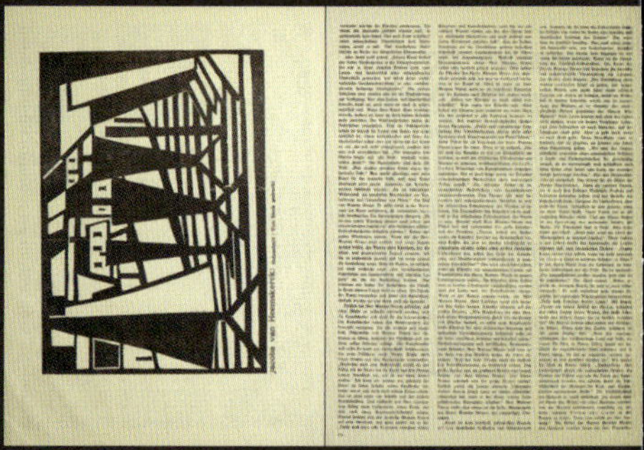

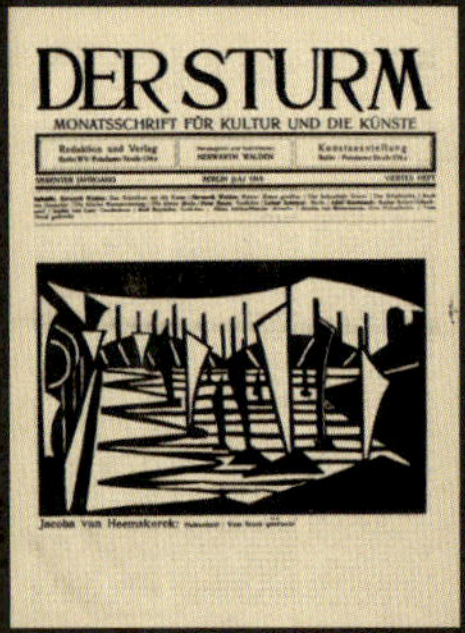

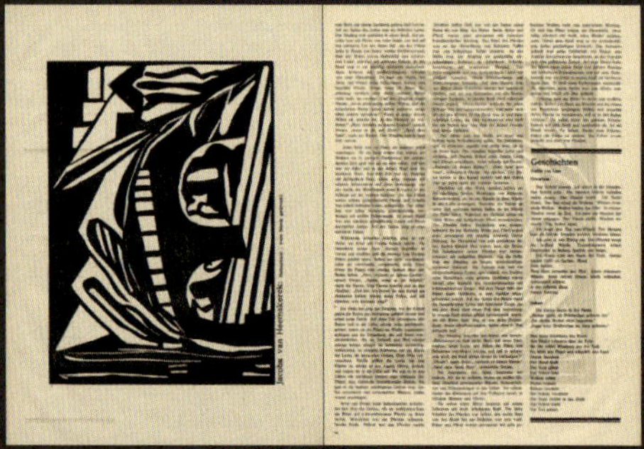

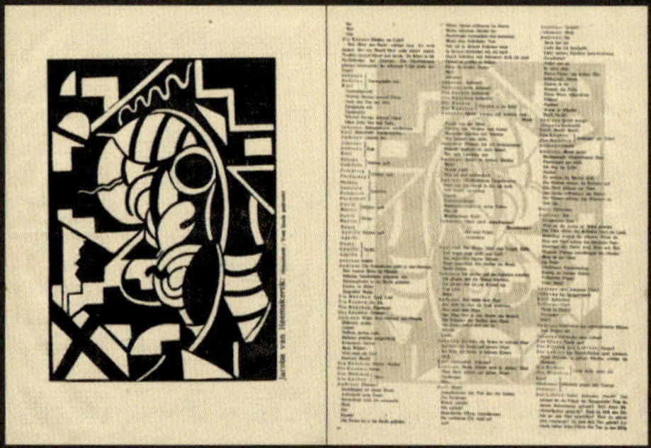

1917

1915 vol. 6, no. 15/16
Cover Oskar Kokoschka; fig. Jacoba van Heemskerck; texts Salomo Friedlaender, Adolf Knoblauch
1916 vol. 6, no. 19/20
Cover Max Ernst; figs. Jacoba van Heemskerck; texts Wilhelm Runge, Adolf Knoblauch

1916 vol. 6, no. 21/22
Cover Heinrich Campendonk; figs. Jacoba van Heemskerck; text Herwarth Walden
1916/17 vol. 7
Cover Jacoba van Heemskerck
1916 vol. 7, no. 1
Cover Paul Klee; fig. Jacoba van Heemskerck; texts Hermann Essig, Wilhelm Runge

1916 vol. 7, no. 4
Cover Jacoba van Heemskerck; figs. Jacoba van Heemskerck; texts Lothar Schreyer, Adolf Knoblauch, Sophie van Leer
1917 vol. 7, no. 10
Cover Georg Schrimpf; fig. Jacoba van Heemskerck; texts Hermann Essig, Kurt Striepe, Adolf Knoblauch

1917 vol. 7, no. 12
Cover Paul Klee; fig. Jacoba van Heemskerck; text Herwarth Walden

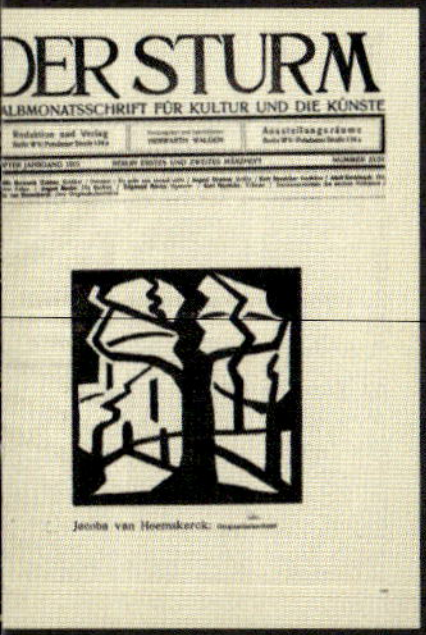

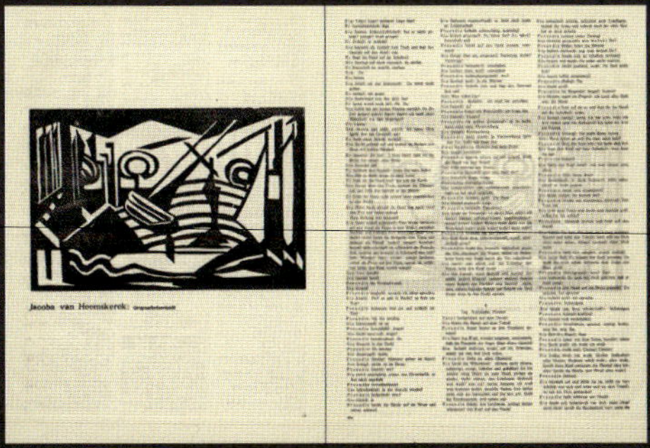

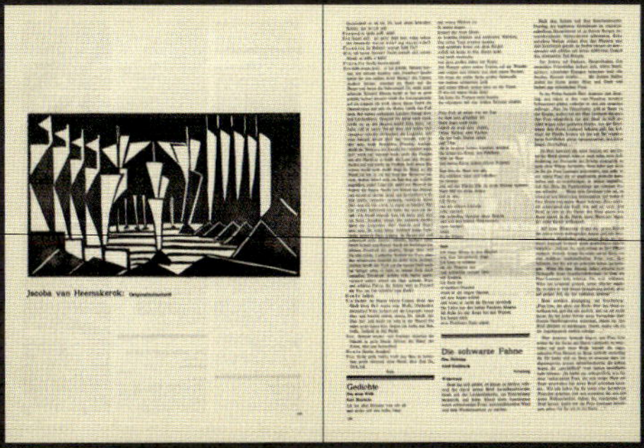

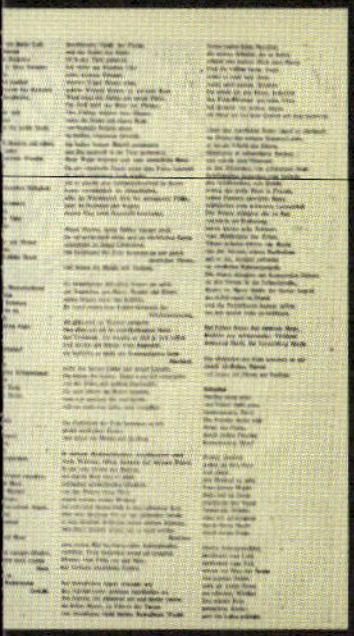

1916

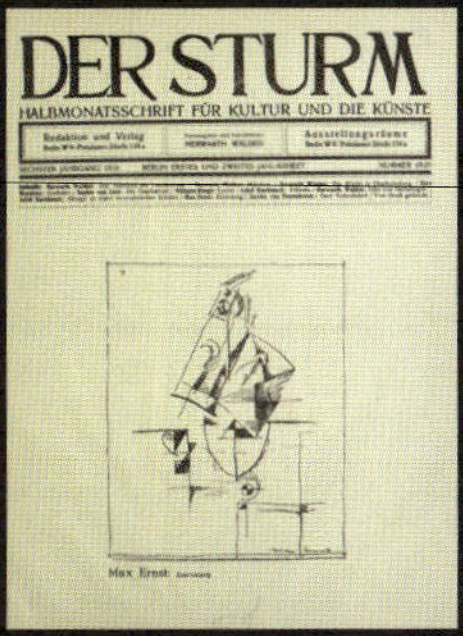

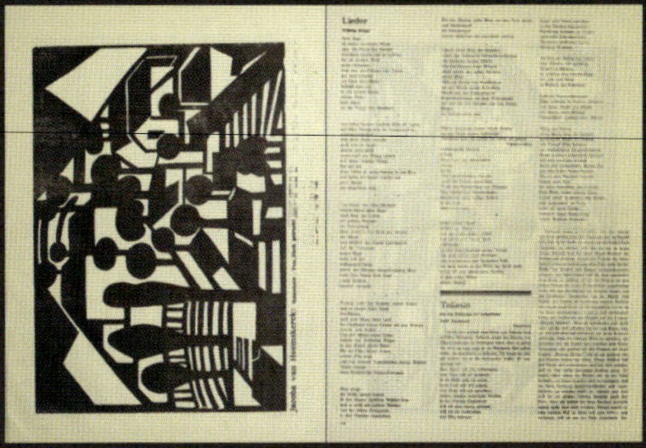

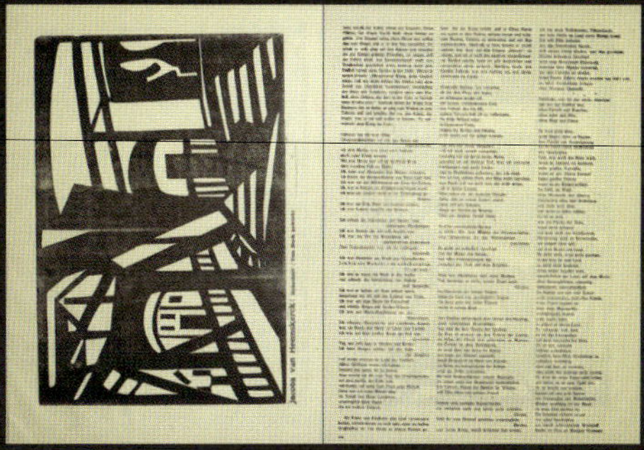

1916/17

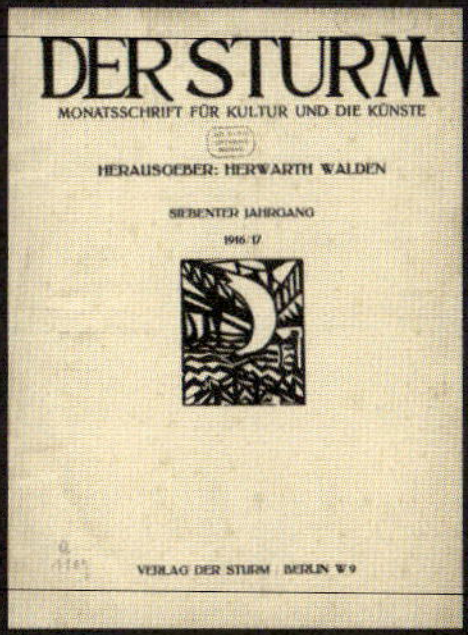

1916

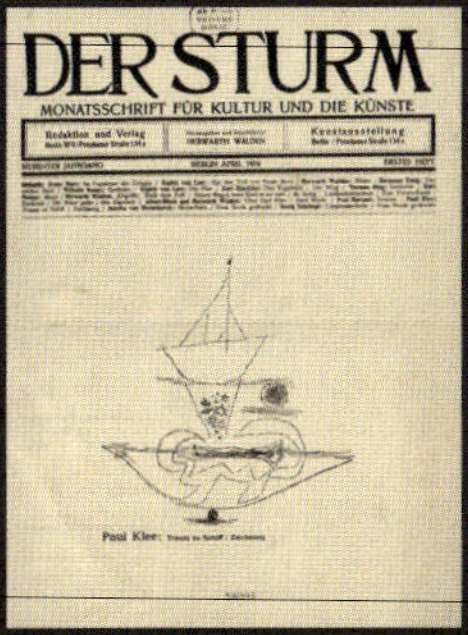

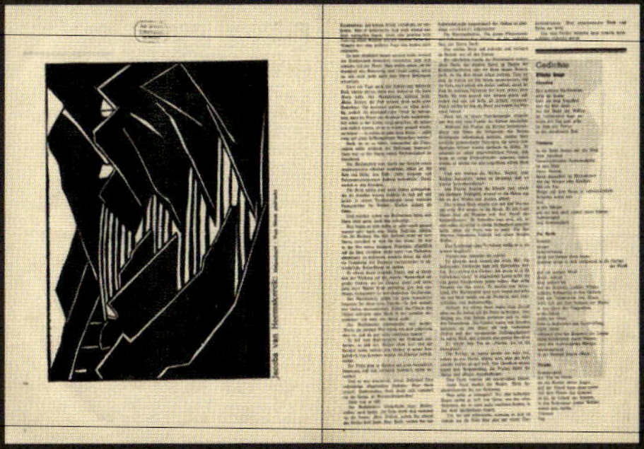

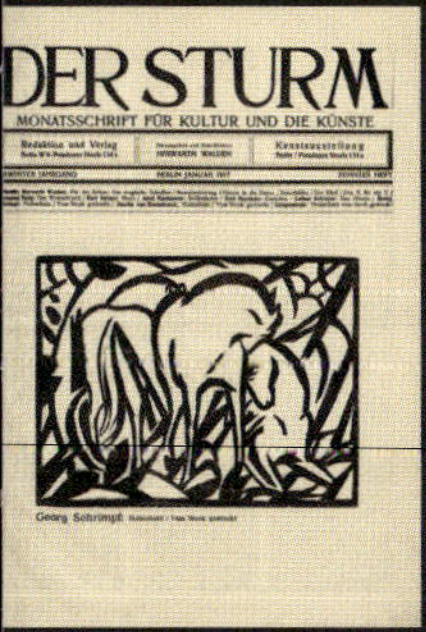

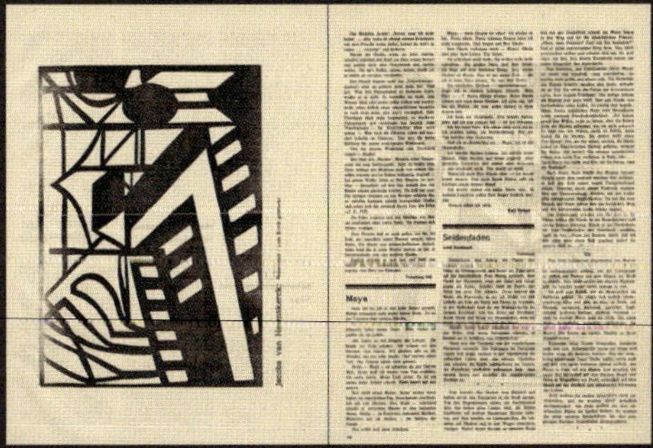

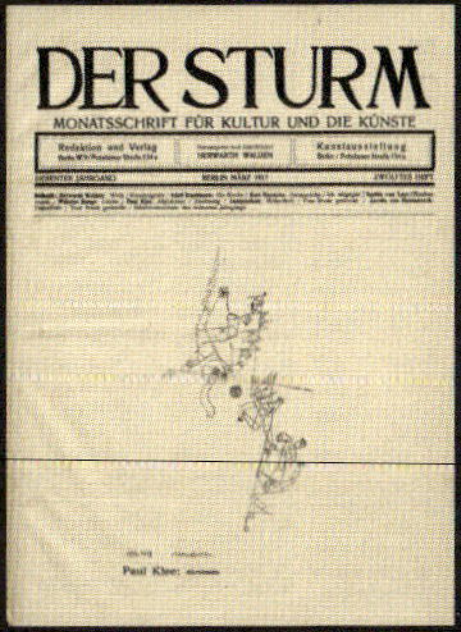

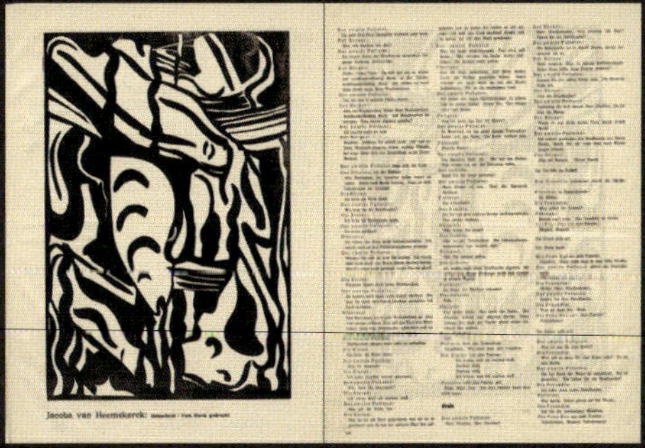

From above left to below right

1917/18 vol. 8
Cover Jacoba van Heemskerck
1917 vol. 8, no. 1
Cover Bohuslav Kokoschka; fig. Jacoba van Heemskerck; texts Thomas Ring, Oskar Graf-Berg

1917 vol. 8, no. 3
Cover Georg Schrimpf; figs. Jacoba van Heemskerck; texts Lothar Schreyer, Franz Richard Behrens, Adolf Knoblauch
1918 vol. 8, no. 10
Cover Georg Schrimpf; figs. Jacoba van Heemskerck; text Lothar Schreyer

1917/18

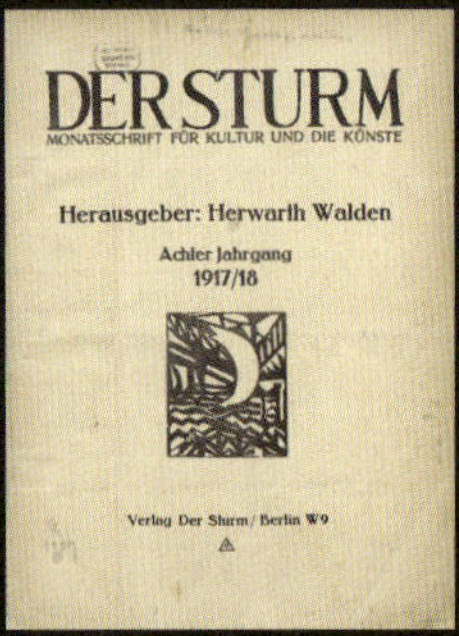

1917

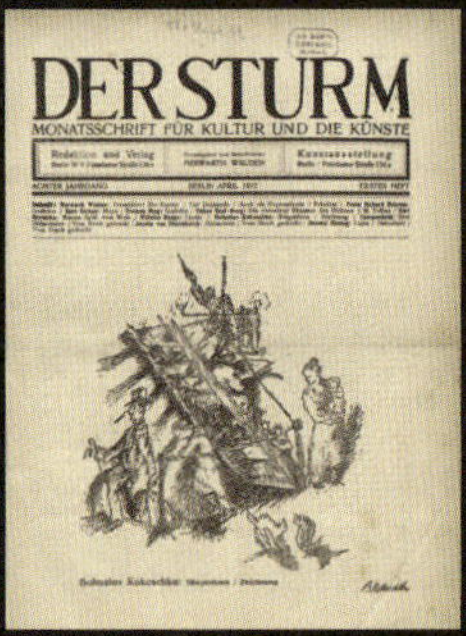

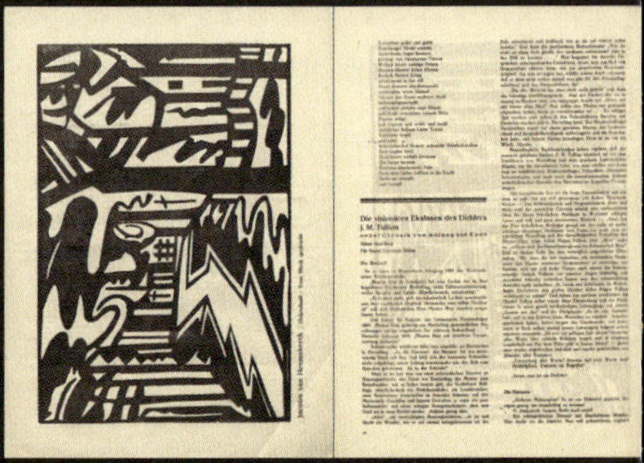

1918

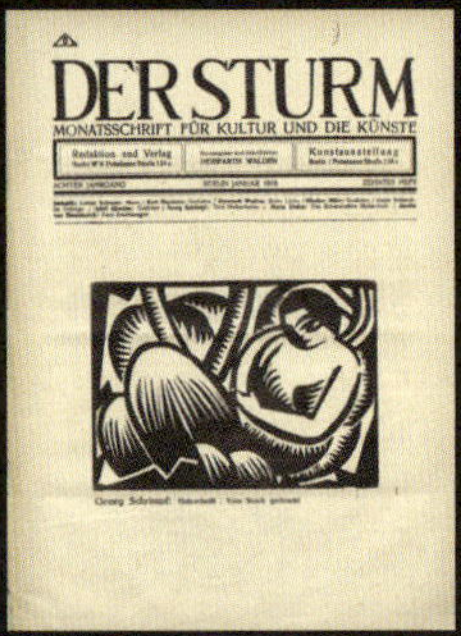

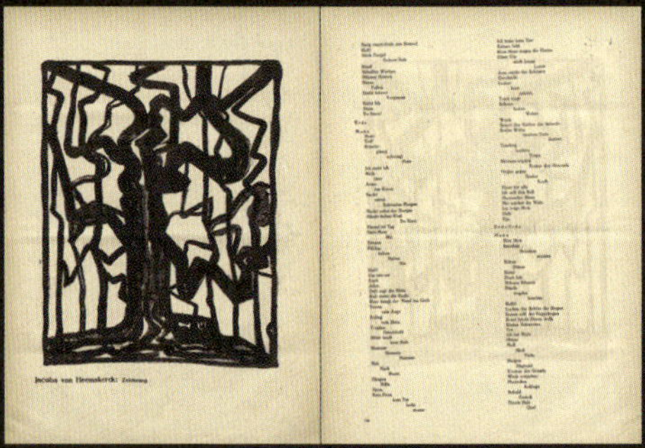

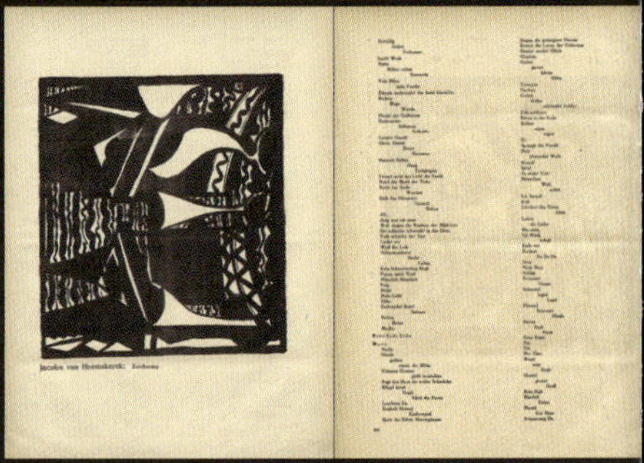

1920

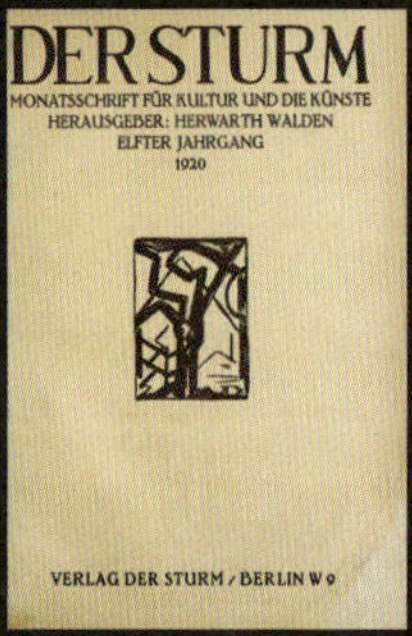

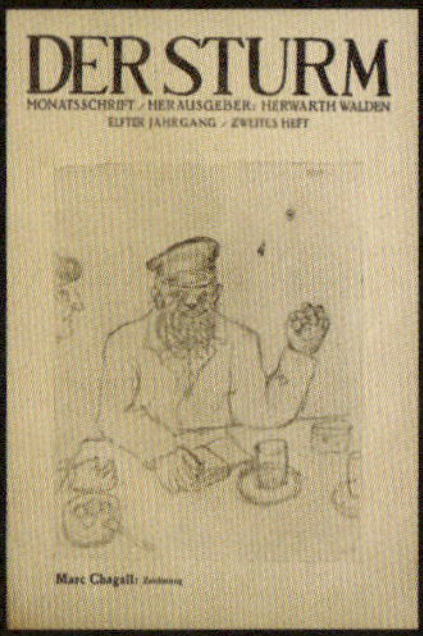

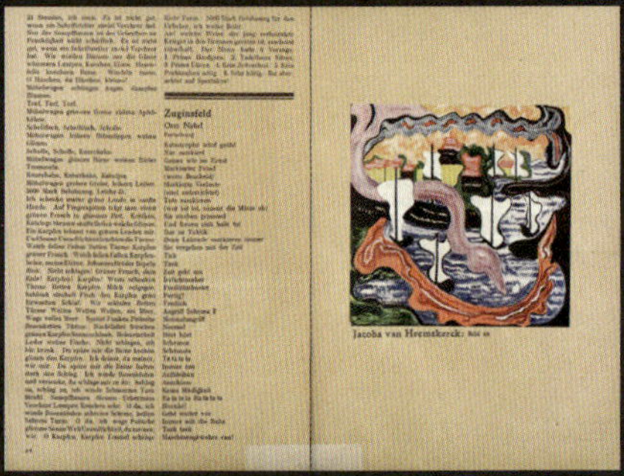

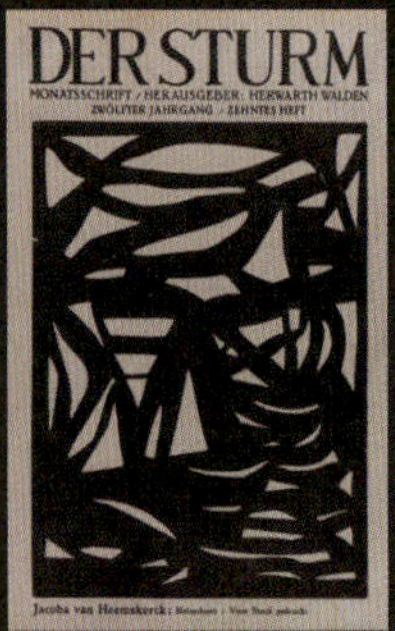

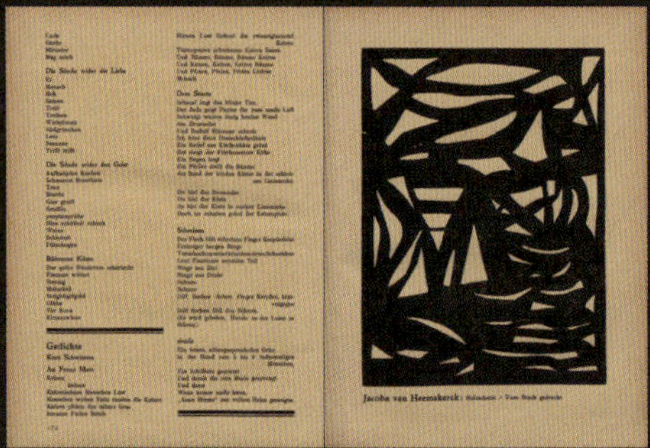

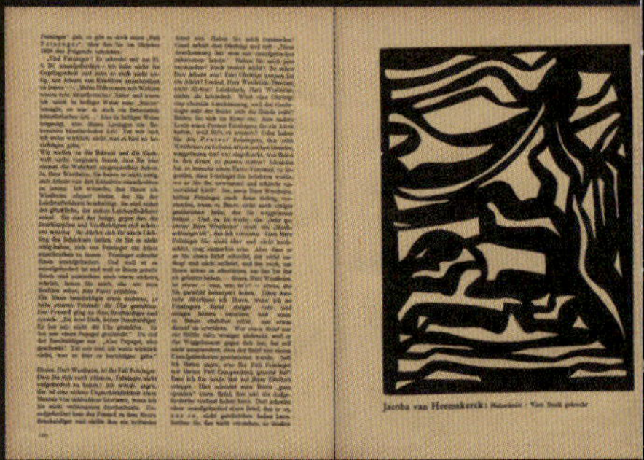

1918/19 vol. 9
Cover Jacoba van Heemskerck
1918 vol. 9, no. 2
Cover Jacoba van Heemskerck
1919/20 vol. 10
Cover Jacoba van Heemskerck
1920 vol. 11
Cover Jacoba van Heemskerck

1920 vol. 11, no. 2
Cover Marc Chagall; texts Kurt Schwitters, Otto Nebel; fig. Jacoba van Heemskerck
1921 vol. 12
Cover Jacoba van Heemskerck
1921 vol. 12, no. 9
Cover Jacoba van Heemskerck; text Lothar Schreyer; figs. Jacoba van Heemskerck;

1921 vol. 12, no. 10
Cover Jacoba van Heemskerck; texts Franz Richard Behrens, Kurt Schwitters, Rudolf Blümner; figs. Jacoba van Heemskerck
1922 vol. 13
Cover Jacoba van Heemskerck
1923 vol. 14
Cover Jacoba van Heemskerck

1923 vol. 14, no. 10
Cover László Moholy-Nagy; text Tibor Déry; fig. Jacoba van Heemskerck

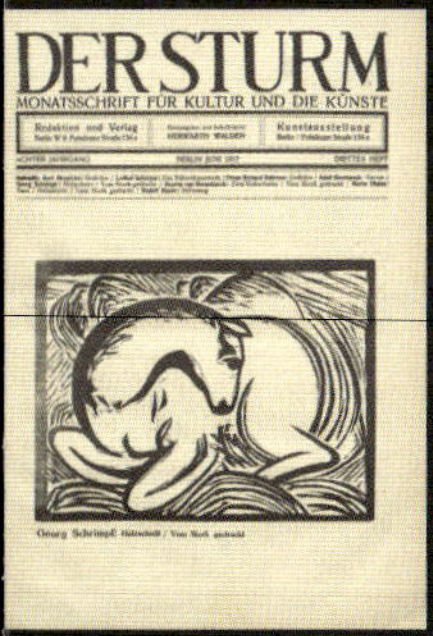

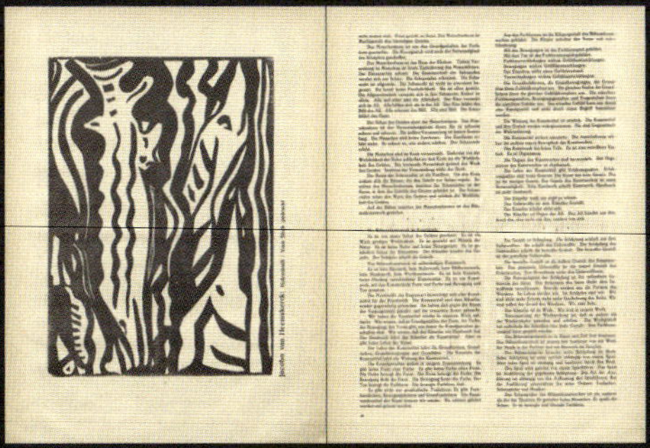

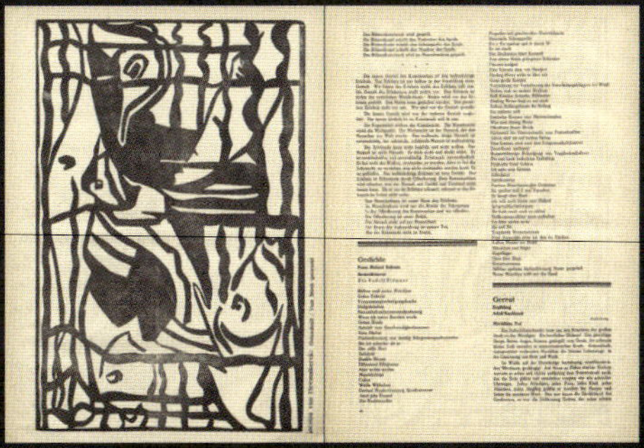

1918/19

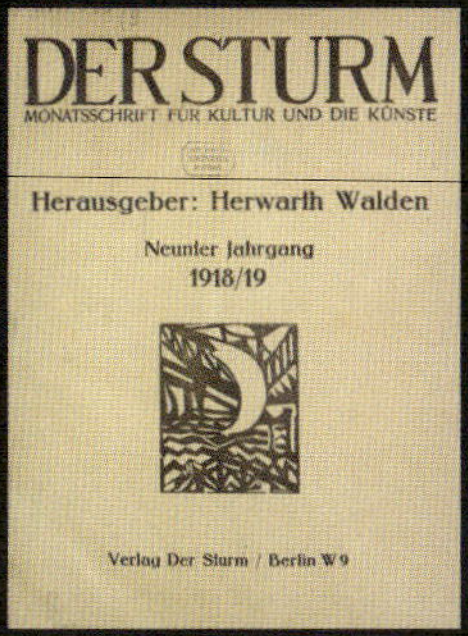

1918

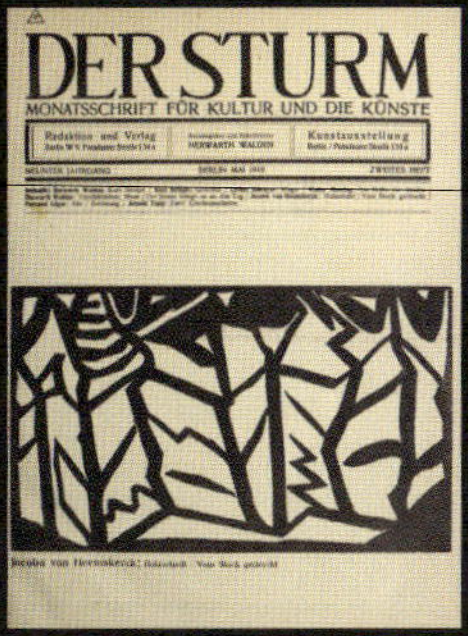

1919/20

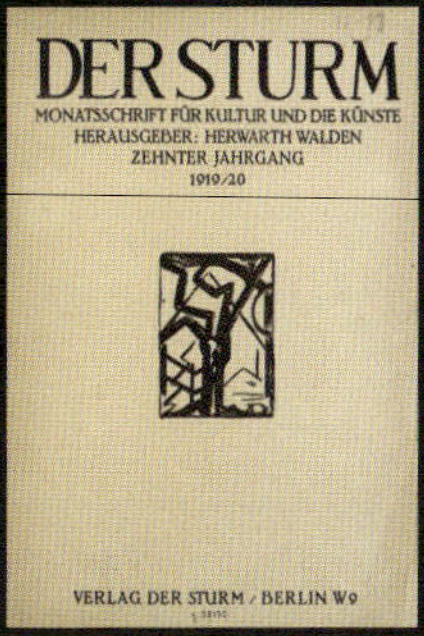

1921

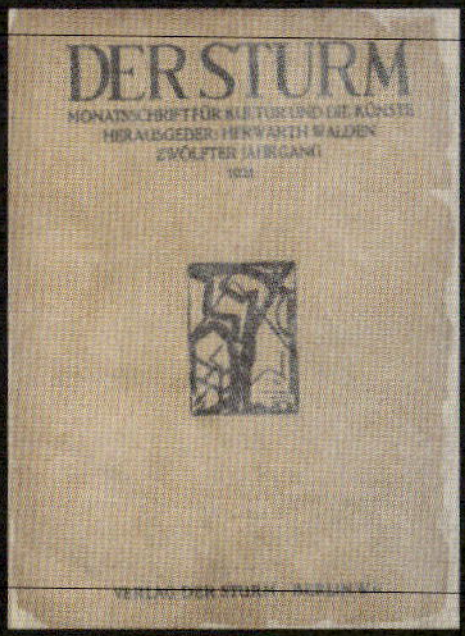

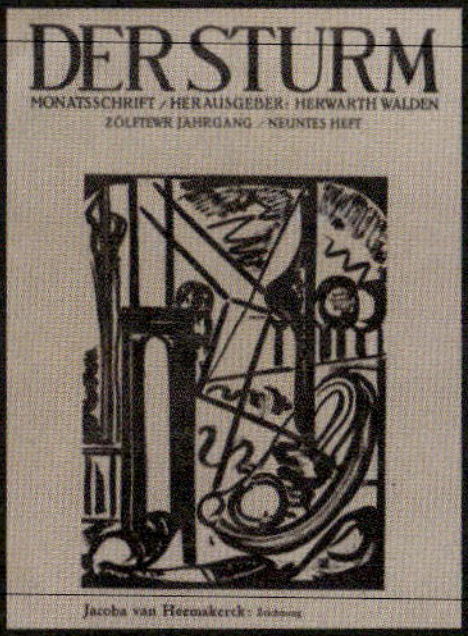

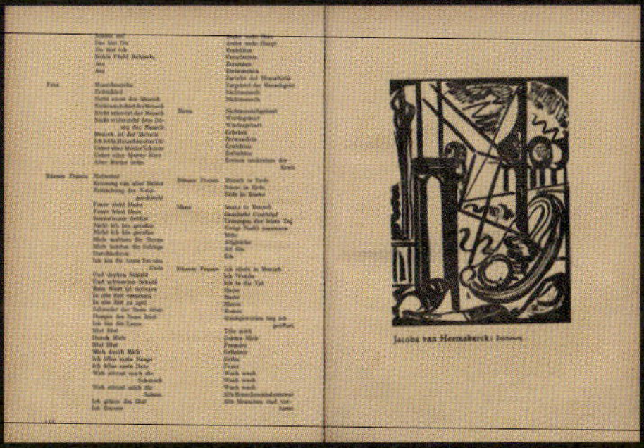

1922

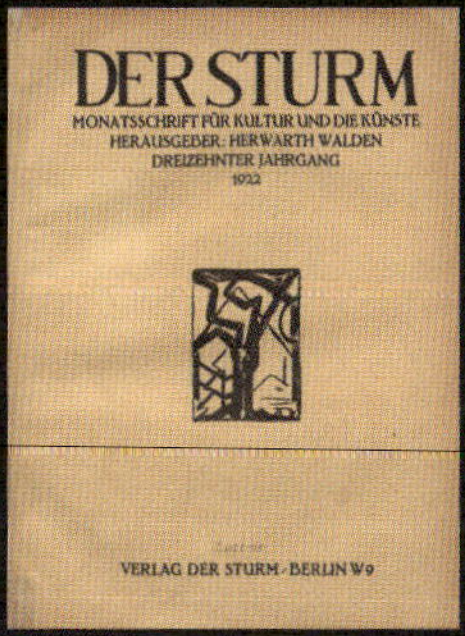

1923

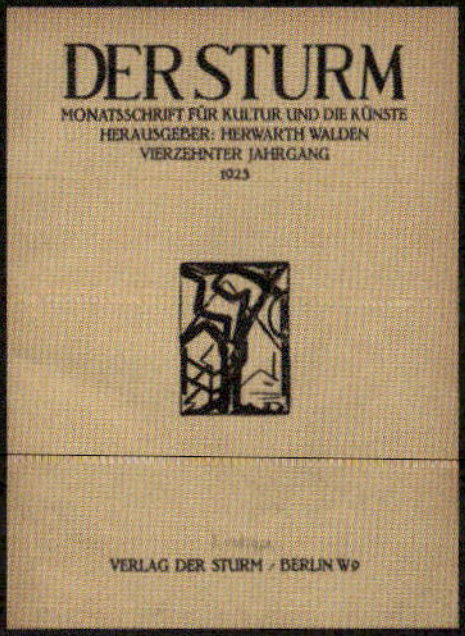

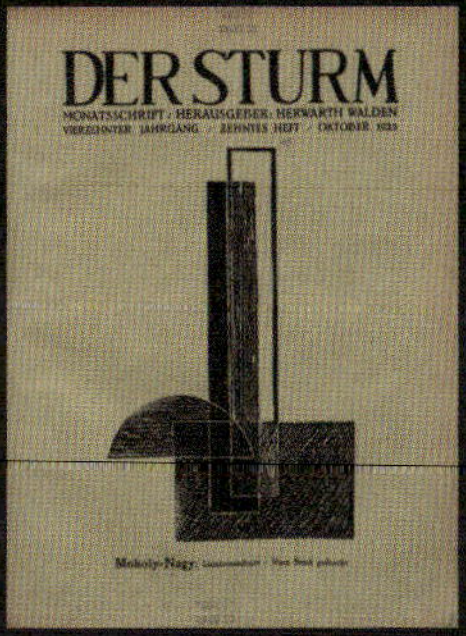

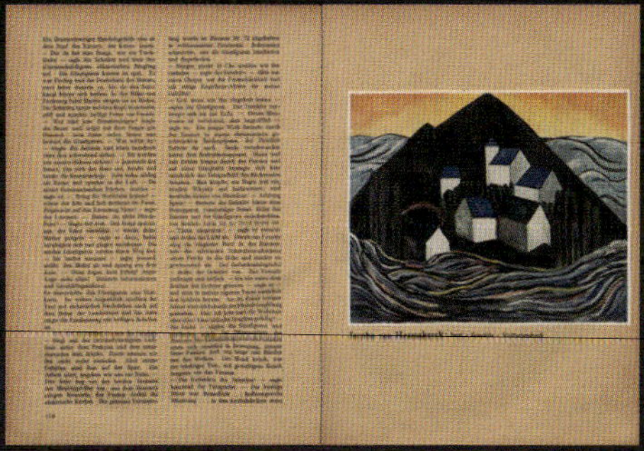

Exhibitions 1904–2020 (selection)

February – March 1904
Salon de l'Union des Femmes Peintres et Sculpteurs › number of works unknown
Paris, Grand Palais

14.5.–1.7.1905
15 jaarlijksche tentoonstelling van kunstwerken van leden der vereeniging in het Stedelijk Museum te Amsterdam [Sint Lucas] › 1 work
Amsterdam, Stedelijk Museum

October – November 1905
Arti et Amicitiae. Tentoonstelling van tekeningen en beeldhouwwerken › 1 work
Amsterdam

May – July 1906
Tentoonstelling ter gelegenheid van het 25-jarig jubileum van Sint Lucas › 1 work
Amsterdam, Stedelijk Museum

1.4.–15.5.1907
Zeventiende jaarlijksche tentoonstelling van kunstwerken van leden der vereeniging [Sint Lucas] › 1 work
Amsterdam, Stedelijk Museum

June – July 1907
Arti et Amicitiae. Tentoonstelling van origineele etsen, gravures, lithografieën en houtsneden › 1 work
Amsterdam

7.9.–30.9.1907
Stedelijke tentoonstelling van kunstwerken van levende meesters › 1 work
Amsterdam, Stedelijk Museum

October – November 1907
Arti et Amicitiae. Tentoonstelling van tekeningen en beeldhouwwerken › 1 work
Amsterdam

3.5.–15.6.1908
18e jaarlijksche tentoonstelling van kunstwerken van leden der vereeniging [Sint Lucas] › 1 work
Amsterdam, Stedelijk Museum

1.6.– [?].10.1909
X. Internationale Kunstausstellung: Münchener Künstlergenossenschaft und Münchener Secession › 1 work
Munich, Königlicher Glaspalast

10.7.–22.8.1909
Gemeentelijke tentoonstelling van kunstwerken van levende meesters › 1 work
Arnhem, Musis Sacrum

24.4.– [?].6.1910
20ste jaarlijksche tentoonstelling van kunstwerken van leden der vereeniging [Sint Lucas] › 5 works
Amsterdam, Stedelijk Museum

30.7.–21.8.1910
[Tentoonstellung] IVe Salon Doe Stil Voort › 7 works
Brussels, Musée Moderne

2.4.–13.6.1911
27ème Exposition de Société des Artistes Indépendants › 3 works
Paris, Quai d'Orsay, Pont de l'Alma

16.4.–30.6.1911
XXe Exposition de Société des Beaux-Arts › 1 work
Paris, Grand Palais

30.4.–11.6.1911
21e jaarlijksche tentoonstelling van kunstwerken van leden der vereeniging [Sint Lucas] › 1 work
Amsterdam, Stedelijk Museum

July – August 1911
Tentoonstelling van schilderijen en teekeningen van Walchersche schilders › 7 works
Domburg, Tentoonstellingszaal

6.10.–5.11.1911
Internationale tentoonstelling van moderne kunst. Moderne Kunst Kring › 1 work
Amsterdam, Stedelijk Museum

20.3.–16.5.1912
28ème Exposition de Société des Artistes Indépendants › 3 works
Paris, Quai d'Orsay, Pont de l'Alma

July – August 1912
Kunst Nijverheid Sport › number of works unknown
Nijmegen, Feestterrein Oud Heidelberg

28.7.–19.8.1912
Tentoonstelling van schilderijen › 7 works
Domburg, Tentoonstellingszaal

6.10.–7.11.1912
Moderne Kunst Kring (Cercle de l'art moderne). Ouvrages de peinture, sculpture, dessin, gravure › 3 works
Amsterdam, Musée Municipal Suasso [Stedelijk Museum]

9.3.–18.5.1913
29ème Exposition de Société des Artistes Indépendants › 3 works
Paris, Quai d'Orsay, Pont de l'Alma

May – June 1913
De Onafhankelijken.
Eerste tentoonstelling › 3 works
Amsterdam, Gebouw Willaertstraat

20.5.–30.9.1913
De Vrouw 1813–1913 › 5 works
Amsterdam, Meerhuizen

July – August 1913
Tentoonstelling van schilderijen › 6 works
Domburg, Tentoonstellingszaal

20.9.–1.12.1913
Der Sturm. Erster Deutscher Herbstsalon › 4 works
Berlin, Potsdamer Straße 75

7.11.–8.12.1913
Moderne Kunst Kring (Cercle de l'art moderne) › 1 work
Amsterdam, Stedelijk Museum

15.11.–15.12.1913
Tweede internationale jury-vrije tentoonstelling De Onafhankelijken › 5 works
Amsterdam, Gebouw Amstelveenschenweg

21.12.1913–21.1.1914
Tentoonstelling van schetsen en studies, grafische kunst, zwart en wit en beeldhouwwerken van leden van de vereeniging Sint Lucas › 2 works
Amsterdam, Stedelijk Museum

March 1914
Jacoba van Heemskerck,
Arthur Segal, Marianne von Werefkin (23. Sturm-Ausstellung) › 21 works
Berlin, Potsdamer Straße 134a

1.3.–30.4.1914
30me Exposition de Société des Artistes Indépendants › 3 works
Paris, Champ de Mars

April – October 1914
Jacoba van Heemskerck. Sturm-Ausstellung › number of works unknown
Hamburg

July – August 1914
Tentoonstelling van schilderijen › 6 works
Domburg, Tentoonstellingszaal

November – December 1914
Heinrich Campendonk, Jacoba van Heemskerck (29. Sturm-Ausstellung) › 11 works
Berlin, Potsdamer Straße 134a

January – February 1915
Severini, Campendonk, Marc, Münter, Mense, van Heemskerck, Kokoschka (30. Sturm-Ausstellung) › 1 work
Berlin, Potsdamer Straße 134a

March 1915
Jacoba van Heemskerck
(31. Sturm-Ausstellung)
› number of works unknown
Berlin, Potsdamer Straße 134a

November 1915
Sammlung Walden. Gemälde, Zeichnungen, Plastiken › 16 works
Berlin, Potsdamer Straße 134a

14.11.–30.11.1915
Der Sturm. Neue Kunst.
Gemäldeausstellung › 3 works
Brandenburg/Havel,
St. Annen Straße 30

December 1915
Graphische Werke
(36. Sturm-Ausstellung) › 25 works
Berlin, Potsdamer Straße 134a

February 1916
Jacoba van Heemskerck. Gemälde und Zeichnungen (38. Sturm-Ausstellung) › number of works unknown
Berlin, Potsdamer Straße 134a

17.3.–16.4.1916
Expressionisten, Kubisten
(2. Sturm-Ausstellung) › 11 works
The Hague, Kunstzalen d'Audretsch

April – May 1916
Jacoba van Heemskerck. Sturm-Ausstellung › number of works unknown
Hagen, Folkwang Museum

7.5.–31.5.1916
Expressionisten, Kubisten
(1. Sturm-Ausstellung) › 7 works
Braunschweig, Herzogliches Museum

20.6.–5.7.1916
Expressionisten, Kubisten
(1. Sturm-Ausstellung) › 7 works
Potsdam, Potsdamer Kunstverein

1.7.– [?].8.1916
Expressionisten, Futuristen, Kubisten. Gemälde und Zeichnungen (43. Sturm-Ausstellung) › 4 works
Berlin, Potsdamer Straße 134a

15.9.–15.10.1916
Expressionisten, Futuristen, Kubisten. Gemälde und Zeichnungen (1. Sturm-Ausstellung) › 10 works
Brno, Mährischer Kunstverein Brno, Kaiser Franz Joseph-Jubiläums-Künstlerhaus

January 1917
Jacoba van Heemskerck. Gemälde, Aquarelle, Zeichnungen, Holzschnitte (48. Sturm-Ausstellung) › 64 works
Berlin, Potsdamer Straße 134a

7.2.–7.3.1917
Sturm-Ausstellung › 10 works
Basel, Galerie Corray

March 1917
Sturm-Gesamtschau. Gemälde, Aquarelle, Zeichnungen (50. Sturm-Ausstellung) › 3 works
Berlin, Potsdamer Straße 134a

1.3.–1.4.1917
Jacoba van Heemskerck. Sturm-Ausstellung › number of works unknown
Dresden

17.3.–7.4.1917, 9.4.–30.4.1917
Sturm-Ausstellung, 1. und 2. Serie › 10 works
Zurich, Galerie Dada

June 1917
Sturm-Gesamtschau. Gemälde, Aquarelle, Zeichnungen (53. Sturm-Ausstellung) › 2 works
Berlin, Potsdamer Straße 134a

July – August 1917
Sturm-Gesamtschau. Gemälde, Aquarelle. Zeichnungen (5. Sturm-Ausstellung) › 3 works
Hamburg, Galerie Louis Bock & Sohn

September – October 1917
Der Sturm Kunstnere (2. Sturm-Ausstellung) › 10 works
Copenhagen, Kunstnerkabaretten “Edderkoppen“

15.10.–30.11.1917
Jacoba van Heemskerck. Sturm-Ausstellung › number of works unknown
Frankfurt am Main

December 1917
Jacoba van Heemskerck › number of works unknown
Frankfurt am Main, Vereinigung für Neue Kunst

March [recte. April 1918]
Jacoba van Heemskerck. Gemälde, Aquarelle, Zeichnungen, Holzschnitte (62. Sturm-Ausstellung) › 68 works
Berlin, Potsdamer Straße 134a

16.6.–14.7.1918
Sturmgraphik › 5 works
Jena, Kunstverein Jena

10.10.– mid-November 1918
Sturm-Ausstellung › 8 works
Wrocław, Galerie Ernst Arnold

December 1918
Der Sturm. International Kunst. Ekspressionister og Kubister. Malerier og Skulpturer › 12 works
Copenhagen, Georg Kleis Kunsthandel

February 1919
Gesamtschau (71. Sturm-Ausstellung) › 3 works
Berlin, Potsdamer Straße 134a

April 1919
Sonderausstellung Der Sturm. Expressionisten, Futuristen, Kubisten (2. Expressionistische Ausstellung) › 48 works
Dresden, Galerie Ernst Arnold

8.5.1919– [?]
Nell Walden, Hans Brass + Gesamtschau (74. Sturm-Ausstellung) › 5 works
Berlin, Potsdamer Straße 134a

9.6.1919– [?]
Oswald Herzog, Oskar Fischer, Heinrich von Boddien + Gesamtschau (75. Sturm-Ausstellung) › 2 works
Berlin, Potsdamer Straße 134a

July – August 1919
Gesamtschau Expressionisten. Gemälde, Bildwerke, Aquarelle, Zeichnungen (1. Sturm-Ausstellung) › 4 works
Berlin-Osten, Petersberger Straße 39

21.7.1919– [?]
Kurt Schwitters, Magda Langenstraß-Uhlig + Gesamtschau (76. Sturm-Ausstellung) › 1 work
Berlin, Potsdamer Straße 134a

29.7.– [?].9.1919
Ausstellung Neuer Kunst 1919. Expressionisten, Kubisten, Futuristen › 8 works
Zurich, Kunstsalon Rembrandt

August 1919
Maria Uhden – Gedächtnisausstellung, Paul Busch, Paul Nietsche + Gesamtschau (77. Sturm-Ausstellung) › 1 work
Berlin, Potsdamer Straße 134a

September 1919
Georg Muche, Hans Sittig + Gesamtschau (78. Sturm-Ausstellung) › 2 works
Berlin, Potsdamer Straße 134a

11.10.1919– [?]
Johannes Molzahn, Karl Herrmann, Jacoba van Heemskerck – Entwürfe für Glasfenster, Gemälde, Bildwerke, Aquarelle, Zeichnungen + Gesamtschau (79. Sturm-Ausstellung) › 13 works
Berlin, Potsdamer Straße 134a

25.10.–30.11.1919
Der Sturm und Üecht-Gruppe (1. Herbstschau neuer Kunst) › 10 works
Stuttgart, Kunstgebäude Stuttgart

November 1919
Hugo Händel, Oskar Fischer + Gesamtschau (80. Sturm-Ausstellung) › 2 works
Berlin, Potsdamer Straße 134a

December 1919
Arnold Topp + Gesamtschau (81. Sturm-Ausstellung) › 1 work
Berlin, Potsdamer Straße 134a

February 1920
Jacoba van Heemskerck + Gesamtschau (83. Sturm-Ausstellung) › 37 works
Berlin, Potsdamer Straße 134a

March 1920
Sonja [sic.] Delaunay-Terk + Gesamtschau (84. Sturm-Ausstellung) › 5 works
Berlin, Potsdamer Straße 134a

April 1920
Kurt Schwitters + Gesamtschau (85. Sturm-Ausstellung) › 2 works
Berlin, Potsdamer Straße 134a

May 1920
Rudolf Bauer + Gesamtschau (86. Sturm-Ausstellung) › 1 work
Berlin, Potsdamer Straße 134a

June 1920
Nell Walden, Tour Donas + Gesamtschau (87. Sturm-Ausstellung) › 1 work
Berlin, Potsdamer Straße 134a

July – August 1920
Tentoonstelling van schilderijen › 11 works
Domburg, Tentoonstellingszaal

August 1920
Reinhard Goering, Thomas Ring, Walter Selle – Gedächtnisausstellung + Gesamtschau (88. Sturm-Ausstellung) › 2 works
Berlin, Potsdamer Straße 134a

September 1920
Reinhard Goering, Paul Klee + Gesamtschau (89. Sturm-Ausstellung) › 2 works
Berlin, Potsdamer Straße 134a

2.9.–10.9.1920
Jacoba van Heemskerck. Geschilderd gebrand glas › number of works unknown
The Hague, Haagse Kunstkring

October 1920
Graphische Gesamtschau, Aquarelle, Zeichnungen, Holzschnitte, Lithos, Radierungen, Glasbilder (90. Sturm-Ausstellung) › 14 works
Berlin, Potsdamer Straße 134a

October – November 1920
Üecht Gruppe (2. Herbstschau neuer Kunst) › 3 works
Stuttgart, Kunstgebäude Stuttgart

November 1920
Johannes Molzahn + Graphische Gesamtschau (91. Sturm-Ausstellung) › 5 works
Berlin, Potsdamer Straße 134a

December 1920
Paul Busch, Johannes Molzahn + Graphische Gesamtschau (92. Sturm-Ausstellung) › 3 works
Berlin, Potsdamer Straße 134a

December 1920
Junge niederländische Kunst
(Die Kornscheuer)
Berlin, Nationalgalerie
(Kronprinzenpalais)

1921
Ohne Titel [Glasarbeiten]
Amsterdam

February – March 1921
Der Sturm ständige graphische Ausstellung + Heinrich Campendonk + Gesamtschau › number of works unknown
Berlin, Potsdamer Straße 134a

3.4.1921–?
Kurt Schwitters + Gesamtschau
(96. Sturm-Ausstellung) › 1 work
Berlin, Potsdamer Straße 134a

May 1921
Robert Delaunay + Gesamtschau
(97. Sturm-Ausstellung) › 1 work
Berlin, Potsdamer Straße 134a

June –15.7.1921
Rudolf Bauer, Vjera Biller + Gesamtschau
(98. Sturm-Ausstellung) › 1 work
Berlin, Potsdamer Straße 134a

July 1921
Internationale tentoonstelling van graphische kunst te Domburg › 8 works
Domburg, Tentoonstellingszaal

17.7.–26.8.1921
Paul Klee, Hans Mattis Teutsch + Gesamtschau (99. Sturm-Ausstellung) › 2 works
Berlin, Potsdamer Straße 134a

September 1921
Zehn Jahre Sturm. Gesamtschau
(100. Sturm-Ausstellung) › 4 works
Berlin, Potsdamer Straße 134a

November 1921
Jacoba van Heemskerck + Gesamtschau
(102. Sturm-Ausstellung) › 53 works
Berlin, Potsdamer Straße 134a

December 1921
Erich Buchholz + Versteigerungsausstellung. Werke der Meister des Staatlichen Bauhauses Weimar + Gesamtschau
(103. Sturm-Ausstellung) › 8 works
Berlin, Potsdamer Straße 134a

January 1922
Arnold Topp, Adolf Bauer-Saar + Gesamtschau (104. Sturm-Ausstellung) › 2 works
Berlin, Potsdamer Straße 134a

21.1.–23.1.1922
2de Kongres van Moderne Kunst
› number of works unknown
Antwerpen, El Bardo-Saal

February 1922
László Moholy-Nagy, László Péri
+ Gesamtschau (105. Sturm-Ausstellung)
› 2 works
Berlin, Potsdamer Straße 134a

March 1922
Willi Baumeister, Fernand Léger + Gesamtschau (106. Sturm-Ausstellung) › 4 works
Berlin, Potsdamer Straße 134a

April 1922
Georg von Poschedajew + Gesamtschau
(107. Sturm-Ausstellung) › 5 works
Berlin, Potsdamer Straße 134a

May 1922
Kurt Schwitters, Ljubov Kosinzova-Ehrenburg + Gesamtschau
(108. Sturm-Ausstellung) › 2 works
Berlin, Potsdamer Straße 134a

28.5.–3.7.1922
Erste Internationale Kunstausstellung Düsseldorf › 6 works
Düsseldorf, Warenhaus Leonhard Tietz

June – July 1922
Albert Gleizes, Walter Krug + Gesamtschau (109. Sturm-Ausstellung) › 4 works
Berlin, Potsdamer Straße 134a

August 1922
Gösta Adrian-Nilsson, Ossip Zadkine
+ Gesamtschau (110. Sturm-Ausstellung)
› 7 works
Berlin, Potsdamer Straße 134a

September 1922
Serge Charchoune, Helene Grünhoff
+ Gesamtschau (111. Sturm-Ausstellung)
› 6 works
Berlin, Potsdamer Straße 134a

October 1922
Louis Marcoussis + Gesamtschau
(112. Sturm-Ausstellung) › 4 works
Berlin, Potsdamer Straße 134a

December 1922
Alexander Bortnyik, Paul Fuhrmann, Oscar Nerlinger + Gesamtschau
(114. Sturm-Ausstellung) › 3 works
Berlin, Potsdamer Straße 134a

1923
International Konst. Ekspressionister och Kubister. Malerier, Grafik och Skulpturer › 7 works
Göteborg, Kunsthochschule Valand

1923
International Kunst. Ekspressionister og Kubister. Malerier og Skulptur
(1. Sturm-Ausstellung) › 5 works
Copenhagen, Ole Haslunds Hus

January 1923
Johannes Molzahn, Robert Michel
+ Gesamtschau (115. Sturm-Ausstellung)
› 5 works
Berlin, Potsdamer Straße 134a

February 1923
László Moholy-Nagy, László Péri
+ Gesamtschau (116. Sturm-Ausstellung)
› 3 works
Berlin, Potsdamer Straße 134a

April 1923
Max Herman Maxy + Gesamtschau
(118. Sturm-Ausstellung) › 4 works
Berlin, Potsdamer Straße 134a

May 1923
Emilio Pettoruti, Robert Storm-Petersen
+ Gesamtschau (119. Sturm-Ausstellung)
› 2 works
Berlin, Potsdamer Straße 134a

July 1923
Gesamtschau (121. Sturm-Ausstellung)
› 4 works
Berlin, Potsdamer Straße 134a

September 1923
Arnold Topp, Wilhelm Wulff, Die jungen Dänen + Sturm-Gesamtschau
(123. Sturm-Ausstellung) › 6 works
Berlin, Potsdamer Straße 134a

November 1923
Ernst Oscar Albrecht, Anne Reibstein-Albrecht + Sturm-Gesamtschau
(125. Sturm-Ausstellung) › 1 work
Berlin, Potsdamer Straße 134a

December 1923
Béla Kádár + Sturm-Gesamtschau
(126. Sturm-Ausstellung) › 1 work
Berlin, Potsdamer Straße 134a

January 1924
Hugo Scheiber, Béla Kádár, Gewebe aus Alt-Peru + Sturm-Gesamtschau
(127. Sturm-Ausstellung) › 1 work
Berlin, Potsdamer Straße 134a

March 1924
Jacoba van Heemskerck Gedächtnisausstellung + Sturm-Gesamtschau
(129. Sturm-Ausstellung) › 53 works
Berlin, Potsdamer Straße 134a, later Vienna, Kunstsalon Würthle, Amsterdam and other Dutch cities

Museum Solo Exhibitions, posthumous

1933–34
Jacoba van Heemskerck
› number of works unknown
The Hague, Gemeentemuseum Den Haag

28.1.–29.2.1960
Jacoba van Heemskerck
› number of works unknown
Amsterdam, Stedelijk Museum

30.4.–27.6.1982
Jacoba van Heemskerck, kunstenares van het expressionisme › 110 works
The Hague, Gemeentemuseum Den Haag

Summer 1983 – February 1984
Jacoba van Heemskerck – Eine expressionistische Künstlerin › 108 works
Berlin, Haus am Waldsee; Stuttgart, Württembergischer Kunstverein, Saarbrücken, Saarlandmuseum, Bonn, Rheinisches Landesmuseum, Erlangen, Städtische Galerie

27.8.–21.11.2005
Jacoba van Heemskerck. Een herontdekking › 81 works
The Hague, Gemeentemuseum Den Haag

19.9.2009–10.1.2010
Jacoba van Heemskerck (1876–1923), vrouwelijke Mondriaan › number of works unknown
Amersfoort, Mondriaanhuis

Imprint

This catalogue has been published on the occasion of the exhibition
Jacoba van Heemskerck.
Truly Modern

Kunsthalle Bielefeld
19 June to 05 September 2021

Museen Stade | Kunsthaus
25 September 2021 to
6 February 2022

Edwin Scharff Museum Neu-Ulm
26 February to 19 June 2022

in cooperation with

KUNSTMUSEUM DEN HAAG

With kind support of the Kingdom of the Netherlands

Kingdom of the Netherlands

Exhibition

Curators
Luisa Pauline Fink, Henrike Mund

Kunsthalle Bielefeld

Director
Christina Végh

Curator and Head of Collection
Dr Henrike Mund

Curator
Dr Linda Walther

Curatorial Assistant
Laura Rehme

Head of Administration
Thomas Kosfeld

Registrar
Hannelore Wahl

Press, Marketing, Communication
Anne Kaestner

Education
Matthias Albrecht, Christiane Lutterkort

Library and Museum Shop
Tania Müller

Reception
Susanne Esdar, Petra tom Felde

Museum Guards
Petra Göke, Bärbel Schütt,
Anja Stetzelberg

Conservation
Dr Marie Althöfer, Gisela Tilly

Head of Technical Team
Viktor Breivogel, Waldemar Schulz

Technical Team
Ingo Bustorf, Rüdiger Freund,
Gunther Grabe, Gerd Kruse,
Fred Rabe, Robert Schlotter

Documentation
Philipp Ottendörfer (photo),
Roman Schauerte (film)

Kunsthalle Bielefeld
Artur-Ladebeck-Straße 5
D – 33602 Bielefeld
www.kunsthalle-bielefeld.de

Museen Stade | Kunsthaus

Director
Dr Sebastian Möllers

Curator and Head of Collection
Luisa Pauline Fink

Curator
Regina Wetjen

Assistant to the Director and Registrar
Julia Schubert

Secretary
Carola Arndt-Vöge

Press, Marketing, Communication
Luisa Pauline Fink, Regina Wetjen

Education
Wiebke Etzold

Conservation
Ulrike Habeck

Visitors' Service
Nicola Blendermann

Technical Team
Klaus Baumgarten, Olaf-Frank Lührs

Reception and Museum Guards
Saeid Behzadpour, Marcus Bohlmann,
Katrin Mielitz, Michael Schmidt,
Hartmut Schwarting

Museen Stade
Wasser West 39
D – 21682 Stade
www.museen-stade.de

Kunstmuseum Den Haag

Director
Benno Tempel

Head of Exhibitions
Dr Daniel Koep

Head of Collection
Doede Hardeman

Curator of Modern and Contemporary Art
Laura Stamps

Administration Collection Modern Art
Vivien Entius

Coordinaton Collections and Conservation
Erica Jonkman

Conservation and Restoration Modern Art
Leonoor Speldekamp

Registrar
Hanneke Modderkolk, Marjolein Prinse

Coordination of Loans
Frans Peterse

Art Handling
Erwin Sutedjo

Kunstmuseum Den Haag
Stadhouderslaan 41
NL – 2517 HV Den Haag
www.kunstmuseum.nl

The catalogue has been realised with the generous support of the
Ernst von Siemens Kunststiftung

The exhibition in Bielefeld is generously supported by the
Kulturstiftung pro Bielefeld

The catalogue and the exhibition in Stade are generously supported by
Brougier-Seisser-Cleve-Werhahn Stiftung

ZEIT-Stiftung Ebelin und Gerd Bucerius

Editors
Luisa Pauline Fink, Sebastian Möllers, Henrike Mund, Christina Végh

Concept
Luisa Pauline Fink, Daniel Koep, Henrike Mund

Graphic Design
Typography Interiority & Other Serious Matters

Lithography
Pieter Reinink (PR Digitaal)

Translation from Dutch
Sue McDonnell (pp. 4, 25–41, 43–56, 131–147)

Translation from German
Allison Moseley (pp. 5–6, 7–23, 57–72, 151)

Translation Copyediting
Keonaona Petersen

Copyediting
Luisa Pauline Fink, Henrike Mund

Copyediting text Laura Stamps
Marleen Blokhuis

Exhibition List
Tania Müller

Image Research
Vivien Entius

Published by
Hirmer Verlag

Project Direction
Kerstin Ludolph

Production
Hannes Halder

Printing and Binding
Passavia Druckservice GmbH & Co. KG

ISBN 978-3-7774-3699-9

Printed in Germany

Front cover:
Jacoba van Heemskerck
Bild no. 46 (Rog) |
Image no. 46 (Ray) 1916

Bibliographical data of the Deutsche Nationalbibliothek
The Deutsche Nationalbibliothek lists this publication in the Deutsche Nationalbibliografie; detailed bibliographic information is available on the Internet at http://www.dnb.de.

Image Credits
For all images not listed here and the images in the catalogue-section: Kunstmuseum Den Haag

bpk 11, 39
bpk / Berlinische Galerie 51
bpk / Kunstbibliothek, SMB, Photothek Willy Römer / Willy Römer 12
bpk / Nationalgalerie, SMB 68
bpk / Rudolf Dührkoop 10
bpk / Staatsbibliothek zu Berlin 60, 61, 64, 65
Courtesy of the Theosophical Society in America Archives 29
Digitaal Fotoarchief Gemeente Wassenaar 15
Forschungsstelle Kulturimpuls 13
Gabriele Münter- und Johannes Eichner-Stiftung, Munich 40
Haags Gemeentearchief 66
J & M Zweerts Fotografie 48
Kröller-Müller Museum, Otterlo 28
Private Collection: 18, 34, 47, 49, 71
Rijksdienst voor het Cultureel Erfgoed 59
RKD – Nederlands Instituut voor Kunstgeschiedenis 2, 8, 14, 19, 20, 21, 58, 70
Rudolf Steiner Archive, Dornach, Switzerland 17
Scan: Jacoba van Heemskerck. Sturm-Bilderbuch VII, Berlin 1924, n. p. 69
Staatsbibliothek zu Berlin – Preußischer Kulturbesitz, Handschriftenabteilung:
Zsn 12 361 R 9, 38
Sturm-Archive 3, 16
Sturm-Archive I: Jacoba van Heemskerck, Bl. 4 (http://resolver.staatsbibliothek-berlin.de/SBB0000DB5A00000000): 50 / Bl. 337 (http://resolver.staats bibliothekberlin.de/SBB0000DA0E00 000000): 62 / Bl. 366 (http:// resolver.staatsbibliothek-berlin.de/ SBB0000DA2900000000): 63
ZB – Planbureau en Bibliotheek van Zeeland: 5, 6, 7, 46

Magazine Der Sturm (pp. 152-155):
https://digi.ub.uni-heidelberg.de/diglit/ sturm1914_1915/0069 / 0104 / 0108 / 0109 / 0127 / 0151 / 0155 / 0156 / 0157 / 0158
https://digi.ub.uni-heidelberg.de/diglit/ sturm1915_1916/0051 / 0057 / 0058 / 0075 / 0086 / 0090 / 0091 / 0109 / 0113 / 0114 / 0115 / 0116 / 0121 / 0125 / 0126 / 0127 / 0128
https://digi.ub.uni-heidelberg.de/diglit/ sturm1916_1917/0003 / 0007 / 0011 / 0012 / 0043 / 0047 / 0048 / 0051 / 0052 / 0115 / 0121 / 0122 / 0139 / 0145 / 0146
https://digi.ub.uni-heidelberg.de/diglit/ sturm1917_1918/0003 / 0007 / 0015 / 0016 / 0039 / 0043 / 0044 / 0045 / 0046 / 0151 / 0155 / 0156 / 0157 / 0158
https://digi.ub.uni-heidelberg.de/diglit/ sturm1918_1919/0005 / 0025
https://digi.ub.uni-heidelberg.de/diglit/ sturm1919_1920/0003
https://digi.ub.uni-heidelberg.de/diglit/ sturm1920/0001 / 0021 / 0028 / 0029
https://digi.ub.uni-heidelberg.de/diglit/ sturm1921/0005 / 0191 / 0193 / 0196 / 0197 / 0211 / 0216 / 0217 / 0224 / 0225
https://digi.ub.uni-heidelberg.de/diglit/ sturm1922/0005
https://digi.ub.uni-heidelberg.de/diglit/ sturm1923/0005 / 0171 / 0184 / 0185